East-West
Tensions in the
Third World

THE AMERICAN ASSEMBLY was established by Dwight D. Eisenhower at Columbia University in 1950. Each year it holds at least two nonpartisan meetings which give rise to authoritative books that illuminate issues of United States policy.

An affiliate of Columbia, with offices at Barnard College, the Assembly is a national, educational institution incorporated in the state of New York.

The Assembly seeks to provide information, stimulate discussion, and evoke independent conclusions on matters of vital public interest.

CONTRIBUTORS

DAVID E. ALBRIGHT, Professor of National Security Affairs, Air War College, Maxwell Air Force Base

JORGE I. DOMINGUEZ, Professor of Government, Harvard University

FRANCIS FUKUYAMA, Political Science Department, The Rand Corporation

WILLIAM B. QUANDT, Senior Fellow, The Brookings Institution

MARSHALL D. SHULMAN, Director, W. Averell Harriman Institute, Columbia University

ELIZABETH KRIDL VALKENIER, Department of Political Science, Columbia University

DONALD S. ZAGORIA, Professor of Government, Hunter College

THE AMERICAN ASSEMBLY
Columbia University

East-West
Tensions in the
Third World

MARSHALL D. SHULMAN
Editor

W·W·NORTON & COMPANY
New York   London

Published simultaneously in Canada by Penguin Books Canada Ltd, 2801 John Street, Markham, Ontario L3R 1B4

Printed in the United States of America.

The text of this book is composed in Baskerville, with display type set in Baskerville. Composition and manufacturing by The Haddon Craftsmen, Inc. Book design by Jacques Chazaud.

First Edition

ISBN 0-393-02310-9

ISBN 0-393-30337-3 {PBK}

W. W. Norton & Company, Inc., 500 Fifth Avenue, New York, N. Y. 10110

W. W. Norton & Company, Ltd., 37 Great Russell Street , London WC1B 3NU

1 2 3 4 5 6 7 8 9 0

Contents

Maps

East-West Tensions in the Third World

Preface

MARSHALL D. SHULMAN
and WILLIAM H. SULLIVAN

After six years of tension, the leaders of the United States and the Soviet Union met in Geneva on November 19 and 20, 1985, to begin a process designed to improve the management of East-West relations. One of the items on their agenda concerned regional conflicts, most of which occur in the lesser developed countries known as the Third World.

On November 21, 1985, the Seventieth American Assembly, cosponsored by the W. Averell Harriman Institute for Advanced Study of the Soviet Union, convened at Arden House in Harriman, New York, to consider *East-West Tensions in the Third World.* This meeting brought together distinguished Americans from various sectors of our society as well as representatives of our closest allies. They discussed an agenda prepared by Dr. Marshall D. Shulman, director of the Harriman Institute, and developed from background papers written for the participants.

MARSHALL D. SHULMAN is director of the W. Averell Harriman Institute for Advanced Study of the Soviet Union. WILLIAM H. SULLIVAN is president of The American Assembly.

At the close of their deliberations, on November 24, 1985, the participants issued a report, which is included as an appendix to this book. It contained findings as to the causes of existing tensions and made recommendations for easing them.

The background papers used by the participants have been compiled into the present volume, which is published as a stimulus to better informed views on a series of international problems that may hold the key to the future destiny of most of mankind. These problems reflect not only the turmoil of development but also the temptations that they present for involvement by states with military capabilities for destruction on a massive scale.

Funding for this project was provided by the Richard Lounsbery Foundation, the Rockefeller Foundation, and the Philip D. Reed Foundation. We are grateful for their support. The opinions expressed in this volume are those of the individual authors and not necessarily those of the sponsors nor of The American Assembly and the Harriman Institute, which do not take stands on the issues they present for public discussion.

1

Overview

MARSHALL D. SHULMAN

I t is both an important and an interesting question to which this volume directs our attention: how may East-West tensions in the Third World be eased?

The importance of the subject stems from the fact that, although the regulation of nuclear weapons may have the most immediacy and urgency on the United States–Soviet agenda, the conflicts that arise in the Third World, sometimes unpredictably and explosively, may be more likely to engage the superpowers in a dangerous confrontation than the intersection of their interests in Europe, which they have learned over the decades to handle with great caution. The greater risk of Third World conflicts getting out of control and escalating, even if neither power intends it, can result from mounting

MARSHALL D. SHULMAN is the director of the W. Averell Harriman Institute for Advanced Study of the Soviet Union and the Adlai E. Stevenson Professor of International Relations at Columbia University. Dr. Shulman is the author of a number of books and articles on international relations, Soviet foreign policy, and military security. Besides extensive academic experience, Dr. Shulman has served as special assistant and special adviser to the secretary of state.

demonstrations of will, from the temptation to resort to nuclear capabilities to compensate for conventional imbalances, and from the volatility of politics in the Third World.

East-West tensions in the Third World are also important because they inevitably affect the totality of East-West relations. As the lesson of the 1970s demonstrated, it is not possible as a practical matter to maintain a calm and businesslike relationship between the United States and the Soviet Union on arms control or other bilateral matters at a time when tensions are inflamed by episodes of conflict and high competition in the Third World. The conclusion is inescapable that if East-West relations are to be put onto a less dangerous footing, ways must be found to keep the competition in the Third World within safer bounds than it has been in the past.

What makes the subject interesting as well is that it involves virtually every aspect of international politics, including the internal politics of all the states concerned. As the following chapters demonstrate, the competition in the Third World between the United States and the Soviet Union has many dimensions: military, political, ideological, and economic. The terrain on which this competition takes place is deeply affected by such fundamental movements as the resurgence of nationalism in both industrial and developing countries and of religious fundamentalism. The terms of the competition are affected by changes in military and communications technology, as is well illustrated in Francis Fukuyama's discussion in chapter 7 of how the increasing range of strategic weapons reduced the dependence of the United States upon foreign bases for its strategic aircraft.

The thought-provoking possibility suggests itself that there may be a link between these two fundamental trends in international politics: that the accelerating pace of technological change, by its disorienting effect upon the way people live, the gap it widens between the experience of one generation and the next, and the challenge to traditional sources of values and authority, may stimulate the return to religious and nationalist fundamentalism we now witness in both industrial and developing societies. Advanced societies seek to adapt their institutions to the requirements of the new phase of the industrial revolution, which puts a primacy on the application of computers, electronics, and information-processing, and which has heightened such nationalist tendencies as protectionism as they compete in a new ordering of power relations between the United States, Japan, Western Europe, and the Soviet Union. In the developing societies, the process of modernization comes inevitably into conflict with traditional values rooted in ancient religion and erupts into fundamentalist backlash religious rebellions, most dramatically illustrated by the overthrow of the Shah of Iran and his replacement by Khomeini's Islamic fundamentalism.

On another plane, the competition in the Third World is also affected by shifts in the configuration of power resulting from changes in military and communications technology. In the early years of the nuclear weapon, the main emphasis in international politics was upon the bipolarity between the two nuclear superpowers. But as the limitations of translating strategic power into political influence became clearer and as the movement for national independence gathered force in the Third World, it has become clearer that bipolarity in strategic power was tempered by regional multipolarity and that events in the Third World took on a life of their own, subject in only a limited degree to the will of the Great Powers.

A concomitant development in international politics affecting our subject has been the shift in its geographic focus. In the early postwar years and up until the partition of Germany after the Berlin Blockade of 1948–49, Europe was the central territorial concern in the East-West competition. As Europe became relatively stabilized after the partition, attention shifted to the Third World as the battleground. Nikita Khrushchev, in refuting Chinese charges of the loss of revolutionary zeal by the Soviet Union, affirmed Soviet interest in and support of "National Liberation Movements," and it was this flagging of Soviet intent that led President John F. Kennedy to see the "strategic importance" of the civil war in Vietnam, as described in Fukuyama's chapter. In recent years, moreover, the concentration of geographic attention has been toward Asia and the Pacific. As Donald Zagoria points out in chapter 4, both the Soviet Union and the United States have been shifting, in some degree, the focus of their attention and their efforts in this direction, with possible portentous consequences in the coming decade.

Another respect in which the East-West competition in the Third World has been changing, and one which has not received sufficient attention, is that the policies of the Soviet Union and the United States toward the Third World have gone through a considerable evolution during the four decades since the end of the Second World War. In different ways, each of the following chapters illustrates the point.

Although Soviet leaders from the time of Lenin had drawn attention to the colonial dependencies as the weak link in the imperialist chain, it was a surprisingly long time before the Soviet Union appreciated the opportunities opened up by the rapidity of the decolonization process after World War II. It was not until the early Khrushchev period that the Soviet Union perceived the newly independent states as targets of opportunity. There were, however, many setbacks in early Soviet efforts to exploit these opportunities, resulting in part from the limited Soviet knowledge of these areas and the insensitivity of Soviet representatives to local cultures and politics. Research institutes were established or strengthened and specialists were trained on a large scale, so that Soviet efforts were more effective when they returned to the Third World in a subsequent period. Soviet capabilities were also increased by their growing military strength: the growing Soviet navy had made the Soviet Union a maritime power with a global reach and global interests, and their sea power and increasing airlift capabilities enabled them to overcome the logistic limitations that had hampered their earlier efforts and to use military instrumentalities—from arms transfers to military advisers and proxy combat troops—as a major element in their Third World activities. On the other hand, problems in the Soviet economy hampered Soviet efforts to use economic assistance as an instrument in the Third World and even led the Soviet Union to emphasize relations with Third World countries that could benefit the Soviet economy, as Elizabeth Valkenier demonstrates in chapter 6. Even further, she suggests that involvement of the Soviet Union in the world economy has reached the point at which the Soviet Union sees a self-interest in encouraging Third World countries to attract Western investment to aid in their development. If this proves to be a dominant and lasting element in Soviet policy, it will have a bearing on modes by which tensions might be reduced in the East-West competition.

A comparable evolution in United States policy toward the Third World, but in a different direction, is traced in the Fukuyama chapter, among others. After an initial period in which the United States sought to develop a network of pacts with Third World countries to contain the Soviet Union and China, this effort was not pursued because political upheavals made foreign bases and some alliances untenable and because the longer range of new strategic weapons made foreign bases less necessary. More recently, the protection of Western access to Middle Eastern oil led to the creation of forces for rapid deployment abroad and the effort to gain contingency access to facilities abroad in times of crisis, a more modest purpose which took account of local sensitivities to the presence of foreign military installations. Paralleling this change on the military plane, the optimism of early expectations regarding the process of economic development in the Third World was tempered by the growing realization of the massive problems of nation-building, of keeping a balance between growing populations and diminishing food supplies, and of multiple sources of continuing political turbulence. The tendency to see Third World crises predominantly in terms of the East-West competition, however, served to obscure local causes of instability and gave greater emphasis to perceived strategic interests than to the commitment to the process of economic and social development that had elicited enthusiasm and support during the earlier period.

No one who lived through the Vietnam experience in the United States needs to be reminded how deeply it influenced subsequent discussion of how much interventionism Ameri-

cans were willing to accept, and even in the more recent period
of a heightened nationalism and activism in foreign policy, the
question continues to be contended in American politics, as is
evident in Jorge Dominguez's account in chapter 3 of the
American dilemmas in Central America.

Turning now from a consideration of the general issues
involved in the East-West competition and some of the
changes that have characterized Soviet and American approaches to that competition, we observe from the following
chapters how important are the differences in the various regions of the Third World.

In his chapter on the Middle East, William Quandt draws
our attention to the fact that in this area of the most intense
and perhaps the most imminently dangerous competition between East and West, the major factors governing the competition are to be found *within* the area and are only in a limited
degree subject to Great Power control. Quandt emphasizes
the importance of regional nationalism and the overarching
issue of the Arab-Israeli conflict as factors dominating Middle
Eastern politics, frustrating American efforts to draw these
states into a "strategic consensus" against the Soviet Union,
and equally limiting Soviet influence in the area.

Although strategic, economic, and ideological elements are
involved in the Soviet-American competition in the Middle
East, Quandt observes that these elements may be significant
primarily to the extent that they shape the reaction of the
United States and the Soviet Union to the volatile and unpre-
dictable situation that will follow the passing of the Khomeini
regime in Iran.

David Albright, in his chapter on East-West competition in
Africa, assigns primary emphasis to Soviet global power aspirations and to Soviet reliance upon military instruments as
exacerbating factors, with secondary importance assigned to
ideological factors. In North Africa, Albright traces the rise
and fall of Soviet influence and expresses concern that Soviet
military assistance to Libya, rendered in spite of reservations
about the unpredictability of Mu'ammar al-Qadhafi, contains
the major potential for disruption and the exacerbation of

East-West tensions in the area. In the Horn, he warns of the disruptive effect of the large-scale Soviet involvement in Ethiopia because of Western apprehensions of its potential strategic position astride vital sea lanes. In Southern Africa, says Albright, the greatest danger lies in the equivocal Soviet attitude toward armed struggle between black nationalists and white minority governments, tempered only by Soviet concern for the spillover effect of this armed struggle on the Marxist governments of Angola and Mozambique. Only if the West is able to resolve African disputes and conflicts through effective diplomacy, he believes, is there any prospect of reducing East-West tensions in the area.

The aspect of East-West competition most hotly debated in the United States in the present period is the extent and nature of Communist support for revolutionary movements in Central America. In chapter 3, Jorge Dominguez sifts the evidence for Soviet and Cuban involvement in the area, and suggests several conclusions that bear on U.S. policy and on the prospects for the reduction of tensions in this aspect of the competition in the Third World. From his account of the successive shifts in Cuban and Soviet policy toward Central America and the shifting differences in their policies, he concludes that any successful U.S. effort to deal with the problem must start with the realization that it is both a Soviet and Cuban problem, and perhaps more Cuban than Soviet. Any effort to reduce external support for revolutionary movements in Central America, he argues, must address Cuba as well as the Soviet Union. Although the area is not one of high priority for the Soviet Union, he finds that the Soviets have accelerated weapons deliveries to Nicaragua in response to that country's alarm over the perceived threat of United States military intervention, whereas the Cubans, despite their long history of active support for revolutionary movements, have in the recent period been counseling moderation and support of the Contadora process. But the answer to the Central American problem, Dominguez argues, lies largely inside these countries.

The thorny problem of Cuba in U.S. policy, as a break in the long tradition of the Monroe Doctrine and as a source of military support for Angola and Ethiopia (and Dominguez cites mounting evidence that the decision to send Cuban troops to Angola in 1975 was more Cuban than Soviet), is one that calls for more direct attention to Havana. He notes the emergence of a practical U.S.–Soviet security regime over Cuba and the clear understanding between Havana and Moscow that the Soviet Union would not fight if war broke out in the Western Hemisphere.

Taking account of apprehensions expressed in the United States that, in the event of a conventional war in Europe, Cuba might be a threat to lines of resupply to Europe from ports in the Gulf of Mexico, Dominguez suggests a number of measures by which reciprocal security concessions might assure Cuban neutrality in the event of such a conflict.

With regard to Mexico and South America, Dominguez notes that although the area appears to represent a relatively low priority for the Soviet Union, it has substantially increased its trade with the area in recent years, without apparent regard for ideological considerations. Although the Soviet Union has supplied weapons and military training to Peru, it has received in return some economic, but few political, benefits.

In the Latin American area as a whole, Dominguez concludes that the greatest danger stems from the possibility that the United States may be more panicky than judicious. The great diversion of U.S. military resources to the area is not only costly to our military requirements elsewhere, but in his judgment worsens the situation in Central America and reduces the possibility that military activities by all parties concerned could be more effectively limited by negotiations.

In contrast, Donald Zagoria's survey of the East-West competition in Asia draws our attention to the strategic aspect of the competition as a major, and growing, factor. As we noted earlier, both the United States and the Soviet Union are giving increasing attention to the Pacific theater in the strategic competition, but he points out that the economic dynamism of the area has also been attracting an increasing proportion of United States trade and investment, to the detriment of Soviet influence in the area.

Zagoria's account illustrates the difficulty of drawing up a balance sheet of the relative strengths and weaknesses of the Soviet Union and the United States in Asia. America's long-term strategic supremacy in the Pacific is challenged by the growth of Soviet military power in the area over the past fifteen years and by its access to Cam Ranh Bay, but neither the Soviet Union nor the United States has been able to translate its strategic power into political influence, and both face the prospect of serious potential developments that could affect their relative positions dramatically. On the Soviet side of the ledger, the limitations in its economy, the adverse effects of its invasion of Afghanistan and its support of Vietnam's encroachment into Cambodia, its unwillingness to deal with Japan's northern island issue, and its inability to prevent a growing military collaboration between China and the United States are serious liabilities. Equally, the United States faces the prospect of increasing economic tensions in its relations with Japan, the growing antinuclear sentiment in the South Pacific, instabilities in the Philippines that could threaten U.S. bases at Subic Bay and Clark airfield, and growing Soviet pressures on Pakistan.

Given these and other uncertainties, Zagoria asks, might the time be propitious for the United States to engage the Soviet Union in a broad dialogue on Asian security issues? He takes note of recent Soviet feelers to interested powers to begin discussions on security issues. Without illusions about the cross-cutting competitive interests involved, Zagoria proposes that the United States, after consultation with its allies and friends in the area, explore the possibility that some mutual or overlapping interests might lend themselves to productive arrangements. He cites as a possible example the problem of Korea, detecting in Soviet and North Korean behavior a possible interest in the easement of tension on that peninsula.

Perhaps the recent negotiations to improve air traffic safety in the Pacific area, following the tragedy of Korean Airlines flight 007, might be another pointer in this direction, and conceivably the efforts of the secretary general of the United Nations to explore generally acceptable terms for the settlement of the conflict in Afghanistan might be assisted by such discussions.

Cutting across these four regional chapters, those by Francis Fukuyama and Elizabeth Valkenier examine two important functional aspects of the East-West competition, military and economic.

The military factor, Fukuyama reminds us, occurs both as ends and means in the competition. The pursuit of strategic advantage has been, and in some areas continues to be, a major motivation for the rivalry of the Great Powers in the Third World, but it has so frequently been frustrated by intractable local political conditions that it has become a less impelling motivation than in the past. On the other hand, the military instrumentality—particularly arms transfers, but extending across a spectrum which includes military training, logistical support, the use of allied or proxy combat forces, and, at its extreme end, direct military involvement—although it too has often proved costly, dangerous, and frequently counterproductive, is still a common currency in the competition.

Is the military instrumentality subject to tension-reduction measures? Fukuyama is skeptical. He believes that the prudent and selective application of military force, in conjunction with other instruments of policy, may in some cases be necessary, and that the Great Powers find it too valuable a tool to renounce. He is clearly worried that scruples about the use of military means might unilaterally limit U.S. efforts to impose costs on the Soviet use of force. But the interesting question he leaves open to further examination is whether, in particular cases, explicit or tacit limits on the degree of various forms of military intervention could be useful where both powers share an interest in containing a local conflict situation.

Several interesting and suggestive points emerge from Elizabeth Valkenier's chapter on economic aspects of the East-West competition in the Third World, the product of her familiarity not only with the Soviet source materials, but also with the broader range of discussion and debate among Soviet scholars and policy makers. First of all, she emphasizes the extent of the changes that have taken place in Soviet policy toward the Third World, to which we have alluded earlier. But what is more important in her analysis is the direction of that

change. Increasingly, she finds, pragmatic economic considerations tend to drive Soviet efforts in the Third World, to a
greater degree than has been appreciated in the West. If this
reflects, as she believes, a growing Soviet self-interest in
becoming integrated into an interdependent world economy,
then it should follow, she argues, that a rational response on
the part of the United States would be to encourage Soviet
efforts in this direction. She cautions, however, that the issue
may not be a settled one within the Soviet Union, and she
makes the point that the nature of our reaction inevitably
affects the debate. The thrust of her analysis leads to guard-
edly hopeful expectations for consultations and cooperation
between the two powers in supporting economic growth at
least in some areas of the Third World, as part of a long-term
effort to draw the Soviet Union into finding a self-interest in
playing a more responsible role in international development
and stability.

The six papers in this volume cannot, of course, cover all
aspects of this complex subject or all points of view. They have
been selected to offer within a reasonably short scope a stimulus to discussion and thought about some of the more salient
considerations that would have to be taken into account in any
effort to reduce tensions in the East-West competition in the
Third World. They were written independently, and it is striking how great is their range of differences as to the possible
effectiveness of tension-reduction measures. These differences reflect, first of all, the important point that the problem
differs in significant ways in various parts of the world. They
also reflect differences in the underlying assumptions, not always articulated, about the motivations driving Soviet policy in
the Third World and also about its capacity for change. This
is true of all policy preferences about policy toward the Soviet
Union. The most one can hope to do is to make these underlying assumptions as explicit as possible so that they can be
tested against such evidence as is available to us.

In the past, efforts to find ways to reduce the tensions and
the dangers of the East-West competition in the Third World
have generally followed one of three paths.

The first path has been toward some form of "spheres of

influence" settlement. In a sense, of course, each nation has recognized that certain areas are more vital and sensitive to the other side than other areas, and, as a practical matter, has treated them with greater caution. The Soviet Union has not seemed averse to a more formal "spheres of influence" settlement, but the United States, notwithstanding its attachment to the Monroe Doctrine, has regarded a spheres settlement unacceptable as a matter of principle. In Eastern Europe, for example, the United States has in numerous instances abstained from the use of force in critical situations, but has withheld formal recognition of the area as being within a Soviet sphere, and has relied upon political, economic, and cultural links to encourage a greater degree of autonomy in the area. In the Third World, it seems clear that an effort to stabilize the relationships on the basis of a formal spheres arrangement, even if it were not for the problem of principle, would be impossibly difficult to define.

The second path has been to try to work out a mutually agreed "code of conduct," or what has sometimes been called "rules of the game," governing the competition in the Third World. These efforts have not been successful, mainly because any across-the-board agreements in principle do not take into account the many kinds of problems that arise in particular cases—the differences in intensity of interest in one or another area, the kinds of opportunities that may arise in unexpected ways, the particularities of local politics. Of course, as a practical matter, greater or lesser degrees of restraint may be influenced by the general character of the relationship between the Great Powers at any one time, but, even then, cost-benefit calculations may produce temptations too attractive to resist, and there may not be agreement—as there has not been in the past—on how sensitive the general relationship may be to what has been regarded as the natural behavior of powerful nations in the absence of a strong international system.

This leaves us with a third path, one that is suggested in a number of the following chapters. This is the effort to work out, explicitly or tacitly, specific limitations on the kind or degree of intervention by outside powers in particular local or regional situations. In practice, this has been done through quiet diplomacy in situations that are competitive but in which both sides have an interest in keeping the conflict contained, or where a settlement may be regarded as a matter of mutual interest. The papers in this volume suggest that some situations may be regarded as "zero sum"—that is, one side gains, the other side loses—but that many other situations exist where both sides could lose or both sides could gain, and these could offer opportunities for a degree of cooperation.

There is a final point that should be made, and perhaps it is the most important one. The very title of this volume, *East-West Tensions in the Third World,* tends to focus our attention upon the problems and crises of the Third World as aspects of the competition between the United States and the Soviet Union. But the key lesson of our experience in recent years is that we need to have a better understanding than we do of the local causes of instability in particular areas. This is not to say that we may not have to deal with the problem of outside intervention, whether military or political, when it occurs, but this can only be the negative side of our approach, which may be necessary on occasion, but is not sufficient, unless it is supplemented by measures that address the sources of disaffection and instability. We simply do not know enough about local cultures, languages, politics, history, and living conditions. To be effective, our responses to troubled local situations must also be timely; if we direct our attention to these areas only after they have erupted in a revolutionary upsurge, the political middle ground is destroyed, and the only solution that is left is a military arbitration between equally unsavory extremes. If democracy, in whatever form, is to have a chance of developing and surviving under the difficult circumstances in which most people in the Third World live, it needs to have understanding and constructive support before things reach a crisis stage. The point is that we cannot allow the East-West competitive aspect of local conflict situations to obscure our understanding of the local circumstances involved in each place where conflict occurs.

2

U.S.-Soviet Rivalry in the Middle East

The Middle East, more than any other region of the Third World, has been the focus of intense and sustained rivalry between the United States and the Soviet Union in the period since World War II. The area reaching from Morocco to Afghanistan has witnessed some of the most dangerous international crises of the past forty years. On numerous occasions, Moscow and Washington have seemed to be on the verge of direct confrontation in the Middle East. Even the use of nuclear weapons has been contemplated. But to date the two superpowers have always pulled back from the brink, generally pursuing their competition through means short of direct military intervention.

During this turbulent period in the Middle East, both superpowers have succeeded on occasions in dramatically extending their influence in the region, often at the expense of the

WILLIAM B. QUANDT is Senior Fellow, The Brookings Institution. Dr. Quandt has written extensively on the Middle East for more than fifteen years; his work includes four books and numerous articles. He has taught at several universities and served as senior staff member, National Security Council (Middle East).

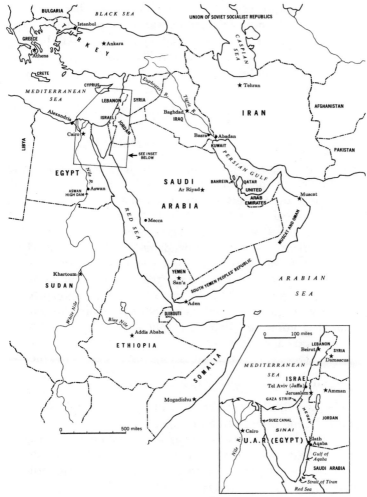

THE MIDDLE EAST

other, but these gains have sometimes proved to be only temporary, and control over events has often remained elusive. Neither superpower can claim to have established a secure sphere of influence, and neither can be sure that the large investments made will assure that vital interests will be protected. Nonetheless, neither seems likely to tire of the game, and, thus, the Middle East will remain an arena of competition, where the rules are not clearly defined and the stakes remain extremely high.

Superpower Interests

Both the United States and the Soviet Union look at the Middle East region with a variety of interests in mind. On one level, the Middle East is just another arena for a rivalry that has become global in the post–World War II world. From this perspective, any gain in influence by one superpower in this region will be seen as a potential danger to the interests of the other and will bring into play some countervailing effort. During periods of particularly acute tensions between Moscow and Washington, the Middle East may become an especially dangerous region. But even in periods of detente, the competition has gone on, tempered only slightly by attempts to define limits and set rules.

Significance in Military Considerations

The Middle East, for reasons of geography, has been of particular importance to both superpowers. The Soviets have thought of the region as contiguous to their borders and, therefore, as an area to be kept free of military threats. For the same reason of proximity to the Soviet Union, the United States has sought to project power from bases and facilities in the Middle East. The United States has, at various times, sought to develop military bases in the region as part of its global policy of countering Soviet military power. In countries such as Iran, Saudi Arabia, Turkey, Libya, Morocco, and Oman, the United States has had, at least for short periods, access to military facilities and intelligence outposts. Some of these are still in operation, and are highly valued. Others have been lost or abandoned as the political tides of the region have changed. Apart from bases, the United States has generally favored the principle of free passage through the waterways of the region, especially the Strait of Gibraltar, the Suez Canal, and the Strait of Hormuz leading into the Persian Gulf. But when the Suez Canal was closed after the 1967 war, the United States was able to adjust quite easily, and some even felt that its closure was more of a burden for the Soviets than for the Americans.

The Soviets have done less than the Americans to develop bases in the region, but they too have found advantage in creating military facilities in countries such as Egypt until 1972, and more recently South Yemen and Ethiopia. In the late 1960s, the Soviets came very close to attaining bases in Egypt, but Egyptian political sensitivities were so strong that in 1972 most Soviet military advisers were obliged to leave Egypt, and soon thereafter relations took a sharp turn for the worse.

Traditionally, the Soviets have been concerned with the waterways of the region, especially the Dardanelles in Turkey, which controls naval movements between the Black Sea and the Mediterranean. Originally the Soviets, and before them the czars, sought to keep hostile powers out of the Black Sea by trying to gain control over the Dardanelles. Later the Soviet interest developed to include access into the Mediterranean for its growing fleet. At a time when a significant portion of the U.S. nuclear deterrent consisted of missiles on Polaris submarines in the Mediterranean, the Soviets placed great emphasis on building up their Mediterranean fleet. During this period, air and naval facilities in Egypt also became a high priority. As technology evolved in the 1970s and the United States developed longer-range missiles for Poseidon and Trident submarines, the Mediterranean ceased to be such an important arena of naval competition.

Much has been made of the supposed Soviet interest in access to warm water ports as a motivating consideration in

Soviet policy toward the Persian Gulf. But the Gulf is a peculiarly poor location for a Soviet naval base, since in wartime the Gulf could be easily closed off. Ports elsewhere suffer from the disadvantage of being far from secure lines of communication. Thus, the Soviets seem to have realized that a secure naval base in the Middle East cannot be readily attained. Instead, a number of facilities in the vicinity of Bab el-Mandeb at the southern end of the Red Sea seem to serve their naval interests and point to a strategic concern that has received comparatively little attention in the West, namely the ability to control shipping by closing the southern end of the Red Sea.

If the global superpower rivalry and clashing strategic interests account for much of the involvement of the two major powers in the Middle East, these facts do not determine the specific way in which their competition has worked itself out. To some degree, both superpowers have been opportunistic, exploiting developments that they had little to do with bringing about. Often they have sought to benefit from the mistakes of one another. This can be seen most clearly in a case like Egypt, where both the United States and the Soviet Union have enjoyed good relations followed by serious problems that have resulted in a reversal of alliances by the Egyptian leaders.

Economic Concerns

On the dimension of economic interests, the United States has clearly developed a much deeper commitment than the Soviet Union. This has taken the form primarily of intensive involvement with the development of the petroleum resources of the region, especially in the Persian Gulf and in Saudi Arabia. Oil has been a commercial and strategic concern for the United States. American oil companies have earned billions of dollars from their operations in the Middle East. The economic recovery of Europe and Japan after World War II was fueled in good measure by inexpensive oil from the Middle East. Even when oil ceased to be inexpensive in the 1970s, and the United States itself became dependent on imports from the Middle East, the United States had a deep interest in how the petrodollar-surplus countries disposed of their sudden new wealth. The volume of American trade with the Middle East soared in the 1970s, as did the level of Arab investment of their new wealth in the United States.

For the Soviet Union, concrete economic interests have counted for less in the Middle East than they have for the United States. Still, the Soviets have shown an interest in developing the gas resources of both Iran and Afghanistan and have tried to work out advantageous terms for importing their gas into the USSR. Arms sales for hard currency to countries like Libya, Syria, and Iraq have also been of some benefit to the Soviets. On balance, however, the Soviet interest in the Middle East cannot be understood primarily in economic terms.

Domestic Concerns of the Superpowers

In somewhat different ways, both superpowers have also been drawn to the Middle East by their own internal concerns. For the Soviet Union, this interest derives from the existence of a very large Muslim population within its own borders with ties of kinship and ethnicity to Muslims in Turkey, Iran, and Afghanistan.

For the United States, it is the existence of an influential Jewish community with a deep commitment to Israel that adds a special dimension to American involvement with the Middle East. No other country retains such a close set of ties to Israel as does the United States, in large measure because of the efforts of the American Jewish community. By contrast, the sizable Jewish population in the Soviet Union is more a cause of friction between Israel and the Soviet regime, since Moscow has been hostile to the idea that Israel has a special claim to defend the interests of Soviet Jewry.

Added to all of the above impulses to action is the ideological dimension of the U.S.–Soviet rivalry. Both superpowers have sought to promote the interests of political groups that share their values. The Soviets have been active in encouraging the development of Communist parties, and the Ameri-

cans have thrown their weight on occasions behind those who
support free markets and are pro-Western. But the Soviets
often have been willing to overlook the interests of the local
Communist parties if that suited their broader interests, and
the United States has certainly felt free to deal with a variety
of regimes and movements that have had little in common with
American political values. Ideology colors the rivalry, and the
rhetoric of both superpowers is imbued with it, but ideological
zeal does not go very far in explaining either U.S. or Soviet
foreign policy in the Middle East.

Regional Political Dynamics

Both the United States and the Soviet Union have had multiple reasons to seek influence in the Middle East, but competing interests alone do not explain the dynamics of U.S.–Soviet
rivalry in the region. After all, the states in the Middle East
have not been passive pawns in the struggle between the
giants, nor have they always been manipulated and pressured
against their will. Developments within the Middle East have
often caught the superpowers by surprise, sometimes creating
opportunities, other times posing difficult dilemmas.

The ability of the superpowers to intervene in the Middle
East has been facilitated by widespread instability and persistent regional conflicts. The root causes of the turmoil in the
Middle East region are complex, but in one sense this is a
region that has witnessed the demise of the broad organizing
principle of imperial control that was upheld in different ways
by both the Ottoman Empire and the subsequent period of
European colonial rule. A viable new formula has not yet been
fully developed, although the modern state system seems to
have taken root and has developed a dynamism and an equilib-
rium of its own.

Anticolonialism and Nationalism

What the Ottomans and the colonial powers had in common
was that they provided a system of control and a set of rules

that kept a semblance of order among the competing ethnic and religious groups of the region. In time, of course, both collapsed because of their own weaknesses and limitations as well as their inability to meet growing demands for political participation on the part of increasingly self-conscious populations. Nationalism became the new rallying cry, and it proved to be enormously successful in mobilizing support against the colonial systems of rule. It promised not only independence, but also social justice.

The first phase of anticolonial struggle for many in the Middle East was against the Ottoman caliphate centered in Istanbul. For many Muslims this proved to be a difficult political choice, since the Ottomans had represented Islamic legitimacy for at least 400 years. Still, young Turks took the lead in breaking with the sultanate after World War I, and young Arab nationalists in Egypt, Syria, Iraq, and Palestine were not far behind in mounting their own movements for political independence.

Drawing on quite different sources, at about the same time, Jewish nationalism, or Zionism, came to the Middle East with the dream of recreating a Jewish state in the Holy Land. Lagging a bit behind were the nationalist movements of North Africa, but by the 1930s they too were in full swing. By the 1920s and 1930s, it was British and French colonial rule, which had succeeded the Ottoman Empire, that was the main target of nationalist agitation.

Neither the United States nor the Soviet Union was much involved in Middle Eastern affairs during the period of intense anticolonial struggle in the 1930s. It was only after World War II, with the weakening of the systems of British and French rule in much of the region and the emergence, over the opposition of the Arabs, of a Jewish state in part of Palestine, that both superpowers began the relentless search to fill what they mistakenly believed to be a political vacuum.

Each in its own way, Moscow and Washington had postured as anticolonial and sympathetic to the aspirations of the newly independent countries. Both tried to evoke their own revolutionary traditions and more recent experiences of governing and building industrial economies as somehow relevant to the problems facing the new leaders of the region. Some Middle Easterners, no doubt, were drawn to Marxism-Leninism and naturally turned to the Soviets for assistance; others upheld liberal democratic values and found in Washington a natural ally.

The Challenge of Independence

It was not just the ideas of the superpowers that found a market in the newly independent polities of the Middle East. Leaders wanted economic aid, and they very quickly developed an enormous appetite for guns as well. Inevitably, the two strongest powers in the world were seen as the most likely sources of both. Money and technology might bring development and enhance legitimacy by redeeming some of the promises of a better life raised by the struggle for independence; arms could insure that regimes could keep themselves in power against challenges from without and within.

It took some time for the superpowers to learn how to turn the ambitions of new leaders to their advantage, but before long they proved more than willing to play the "game of nations," as one participant labeled it. Sometimes Moscow and Washington found themselves briefly on the same side, as in their simultaneous decisions to recognize the state of Israel in 1948. Sometimes they competed for influence, as with Egypt in the early period of President Gamal Abdel Nasser. Some countries, such as Iran under the Shah, seemed to be the preserve of Washington; while in recent years South Yemen has appeared to be a Soviet outpost. Others, such as Algeria and Iraq, try to maneuver between the superpowers, taking from both without giving too much.

If the collapse of the colonial empires and the emergence of nationalism set the stage for the entry of the superpowers into the Middle East, nationalism has also been a barrier against either power's gaining a firm sphere of influence. Local leaders may often be weak and dependent, but they cling tenaciously to their prerogatives and gain stature by showing that they can stand up to bigger powers. Yet they cannot shake their dependency, however proud and independent they may be. They need capital, investment, technology, markets, and arms. Their internal weakness makes them susceptible to outside influence; their persistent quarrels with their neighbors create another form of dependency. Rare is the country in the Middle East that turns its back on both superpowers and strives for self-sufficiency.

Islamic Revival

The one political current in the region that has tried hardest to break the grip of dependency on the superpowers has been militant Islam. The most notable example of this ideology in action has been the Islamic Republic of Iran, with its slogan of "neither East nor West" and its description of both the United States and the Soviet Union as satanic powers. Since coming to power in 1979, Ayatollah Khomeini has kept his distance from both major powers, and despite an enormously costly war with Iraq he has not turned to either for significant quantities of weapons.

Neither outside power has quite known what to make of the resurgence in the power of Islam. It hardly fits classical Marxist theory to see revolution carried out in the name of religion by men whose inspiration lies in the seventh century and whose social codes are seemingly medieval. Nor do Americans, with their pragmatism and secularism, know quite what to make of true believers who are prepared to die for their religion. The Soviets were doubtless pleased to see the Islamic revolution topple the Shah, who had been such a close ally of the United States, but they were considerably less happy a few years later when the Communist party of Iran, the Tudeh, was decimated and its leaders accused of spying for the Soviet Union.

On occasions, Americans have indulged the illusion that the Islamic movement could be turned to pro-Western purposes. After all, some said, militant Muslims believe in God, and thus must be more opposed to atheistic communism than to Western societies, which accord religion a place of respect. In Afghanistan, where resistance against Soviet occupation is carried out by nationalists who invoke Allah's name, the Americans have found it convenient to support an Islamic resistance movement. However, the contemporaneous example of Shiite anger in Lebanon being turned against American targets in the mid-1980s should help to dispel the notion that the Islamic movement in the Middle East is more anti-Soviet than anti-American. Both superpowers, depending on circumstances, can find themselves the targets of Muslim anger, and on occasions both may be able to benefit from Muslim militancy. But the point about the current wave of Islamic sensitivity in the Middle East is that it rejects the models and support of both superpowers. It looks for inspiration from within its own traditions, and it fears the manipulative intentions of outside powers.

In this sense, Islamic militancy is quite different from the nationalist period that preceded it and whose failures are one of the reasons for its rise. As much as the nationalist leaders were suspicious of the East and West, they still drew most of their political and economic ideas from them.

Shifting Patterns of Superpower Competition

While the two superpowers have been rivals for influence in the Middle East since World War II, the focus of their rivalry has shifted several times. In part this has been the result of changes in perceived interests, and in part it has reflected changes in regional alignments and in the balance of power.

In the immediate postwar period, the United States and the Soviet Union engaged in some of the first skirmishes of the so-called cold war in the Middle East. Out of these contests the United States developed a policy of "containment" of Soviet influence, codified in the Truman Doctrine of 1947.

The "Northern Tier"

Iran and Turkey, two countries bordering on the Soviet Union, were at the center of the developments that pitted the

United States against the USSR in the immediate aftermath of
World War II. As part of a wartime agreement, Soviet troops
had occupied part of northern Iran, but were pledged to leave
once the war was over. In due course, and after considerable
hesitation, the Soviet troops were removed, but they left behind pro-Soviet governments in the provinces of Azerbaijan
and Kurdistan. With some encouragement from the United
States, Iran's young Shah ordered his troops into Azerbaijan
to depose the Communist regime there. The move was successful and Soviet troops stayed on their side of the border.
For the Truman administration, this was an early and inexpensive demonstration that Soviet expansion could be checked.
When the Soviets subsequently made threats against Turkey,
the United States was quick to respond with support, both
economic and military. Once again, Soviet moves were relatively easily blocked.

In this period, the United States was successful in preventing Soviet expansion into the so-called Northern Tier of the
Middle East. In time, Turkey was made a formal member of
the North Atlantic Treaty Organization (NATO) alliance, and
Iran also became an ally of the United States, especially after
a successful pro-Shah intervention in 1953. For most of the
next two decades, the lines of demarcation between U.S. interests and Soviet interests were fairly clearly drawn in this part
of the Middle East.

Competition in the Arab World

If the Northern Tier could be seen as something of a success
story in postwar U.S. diplomacy, the same could not be said
of the Arab world. There the picture was much more complicated, and the maneuverings of the two superpowers became
intense. World War II had irreparably shaken the hold of the
British and the French over their colonial possessions, including those in the Middle East, although the final dismantling of
empires would be long and painful. Both Washington and
Moscow quickly recognized that a new era was opening in
much of the Arab Middle East after the war, and both sought

to take advantage of the new situation.

The American objective was to ease the transition from colonial rule to independence under pro-Western moderate leaders. The Soviets also wanted to hasten the end of colonial rule, but they were interested in thwarting American plans to organize the Arab world, as had occurred in the Northern Tier, into an anti-Soviet containment zone.

Two central issues emerged in the U.S.–Soviet contest in the Arab world: one involved Israel, and the other centered on efforts to organize a pro-Western defense alliance linked to Turkey and Iran. Zionism had long been a sensitive issue in the Arab world, and a whole series of Arab leaders had been frustrated in their attempts to prevent the creation of a Jewish state in Palestine. Even after the General Armistice Agreements in 1949, Arabs seemed to be unreconciled to Israel's existence.

In 1950 the United States, joined by Britain and France, tried to stabilize the Arab-Israeli arena by pledging support for the borders set by the armistice agreements and by asserting that arms transfers to the region would be carefully controlled. Shortly thereafter, the British took the lead, with general encouragement from the United States, in organizing a region-wide defense effort that would include countries such as Iraq, Jordan, and Lebanon, and perhaps Egypt as well.

The best laid of plans have a way of coming unraveled in the Middle East, often because of internal upheavals in key countries of the region. This was the case in the mid-1950s as a result of developments in Egypt. The monarchy had been overthrown in an army coup in 1952. A Free Officers Movement had come to power, and it soon became clear that the real power was a young colonel named Gamal Abdel Nasser.

Nasser, Soviet Arms, and Suez

By 1955 Nasser had already succeeded in eliminating his rivals and consolidating his power, and he was now ready to turn to his foreign policy agenda. First and foremost he wanted the British to leave their large base at Suez. Second, he wanted to prevent the formation of an Iraqi-centered pro-Western alliance in the Arab world. Third, he wanted arms to rebuild the strength of his army, in part as a counterweight to the increasingly menacing forces of Israel.

Nasser was an ambitious leader who was prepared to seek support for his goals from either the West or East. Initially, he maintained close contacts with the United States and even conducted secret talks with Israel through American inter-mediaries. He also sought American economic and technolog-ical assistance, especially in the form of the Aswan High Dam. And he tried to buy American arms.

Early in 1955, Nasser was confronted by two simultaneous challenges to his regional leadership. Britain proposed that Iraq should join a pro-Western alliance, for which it would be rewarded with substantial quantities of arms, and Israel struck at Egyptian forces in Gaza, ostensibly in retaliation for guer-rilla attacks by Palestinians. Nasser's response was to proceed with a plan for strengthening his armed forces, this time with Soviet assistance. The so-called Czech-Egyptian arms deal was publicly revealed in September 1955, but dates from earlier in the year. Its effect on Washington was substantial.

While President Dwight D. Eisenhower and Secretary of State John Foster Dulles were clearly disillusioned with Nasser after his decision to turn to the Soviets for arms, they re-sponded with one last effort to compete for influence in Egypt. An effort was made once again to engage Nasser in secret peace talks with Israel, with the offer of financing for the Aswan High Dam as a sweetener. Early in 1956, those talks came to an unsuccessful end, and by midyear the Ameri-cans told Nasser that money for the dam would not be forth-coming.

Nasser reacted to Washington's rebuff by announcing that he would nationalize the Suez Canal and use the toll revenues to build the dam. Britain and France decided to teach Nasser a lesson. They secretly conspired with Israel, without inform-ing Washington, and in late October 1956, Israeli forces in-vaded the Sinai Peninsula. Britain and France, citing alleged danger to the Suez Canal, thereupon sent their forces into the

Canal Zone, obviously hoping in the process to unseat Nasser. They had not counted on the American response.

Eisenhower was furious. His closest allies had kept him in the dark and had taken actions that could have disastrous consequences. Eisenhower wasted no time in pressing for an end to the fighting and a withdrawal of British, French, and Israeli forces from Egypt. The Soviets, as well, opposed the tripartite attack on Egypt, but Nasser knew that it was American pressure that had saved him.

Eisenhower had not acted at Suez out of any pro-Egyptian motives. It was not surprising, then, that U.S.–Egyptian relations quickly reverted to hostility, especially in 1957 as the Americans began to see Nasser behind many of their troubles in the region. For most of the next decade, it was the Soviets who built up their position in Egypt, supplying arms and even assisting in the construction of the Aswan High Dam. By the mid-1960s, the Soviets counted Nasser as one of their closest allies in the Third World.

Arab-Israeli Wars: 1967 and 1973

If American policy in the Northern Tier and Soviet policy in Egypt can each be seen as success stories for at least limited periods of time, the next major development, the Arab-Israeli war of 1967, left a much more ambiguous legacy for both superpowers. While it would be wrong to say that either Moscow or Washington wanted to see a Middle East war in 1967 between Israel and Egypt, it is probably fair to say that the Soviets were careless in planting some of the seeds that grew into a full-fledged crisis in May 1967, and that the Americans did not do as much as they might have to prevent war in the first week of June 1967.

In military terms, the war was a clear-cut Israeli victory. Egyptian, Jordanian, and Syrian forces had all been routed, and Israel was in occupation of the Sinai, the West Bank, Gaza, and the Golan Heights. Soviet threats had done little to check the Israeli advances, especially since the Americans stood firmly with the Jewish state.

Nasser survived the war, but his prestige was badly tarnished, and his vision of pan-Arabism had suffered a nearly fatal blow. Many Arabs resented the Soviets for their lack of effective support, but they were even more angered by U.S. assistance to Israel. Egypt, Syria, Iraq, and Algeria all broke diplomatic relations with Washington. The Soviets quickly moved to rebuild their ties to their Arab allies, and arms and diplomatic support began to flow in late 1967 in large quantities. More than ever, the Arab-Israeli conflict was beginning to reflect the superpower rivalry.

Washington and Moscow were, however, able to agree on one aspect of the Arab-Israeli dispute: if a peaceful settlement were to be achieved, it should be based on United Nations Resolution 242, which called for the return of lands occupied by Israel in the 1967 war in exchange for Arab commitments to peace and recognition of secure borders for Israel. Apart from this limited area of agreement, the United States and USSR seemed to be on a collision course.

At least three times between 1969 and 1974 the two powers seemed to be on the verge of direct military confrontation. The first time involved Soviet forces in the air defense of Egypt during the "War of Attrition" in 1969–70. The second took place in September 1970, when Syrian forces crossed the Jordanian border in support of Palestinians who were in confrontation with King Hussein. The third and most dangerous came during the October 1973 war, when President Richard Nixon responded to Soviet threats to intervene in the region by declaring a worldwide military alert.

The 1973 war turned out to be a major watershed in the competition between the superpowers. Soviet influence in Egypt had now peaked, and in the period following the October war it was quickly replaced by American influence. Egypt's President Anwar Sadat had clearly decided to gamble on the United States as best able to help Egypt solve its internal and external problems. This meant, of course, doing without Soviet arms, a decision of great consequence for Egypt, because it meant that Sadat could not hope to win Egypt's Israeli-held territory through war. Diplomacy offered the alternative, and after five years of intensive negotiations, including the historic Camp David Accords of September 1978, an Egyptian-Israeli peace treaty was signed in March 1979 in Washington, D.C. Rarely has one superpower replaced another so quickly.

Syria, however, remained firmly tied to the Soviets and adamantly opposed to Sadat's diplomatic strategy. Inter-Arab relations came to reflect not only the polarization between Washington and Moscow, but also that between Cairo and Damascus.

Iran in Revolution

The Egyptian-Israeli treaty was signed against a background of anxiety caused by the success of the Islamic revolution in Iran in February 1979. The previous month, the long-time ally of the United States, the Shah of Iran, had left his country, never to return. The forbidding figure of Ayatollah Khomeini returned to Tehran to claim power, and in ensuing years seemed determined to root out all signs of American influence from his country. American facilities were closed down, the embassy was occupied, American diplomats were held hostage for over one year, and political, economic, and military links were almost entirely severed.

The year 1979 turned out to be of historic importance not only because of the Iranian revolution. Toward the end of the year, the Soviets, unable to maintain political influence in Afghanistan, launched a massive military invasion of the country. As many as 100,000 Soviet troops were garrisoned around the major cities in order to keep an unpopular Communist government in power. Meanwhile, much of the countryside came under the control of various resistance groups. In time, the United States and its allies found themselves in the somewhat novel position of encouraging Islamic guerrilla fighters against a Soviet-supported government.

The events in Iran and Afghanistan in 1979 drew attention to the Persian Gulf region as an emerging zone of superpower competition. Long a British-dominated area, the gulf in the 1970s was largely influenced by the fact of Iran's military build-up, a development which had full U.S. support under the so-called Nixon Doctrine. When the Shah's regime collapsed, a new balance of power emerged. For a while, Iraq seemed to be the regional power to reckon with, but its decision to invade Iran in 1980 proved to be based on faulty premises about the strength of the Khomeini regime. By 1982 Iran had expelled most Iraqi troops from Iran, and the stage was set for a prolonged and bloody military stalemate.

Both the United States and the Soviet Union were somewhat unsure of how to react to the new situation in the Persian Gulf. Iran's new regime was an enigma, although both powers clearly maintained a long-term interest in Iran. For quite different reasons, however, by 1984 they both found themselves backing the Iraqi regime, although without great enthusiasm.

For the Americans, the turmoil in the gulf region and the Soviet invasion of Afghanistan raised the fear of a Soviet military move toward the gulf oil fields. In January 1980 President Jimmy Carter lent his name to a statement of policy that made clear that the United States would use force if necessary to defend its interests in the region. The problem, however, was that such forces were not readily available and would have difficulty overcoming the formidable logistical problems of projecting military power halfway around the world without secure bases in the region itself. Nonetheless, a start was made, originally with a rapid deployment force, soon to be renamed and reorganized as the "Central Command."

By the mid-1980s, American forces had gained some experience with Middle Eastern contingencies; exercises had been held in the region; access to facilities in Egypt, Somalia, Kenya, and Oman had been negotiated; and improvements had been made in mobility and the pre-positioning of heavy equipment near the gulf. Still, no one thought that the United States was in a position to prevail in a conventional war in the gulf against an all-out Soviet effort. After all, the Soviets could call on more than twenty divisions stationed to the north of Iran, plus approximately seven airborne divisions, as well as large numbers of combat aircraft capable of operating from bases within the Soviet Union itself.

The Reagan Era

President Carter had been slow in coming to view the Middle East as part of the global arena of U.S.–Soviet rivalry. His successor, Ronald Reagan, initially saw the region almost exclusively in those terms. During the election campaign of 1980, Reagan was quoted as saying that there would be no problems anywhere in the world unless the Soviets were involved. To some degree this may have been rhetorical, but it also seemed to reflect a genuine concern that Soviet power had grown to the point where it could threaten U.S. interests anywhere in the world.

With such an outlook, the Reagan administration naturally began to try to organize its friends in the Middle East into a loosely structured anti-Soviet alliance. In the words of Secretary of State Alexander Haig, a "strategic consensus" should be forged to contain Moscow's influence in the region. Traditional adversaries such as Israel and Saudi Arabia should be brought to recognize their overriding common interest in checking Soviet expansion.

The main problem with the idea of "strategic consensus" was that it did not accord well with the realities of the Middle East. Israel and Saudi Arabia, for example, both were more concerned with threats closer to home than with plots hatched in Moscow. So when the Reagan administration put its theory to the test by trying to sell sophisticated military equipment to the Saudis, the Israelis were vehement in their opposition. Before long, many in the Reagan administration were saying that further progress would have to be made in resolving regional conflicts before an effective anti-Soviet alliance could be created.

The regional conflict that proved to be most threatening to regional stability in the early 1980s was Lebanon. For years Israel and the Palestine Liberation Organization (PLO) had sparred with one another in south Lebanon, and on numerous occasions the situation seemed ready to explode. Finally, in June 1982 the Israeli government decided to go to war in

Lebanon to crush the PLO. The architect of the Israeli plan, General Ariel Sharon, also seemed to believe that Syria could be defeated in Lebanon and forced to withdraw its substantial military presence. Some in Washington apparently shared Sharon's vision and hoped that an Israeli victory over the PLO and the Syrians would deal a heavy blow to Soviet influence in the Middle East.

By the second week of the war, it was clear that Israel could easily occupy all of south Lebanon and force the PLO to retreat to Beirut. Syrian forces were unable or unwilling to do much to help the PLO, but did fight tenaciously on the ground when attacked by the Israelis. When it seemed as if Sharon were intent on destroying Syria's armored strength in Lebanon, the Soviet leadership began to react. General Secretary Leonid Brezhnev contacted Reagan several times, warning that Israel should stop its onslaught against Syria's forces. Reagan passed this message on to the Israelis, and by the end of the second week a shaky cease-fire had emerged between Israel and Syria. As in 1967 and 1973, the superpowers had shown that they were sensitive to the possibility of local conflicts escalating to dangerous levels.

The Israeli war in Lebanon had several unintended consequences. First, it made the American leadership more aware of the danger of leaving regional issues to fester. In particular, it reminded the Reagan administration of the need to address the Palestinian question in a new way. On September 1, 1982, Reagan gave a speech on the Middle East in which he spelled out the U.S. view on a negotiating process that should result in the return of most of the West Bank to joint Jordanian-Palestinian authority as part of an overall peace settlement with Israel. The Israeli government under Menachem Begin's leadership immediately rejected the American proposal.

In time, the Reagan initiative faded as American efforts were devoted to a plan for an Israeli-Lebanese peace agreement, coupled to the withdrawal of Syrian troops from Lebanon. The Americans did not take adequately into account, however, the Syrian determination to resist such designs, nor did Reagan realize until it was too late that the Soviets were determined to back their Syrian ally to the hilt. Throughout much of 1983, the United States and Israel sought to impose their plans on Lebanon, while Syria, with Soviet support, tried to thwart them. By year's end, the United States and Syria were on the verge of a military confrontation.

American public opinion seemed to have little understanding of Reagan's policy, and pressures began to grow, especially in Congress, for a disengagement from Lebanon. In February 1984, just as the electoral campaign was beginning, and in the face of a collapse of the Lebanese army, Reagan decided to withdraw the U.S. Marine contingent that had been dug in around the Beirut airport.

The Lebanon war taught harsh lessons to the United States. It was a reminder that ambitious strategies cannot be built on weak foundations. It also reinforced the view that the United States should use some of its influence in the Middle East to promote diplomatic solutions to problems such as the Israeli-Palestinian conflict. Finally, it drove home the dangers of armed conflict between clients of the two superpowers.

The Arab-Israeli arena saw the two superpowers on the brink of confrontation, but, surprisingly, this was not the case in the Persian Gulf, where just such a confrontation had been feared. Instead, the Iranian revolution and the Iran-Iraq war both unfolded without significant involvement by either Moscow or Washington. Both powers showed caution and restraint, perhaps out of an awareness of how quickly tensions could grow in such a strategically important area.

The relative caution shown by both superpowers in the gulf in the early 1980s, however, did not seem to portend long-term stability there. Instead, it was as if both powers were seeking to keep their options open, not wanting to take excessive risks, but certainly not preparing to abandon interest in the region. With Iran still under the leadership of Khomeini, neither the United States nor the Soviet Union had good prospects of gaining a position of influence in Iran, but after Khomeini the competition easily could resume. This raised the question of how effectively the ideology of Islamic revival could guide Iran on a genuinely nonaligned course.

Patterns of Influence

By the mid-1980s, the Middle East presented a complex mosaic in terms of the superpower rivalry. In some regions, such as the Maghreb states of Morocco, Algeria, and Tunisia, the rivalry was muted, and nationalism and nonalignment remained serious political themes. Libya, however, was a different matter. There, Soviet influence was strong, and President Mu'ammar al-Qadhafi was a force for instability throughout the Middle East and Africa.

By contrast, Egypt was closely aligned with the United States but, nonetheless, determined to demonstrate independence on some regional issues. The scale of the U.S. economic and military programs in Egypt was vast, approaching two billion dollars per year in the mid-1980s, raising questions about the potential for Egyptian resentment if economic development were to slow or regional conflicts involving Egypt were to increase. The Americans had only to look at the fate of the comparably large Soviet presence in the early 1970s to wonder about the future of the relationship.

To Egypt's south, Sudan represented a potentially troublesome area. An army coup in April 1985 removed a corrupt but pro-Western regime, and the new leaders were slow to define their new policies. To the consternation of the Egyptians, however, Sudanese-Libyan relations seemed to warm up.

In the Arabian Peninsula, the United States still enjoyed a privileged position in Saudi Arabia and most of the small Persian Gulf emirates. The United Arab Emirates, Kuwait, and Oman, maintained diplomatic relations with Moscow as of late 1985, and others could be expected to follow their lead. Moscow was certainly willing and had no inhibitions in courting conservative, monarchical regimes.

In South Yemen, of course, the Soviets had a strong foothold, including access to military facilities, and the United States was completely absent. Coupled with the substantial Soviet presence across the Red Sea in Ethiopia, the Soviets had acquired a strategically important position. North Yemen was an arena of muted competition between the two super-powers, both of whom provided some military assistance to a rather shaky regime.

To the north, the United States was the predominant out-side power in both Jordan and Israel. This relationship should have made it possible for Washington to help broker a peace agreement between the two, but the United States was unwill-ing to include the PLO in the effort, and that placed severe limits on how far the Jordanians could go on their own. In addition, Syria, with strong Soviet support, was opposed to any separate agreement between Israel and Jordan that would leave the remainder of the Arab-Israeli conflict untouched.

Some Americans maintained that Israel, because of its strength and its democratic political system, constituted the only reliable bulwark against Soviet expansion in the area. But by the mid-1980s, that proposition was hardly beyond dispute. The Israeli economy was in serious disrepair, requiring several billion dollars annually in U.S. assistance. In addition, the Lebanon war, while weakening the PLO, had done nothing to dislodge the Soviets from their strong position in Syria or to moderate the policies of the Syrian regime. And Israel's much-vaunted military might had little relevance to the popular dis-content that represented a serious challenge to stability throughout the region.

Iran and Iraq fell into a gray area in the U.S.–Soviet compe-tition. Iraq, desperately trying to ward off threats from Iran, was prepared to turn for help to Saudi Arabia, France, and even the United States. But the Soviets also were providing arms, and there was no reason to conclude that Iraq would follow Egypt in making a full break with Moscow. Meanwhile, Iran remained essentially aloof from the superpower rivalry.

The eventual outcome of the Iran-Iraq war could have sig-nificant consequences for how the United States and the USSR compete in this region. To date, the two superpowers have demonstrated a surprising degree of restraint. This suggests that it may be possible for tacit understandings to emerge which will help to limit the danger of superpower confronta-tions in future regional crises. However, one could just as well argue that restraint has been imposed by the lack of opportunity to make significant gains in influence without incurring major risks. Once Iran enters the post-Khomeini era it will be easier to judge the intentions of both Moscow and Washington in this region.

Of the countries under review, Afghanistan seemed most firmly under the control of an outside power as of the mid-1980s. It was the only country in the Middle East that was literally occupied by the military forces of one of the superpowers. Although the Soviets were clearly having difficulty subduing the resistance in the countryside, and the Communist government in Kabul seemed to have little support, it was hard to imagine any reduction of Soviet control in the near future. A withdrawal of Soviet forces would mean the collapse of a pro-Soviet regime, and its replacement would not necessarily be neutral. The Soviets had invested heavily in bringing Afghanistan into their sphere of influence, and the United States reluctantly had acquiesced. Apart from trying to make the price of occupying Afghanistan high for the Soviets, Washington seemed unable to do much.

Unlike Afghanistan, the political orientation of several key Arab states is still an open question, dependent to some extent on how the Arab-Israeli conflict evolves. Throughout much of the 1950s and 1960s, this dispute provided the opening wedge for much of the superpower intervention in the Middle East. With the achievement of peace between Egypt and Israel, many expected that Soviet influence would begin to fade throughout the Arab world. This assumption, however, was based on the belief that further Arab military challenges to Israel were impossible once Egypt had made peace. In time, other Arab countries would presumably follow Sadat's lead and make peace on whatever terms were available. To date, however, this has not happened, and Syria, at least, seems to be trying to develop a military capability, with Soviet support, to stand up to the Israelis.

If peace negotiations between Israel and her other Arab neighbors fail to produce results, several developments could occur which would affect the positions of both superpowers.

First, the Egyptian-Israeli relationship could come under strain, and this would inevitably weaken American support for Egypt, opening the way for at least a modest improvement in Egyptian-Soviet relations. Second, Jordan, which has counted heavily on U.S. support, could become disillusioned with American-led peace efforts and might revert to a much more intransigent posture. Islamic influences could grow in a number of Arab countries, exploiting the theme that pro-American regimes had failed to recover Palestine and Jerusalem.

In Israel itself, prolonged stalemate on the diplomatic front could strengthen the hand of hard-liners, putting off for the indefinite future any possibility of Arab-Israeli accommodation. It is hard to imagine that the Soviets would not try to exploit such a setback for U.S. diplomacy. Whether Moscow could convince skeptical Arabs that it held the key to recovering captured territories and lost dignity is another matter. Perhaps neither superpower would have much credibility among the heirs to the regimes now in place in the Arab world.

Conclusion

This overview suggests that the Middle East remains a dangerous area between East and West. Washington and Moscow have thus far avoided coming into direct military confrontation in the region, but the danger of miscalculation remains. No clear zones of influence exist. The temptation constantly arises to undercut the somewhat fragile positions of the rival superpower.

Regional conflicts abound, resulting in a massive appetite for weapons that both superpowers, as well as many other countries, seem all too eager to supply. Petrodollars or generous grants make arms purchases possible even for poor countries. Technological sophistication in the region is such that already one country, Israel, is thought to possess nuclear weapons, and others may move in that direction over the next decade.

Neither superpower wants a nuclear confrontation in the Middle East, and neither favors the proliferation of nuclear weapons. This provides a limited, but real, common interest. Beyond this, however, there is little dialogue and little agreement. Conflicts such as those between Syria and Israel could explode quickly and would immediately become matters of utmost concern to both Washington and Moscow. Any fundamental shift in alliances, or in the balance of power, in the Persian Gulf region would also affect U.S.–Soviet relations. In short, dangers are legion in the Middle East, and hopeful signs, such as progress toward Arab-Israeli peace, are faint indeed.

3

U.S., Soviet, and Cuban Policies toward Latin America

JORGE I. DOMINGUEZ

Introduction

The Perspective of the Monroe Doctrine

"We owe it therefore to candor," said President James Monroe on December 2, 1823, "and to the amicable relations existing between the United States and those powers, to declare that we should consider any attempt on their part to extend their system to any portions of this Hemisphere, as dangerous to our peace and safety." No other U.S. president's pronouncement about Latin America's relations with the world's major powers has had such an enduring grip on U.S. policy toward Latin America and on the perspectives of much of the U.S. foreign policy elite. Then, as ever since, the Monroe Doctrine—a unilateral declaration of U.S. prefer-

JORGE I. DOMINGUEZ is the author, coauthor, or editor of many articles, booklets, and books on Latin America, comparative government, and human rights. Dr. Dominguez is a professor in the Department of Government at Harvard University and a member or officer of a number of professional associations.

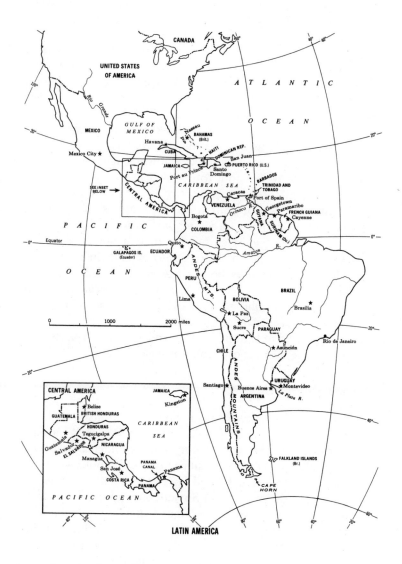

LATIN AMERICA

ences—has shaped U.S. views of the engagement of major powers in the Americas.

The Soviet Union has long understood the significance of this policy world view and, on the whole, has respected it, without acknowledging its legitimacy. In general, Soviet relations with Latin American countries have been correct though not close, mutually beneficial though not central to either partner, and have posed few worries for the United States. Major U.S.–Soviet confrontations have occurred, however, in those exceptional cases when the Soviets have broken these terms of reference or when the U.S. government has believed that the Soviets were about to do so.

The Monroe Doctrine perspective is broad. Monroe's full statement objected, of course, to any establishment of extrahemispheric military forces in the Western Hemisphere, but the statement went well beyond that. It objected specifically to "any attempt on their part to extend their system." The Monroe Doctrine is both a statement of U.S. strategic concerns with its own security and an ideological statement about the types of politics that the U.S. government will tolerate among its weaker neighbors. That ideological component also has endured in U.S. policy toward Latin America, though its significance and specific content have varied.

Central Issues

The issues that emerge from Soviet relations with Latin America touch on many significant aspects of East-West relations worldwide. The world came closer to nuclear war over Cuba in 1962 than at any time since nuclear weapons were first used against Japan. The United States has been concerned as well about the deployment of Soviet conventional forces and about the role of close Soviet allies—specifically Cuba and, increasingly in the 1980s, Nicaragua—in promoting policies that the United States considers hostile to its interests. To stop Soviet and Cuban gains, the United States landed troops on Grenada in October 1983 to overthrow that country's government. The Soviets, for their part, have expanded their diplomatic and political relations throughout the hemisphere.

The central question with regard to Soviet-Latin American relations for the United States and its allies in Europe, East Asia, and Latin America is how to define the legitimate aspects of Soviet relations with Latin America (which strict "Monrovians" surely would set at zero) and identify the steps that might be taken, preferably in concert, to hold the Soviet Union to that permissible standard. For the Soviets and their allies, the central question is how far they can go to challenge a U.S. policy framework for the Western Hemisphere that they necessarily consider illegitimate and identify as well the risks they are prepared to take and the costs they are willing to bear for the sake of "liberating" the Americas from Monroe's heritage.

The Security Regime over Cuba

One of the most enduring arrangements between the United States and the Soviet Union with regard to nuclear weapons and conventional forces has been fashioned to govern permissible Soviet behavior over Cuba. Born in the 1962 missile crisis, it has been tested, amended, refined, and broadened ever since. It is quite unlike any other U.S.–Soviet security understanding. The following are its central characteristics.

Gains for the United States and the Soviet Union

The 1962 missile crisis ended when both sides stopped doing what the other found most objectionable. That was the essence of the bargain. The United States removed its blockade of Cuba. The Soviet Union removed its strategic weapons from Cuba and pledged not to reintroduce them. The joint gain was avoiding nuclear war. But it was not a symmetrical settlement. The Soviet Union recognized U.S. nuclear exclusivity in the Americas—a technological updating of the Monroe Doctrine. The settlement of that crisis humiliated the Soviet Union, leading to an arrangement it recognizes nowhere else in the world. The Soviet Union did gain a conditional U.S. promise not to invade Cuba. But the Cuban government's refusal to accept on-site inspection—the key U.S. condition—negated that gain. As time passed, however, the United States did not invade Cuba, so that Secretary of State Henry Kissinger, on behalf of President Richard Nixon, was prepared to assure the Soviet Union in 1970 that the pledge not to invade Cuba was no longer dependent on on-site inspection but only on Soviet compliance. Revolutionary rule in Cuba was safe. At that moment, and for the first time ever, the U.S. government repealed the Monroe Doctrine with regard to Cuba as unilaterally as it once had issued it.

Problems in the "Understandings"

The arrangements that began in 1962 are often called the "understandings" between the United States and the Soviet Union. They quite literally have taken the following form: "you understand that I understand that I expect you to follow a certain course of action and not another." If the security regime over Cuba is significant, it is also perilously informal. It rests not on formal treaties, not even on the formal exchanges of notes, but on the will of both key participants to abide by its terms.

A further problem is that "its terms" are clearly defined only with regard to a few issues. Beyond what the terms ban, we should be conscious, first, of what they have always permitted. The United States has been prepared since 1962 to accept Cuban military might below the strategic weapons threshold. In particular, the United States accepts Cuba's ownership and operation of advanced MiG-21 and MiG-23F combat aircraft. The United States accepts the emplacement in Cuba, under Cuban ownership and operation, of missiles other than strategic missiles.

The 1962 Settlement and Cuban Support for Insurgencies Abroad

The question has arisen whether Cuban support for insurgencies in other countries was part of the settlement of the

1962 missile crisis. The answer is no. At his November 20, 1962, press conference, President John F. Kennedy took note that Cuba had not agreed to on-site inspection and that, consequently, the United States would continue "to pursue its own means of checking on military activities in Cuba." The president further pledged that the United States would "not, of course, abandon the political, economic and other efforts of this hemisphere to halt subversion from Cuba nor our purpose and hope that the Cuban people shall some day be truly free. But these policies are very different from any intent to launch a military invasion of the island." The president specified that "important parts of the understanding of October 27 and 28 remained to be carried out," especially with regard to verification in Cuba, but even then he did not indicate that an invasion would be forthcoming. The U.S. government in 1962, therefore, considered the question of Cuban support for revolutionary movements elsewhere to be worthy of vigorous opposition, but separate from the arrangements that settled the missile crisis, and to be addressed through other policies.

A revisionist view of the U.S.–Soviet understandings, however, has been put forth. It was summarized in January 1984 by the National Bipartisan Commission on Central America, chaired by Henry Kissinger:

The euphoria surrounding the resolution of the Cuban missile crisis in [1962] seemed to open the prospect that the Cuban revolution would at least be confined to its home territory. . . . This was more than an expectation. It was a declared policy objective of the United States. Obviously it has not been achieved. The problem has been that it was eroded incrementally. This often made it difficult to see the erosion clearly and, as a practical matter, made it even more difficult to halt at any given point. The increases in the Cuban threat were always so gradual that to stop them would have required making a major issue of what was, at the time, only a small change. The total effect of such small changes, however, has been . . . an enormously increased military power and capacity for aggression concentrated on the island of Cuba, and the projection of that threat into Central America (as well as Africa and the Middle East).

In fact, as noted, the original settlement did not include the issue of Cuban support for revolution elsewhere. Nor did it ever forbid the increase of Cuba's military might. Nor did it ban the overseas projection of Cuban military power. It is, therefore, incorrect to imply that such Cuban behavior, which has no doubt occurred, was an erosion of the original settlement.

Perhaps such prohibitions should have been incorporated into the settlement. It would have required extraordinary foresight to have done so. No crystal ball could have foreseen that 36,000 Cuban troops would have been dispatched to fight a war in Angola in 1975–76 or that another very large number would have fought in the Horn of Africa in 1977–78. On the other hand, in 1962 the world was on the brink of nuclear war; insistence on settling secondary issues would have risked sacrificing fundamental objectives for the sake of other worthy but less vital interests. Moreover, the Soviets had limited control over a Cuban government that was willing to go to war. It is doubtful that the proposed maximum U.S. goals could have been reached if they had been raised as a condition for settlement. But, above all, it is a disservice to diplomatic history to neglect to recognize the impressive accomplishment of 1962 and a disservice to diplomatic prospects to suggest the erosion of terms when there was never an agreement on them.

That being said, the Kissinger report did make important points. Support for the overthrow of established governments is against prevailing international treaties including the United Nations Charter. The projection of military power overseas can pose a threat. The point is that policies are needed beyond the framework of the understandings to address these other issues. The security regime is successful but it does not handle every significant and legitimate security concern of the United States and its allies with regard to Soviet-Cuban relations, nor can it be expected to do so.

Updating the Security Regime

The security regime did not stand still after 1962. It has been modified by unilaterally granted nonreciprocal concessions. Mention has been made that Secretary Kissinger in 1970 dropped the previous U.S. insistence on on-site inspection as a condition for observing the no-invasion pledge. In 1975 the Cuban government itself dropped its earlier opposition to the 1962 settlement and dropped its own list of preconditions with regard to these understandings. Since then, Cuba's views and policies on these subjects have been prudent and constructive.

The most significant of the subsequent unilateral nonreciprocal concessions was made by the Soviet Union in 1979. The Soviets agreed that their military forces in Cuba, present there for many years, would not be turned into a self-sufficient combat force. The Soviets promised not to introduce self-sufficient combat troops into Cuba in the future. These promises went beyond anything treated in the security regime in the past. For the first time, nonstrategic forces were covered by the understandings.

Of course, much of the history of the security regime has entailed reciprocal acts and steps to reassess and redefine the meaning of the understandings. For example, the United States and the Soviet Union agreed in 1970 that Cuba would not serve as an operating Soviet naval base for strategic purposes, although that amendment did not rule out Soviet naval calls on Cuban ports (which have continued and have increased in frequency and duration). In 1978 the two governments assessed and accepted the presence of advanced combat aircraft in Cuba, owned and operated by Cuba, and not equipped with nuclear weapons. The security regime, in short, has endured because the parties have found it a reasonable way to avoid war and protect their fundamental interests. The regime still reinforces U.S. primacy in the Americas, but it also institutionalizes the breach of the ideological prohibitions in the Monroe Doctrine.

Perhaps the main Cuban contribution to Soviet defense is to facilitate intelligence gathering. The U.S. government has reported twenty-four Soviet small naval task force deployments to Cuba and some fifty TU-95/BEAR D and TU-142/BEAR F naval reconnaissance and antisubmarine aircraft deployments to Cuba between 1969 and 1985. The U.S. government also reports that the most sophisticated Soviet electronic signal

intelligence facility outside Soviet territory has been established at the Lourdes complex near Havana, apparently targeted at U.S. commercial satellites.

Issues in the 1980s

By the 1980s new issues arose bearing on this security regime. They stemmed from independent sources but led to
convergent outcomes. On the U.S. side, military doctrine
changed. There has been greater concern about a scenario
whereby general war might break out in Europe and remain at
the conventional level. A greater U.S. capability to fight that
war might make it less likely for the United States to have to
use nuclear weapons first. This strategy, therefore, has some
important arms control consequences. Because much of the
resupply of U.S. and allied forces in Europe comes from Gulf
of Mexico ports, there is fear about Cuban or Soviet action to
interrupt it.

On the other side, the successful Cuban interventions in
Angola and in the Horn of Africa between 1975 and 1978 led
to an accelerated modernization of Cuban weapons inventories, including the acquisition of MiG-23 fighter bombers and
of diesel-powered submarines. For the first time, Cuba had the
capability to affect U.S.–European military relations in case of
war.

One frequent suggestion is to attack Cuba early on during
such a conflict. However, the Cuban armed forces are large
and capable. They have demonstrated their skill in wars overseas. There are about 300,000 Cuban troops under arms.
They are well equipped and well trained. There is a militia of
1.2 million people. Very large U.S. assets would have to be
committed to a sideshow at a moment when all U.S. efforts
should focus on the defense of Europe. Therefore, it is worth
exploring further amendments to the historic understandings
that would keep Cuba out of such a war.

Cuba and the Soviet Union have agreed that the Soviets will
not fight if war breaks out involving Cuba in the Western
Hemisphere. The Cuban Communist Party's Central Commit-

tee Plenum Statement of December 1984 conveyed that view to the Cuban people. This agreed-upon decoupling of Cuban from Soviet defense opens the possibility of persuading both the Soviets and the Cubans to permit the Cubans not to join a war in a European theater: reciprocity in Cuban-Soviet relations would permit Cuba to remain outside a conflict between the North Atlantic Treaty Organization (NATO) and the Warsaw Pact. (Cuba does not belong to the Pact.) Procedures need to be worked out between the United States and Cuba to provide for reciprocal security concessions and mutual verification to enable Cuba to stay out of such a war. For example, U.S. war planes in southern Florida may be required to remain on the ground so long as all Cuban war planes do the same, except as otherwise agreed. The United States may be required to refrain from military use of the Guantanamo naval base in such a war, and Cuba may be required to keep its submarines above water.

The specifics of an agreement require further political and technical analysis, but an agreement is desirable and possible for both sides. It is desirable for Cuba in order to enable it to survive such a war. It is desirable for the United States and its allies in order to enable them to resist a Soviet attack on Western Europe. It is desirable for the Soviet Union to preserve its premier ally in the Third World. It is possible because Cuban security is already decoupled enough from Soviet actions. And it is possible because the 1979 amendments to the historic understandings widened their scope from strategic to conventional forces. The time to act is, of course, in advance of a crisis.

The evolution of U.S.–Soviet–Cuban security relations has enshrined U.S. supremacy in the Western Hemisphere but breached the ideological bases of longstanding U.S. policy. This security regime is unlike any other U.S.–Soviet security arrangement. It has institutionalized Soviet subordination, but it has also endured and been amended to meet new security concerns of all three participants. It has served well the interests of the United States, the Soviet Union, and Cuba, for it protects U.S. security while it also guarantees the survival of the Cuban government. It is a tribute to those who fashioned it, but it is also a limited policy instrument that has not served —nor can it serve—to advance all plausible and legitimate U.S. and allied concerns.

"Exporting Revolution"

In December 1982, in a speech reported by the Cuban press, President Fidel Castro speculated about why the Western mass media were so concerned about possible Soviet support for revolutionary movements in Central America:

One of the great lies that the imperialists use concerning Central America is their attempt to impute the revolutions in this area to the Soviet Union.... [The USSR] has had nothing whatsoever to do with Central America. . . . The Soviets did not know even one of the present leaders of Nicaragua . . . during the period of revolutionary struggle. . . . The same holds true for El Salvador . . . with the exception of the Communist party of El Salvador— . . . not one of the major groups—the Soviet Union did not know the leaders of [most Salvadoran] revolutionary organizations and had no contact with them. The same goes for Guatemala. . . . We Cubans . . . have relations with the revolutionary movements; we know the revolutionary leaders in the area. I am not going to deny it.

This is an apt summary of much of the history of Soviet-Cuban relations about the support for revolution in the Americas. The Soviet Union, the formal Mecca of world revolution, was not well connected with revolutionary movements in Central America. The main Soviet links to the region's political left, the orthodox Communist parties, were small and often inconsequential. On the other hand, Cuba has long had relations with revolutionary movements, and it has acted with much autonomy to support them.

To say that Cuba has supported insurgencies on its own does not, of course, make its behavior acceptable. Nor does it mean that the Soviets, at some distance, would not welcome and cheer revolutionary regimes. But it does mean that active Soviet support for such movements is more the exception than the rule and that policies to limit or end external support for the overthrow of governments need to be addressed to those governments that are most engaged in such activity. In Central America in the mid-1980s, that was not the Soviet Union. It was Cuba and the United States.

The Moscow-affiliated Communist Parties

In Central America in the 1960s, left wing splinters from the Moscow-affiliated Communist parties of Nicaragua (the Nicaraguan Socialist party, PSN) and El Salvador (the Communist party of El Salvador, PCES) launched armed struggles. In Guatemala, the Communist party (the Guatemalan Worker's party, PGT) has changed position four times from the 1960s to the 1980s concerning the wisdom of armed struggle as the path to power. The opposition of the PSN and the PCES to armed struggle in the 1960s, and the PGT's hesitancy, well reflected the majority view among Moscow-affiliated Communist parties in Latin America as well as the prevalent views of those Soviets who thought about the prospects for revolution in the Americas.

The Soviets and the Cubans differed in the 1960s on the wisdom and efficacy of armed struggle in Latin America. Cuba strongly supported that path in virtually every case; the Soviets did not. Cuba attacked the passivity of most Soviet-oriented Communist parties, specifically in Central America. The PCES had the audacity to publish Ernesto (Che) Guevara's *Bolivian Diary* and Fidel Castro's prologue, with an added prologue of its own. The PCES prologue noted that for years "dozens of groups have failed in their attempts to successfully create and develop guerrilla *focos.*" The PCES explicitly disagreed with Fidel Castro by name over the armed struggle's significance and over the participation of foreigners, such as Guevara in Bolivia. Revolutions, the PCES averred, "cannot be exported or imported."

At the continental meeting of Latin American Communist parties in 1975, the predominant view still opposed armed struggle. Latin American Communists expressed their judgment on the unsuccessful Popular Unity government, to which the Communists belonged, that was overthrown in Chile in 1973: "The Chilean experience shows clearly that the revolutionary movement cannot discard any way of democratic access to power." Perhaps so, but that democratic path ended in a bloody coup and in the deaths of thousands. But so reluctant were these Communists to be revolutionaries in fact, not just in name, that they drew only partial lessons from the failure of socialist rule in Chile.

In the late 1970s Central America's revolutionary situation changed—and so did the attitudes of many toward it. In 1979 Nicaragua's PSN faced the rise to power of a revolutionary regime that it did not create and that was led by those who had condemned past PSN behavior. General Augusto Cesar Sandino fought against the United States in the 1920s and early 1930s; he was not a Communist. Those who invoked his name to found the Sandinista Front for National Liberation (FSLN) in the 1960s were different. Some came from the PSN; many others came from other sectors of Nicaraguan radicalism. The FSLN's main founder, Carlos Fonseca Amador, rendered a harsh judgment on the PSN: the "traditional Marxist-Leninist sector . . . in practice openly played the game of the Somozaist clique."

By 1980 Guatemala's PGT and El Salvador's PCES joined the armed struggle. PCES swallowed hard. Its secretary general, Schafik Jorge Handal, in 1980 apologized for the past, saying, "We recognized our errors . . . publicly." Indeed, he went on, there are "some elements of truth" to the view that "revolutionary armed organizations arose ten years ago due to the PCES's errors."

Soviet Reconsiderations

These momentous events provoked a debate in the Soviet Union, at least among academics, concerning the lessons to be drawn from Central American revolutions. On balance, the tone of the debate suggested a major change in Soviet understanding of the prospects for revolution in Central America. Yuri Koriolov, for example, in 1984 praised the old PSN's historical role. He noted that the PSN joined the anti-Somoza general strike of January 1978 (led, in fact, by many business firms and other labor leaders) and that a subsequent debate broke out within the PSN. Some left it to join the Sandinistas while others, still deserving of praise, "continued using mainly peaceful means for political struggle."

Tatiana Vorozheikina was bolder. She noted that many "arm chair analysts" spoke ill of the "ultraleft." However, "the Nicaraguan revolution's victory has forced many to abandon those approaches and stereotypes and to revise substantially their attitude toward such movements." In particular, Vorozheikina went on, "the sad experience of the Nicaraguan Socialist Party [the Communist party's formal name] proved that, outside of unity with other forces of the left, a party runs the risk of remaining on the margins of the main path of the revolutionary struggle."

The leading Soviet academic Latinamericanist on the "left," Kiva Maidanik, exulted that from the Nicaraguan revolution, "the first and most important lesson is that revolutionary victory is possible in Latin America." Other key lessons were the need for strategic unity among the forces of the left and the choice of the right path to struggle.

More authoritatively, Sergo Mikoyan, editor of the leading Soviet journal on Latin America, reflected that Fidel Castro's Twenty-sixth of July Movement in Cuba and the Nicaraguan FSLN "have shown (and now it can be said have proven) that under certain conditions they can replace the proletariat's political parties playing the role of the revolutionary vanguard." The disdain for the "ultraleft," he agreed, was wrong, for many so considered had proven able to lead revolutionary movements effectively.

The Soviet Union's earlier theoretical and practical understanding of events in Central America was in a shambles. Soviet-allied Communist parties had been discredited or proven ineffective. The Cuban approach had proven more successful in achieving victory in Nicaragua and more successful in building support for revolutionary change in Nicaragua and El Salvador. Soviet analysts and policy makers revised their view of the prospects for revolution in Central America. Their earlier pessimism was replaced with a new expectation that revolutions could win in Central America and that these new revolutionary regimes could be Soviet allies.

After long ignoring Central America's revolutionary potential, the Soviets in the early 1980s saw fresh opportunities. They supported Cuba's persistently activist policies. This was consistent with the increasing convergence of Soviet and Cuban policies in Africa, especially in Angola and the Horn of Africa in the mid- and late 1970s. The Soviets urged the Communist parties of Central America to take the path of armed struggle. They cajoled their allies to support the Sandinista government and the revolutionary efforts elsewhere. In Central America, the world's two superpowers—each often quite conservative in its own way—were "radicalized." As for the Soviets, for the first time in decades in their Latin American policy, they were talking and, at times, behaving as revolutionaries as the 1980s began.

Cuba's Leadership Role

Cuban support for revolutionary movements began in the first months of revolutionary rule in 1959—well in advance of Cuba's alliance with the Soviet Union and of its confrontation with the United States. Support for revolution is a constitutive ideological dimension of the Cuban revolution. It defines a central concern of that government. It legitimizes Cuba's own regime with a feeling of being on the side of history's march toward the future. It projects Cuba's influence internationally. It creates leverage in Cuban relations with the Soviet Union. It is a powerful weapon to combat the historical enemy, the U.S. government.

Nicaragua. Beginning in the 1960s, Cuba developed a network of relations with revolutionaries in many countries, including in Central America. Among others, some top Sandinista leaders trained in Cuba. Cuba supplied many resources to the Sandinistas, in the end including weapons and ammunition smuggled through Costa Rica with the cooperation of that country's president. However, the Nicaraguan revolution was, above all, a national mutiny against the Somoza family dynasty. It was made in Nicaragua, not in Cuba. By early 1979 most governments, including that of the United States, wanted Anastasio Somoza to step down, as did most Nicaraguans, including the business community and the bishops of the Roman Catholic church. Cuba was one important factor but not the only one; it was significant though not decisive.

The widespread support for Somoza's overthrow had one unanticipated effect. It reduced the barriers against intervention by one country in the internal affairs of another. Those barriers had never been very high in Central America, but they came tumbling down in the late 1970s. In the years that followed, virtually all of the region's governments became involved in supporting the overthrow of a neighboring government, and several external powers (the United States with regard to Nicaragua, and Cuba and probably the Soviet Union with regard to El Salvador) followed suit.

El Salvador. The success of revolution in Nicaragua had a direct impact on El Salvador. The Salvadoran civil war stems from that country's complex history and its mixture of prosperity and repression. Nonetheless, that civil war has also been internationalized as outside powers, above all the United States and Cuba, have supported their internal allies.

Salvadoran revolutionaries sought and got outside help. In 1980 and 1981 Nicaragua, Cuba, and other Communist countries, probably including the Soviet Union, supplied weapons, ammunitions, and other resources to the Salvadoran revolutionaries. The evidence of Nicaraguan and Cuban involvement is persuasive; the evidence of the involvement of several other Communist countries is reasonable though indirect; the evidence of direct Soviet involvement is least conclusive. The evidence of sustained military support after 1981 is not very persuasive for any of them, although there are occasional suggestions of some such aid. The evidence of much external support, short of military supplies, from these countries for.

Salvadoran revolutionaries since 1981 is quite strong. As the internal war in El Salvador turned against the guerrillas in 1984, there has been some circumstantial evidence of increased Cuban support to compensate for increased United States support for the government of El Salvador.

There was no evidence of increased direct Soviet support for the Salvadoran revolutionaries in the mid-1980s although the Soviets welcomed the Salvadoran left's new unity. Applying the lessons from the Nicaraguan revolution, Tatiana Vorozheikina noted the "militarist deviation" of one of the strongest revolutionary forces in El Salvador, the People's Revolutionary Army (ERP), in the 1970s and the "rightist opportunist mistakes committed by the leadership of the Communist party of El Salvador" in the late 1960s. Fortunately, in her view, both deviations were corrected, leading to the "armed struggle against the regime . . . [which] opened for the people the only real possibility to combat rightwing terror."

The Focus of Concern

In conclusion, the only case in Central America where there is some evidence of possible direct but limited Soviet military support for revolutionaries is in El Salvador in 1980–81. The evidence for Cuban support is much stronger, pervasive, and enduring. The evidence of Soviet, Cuban, and Nicaraguan nonmilitary support is much stronger, but the evidence of Soviet-Cuban coordination is, at best, mixed. There was virtually none in the 1960s and through most of the 1970s including the revolutionary process in Nicaragua. To the extent that the Soviets and other Communist governments became involved in supporting the Salvadoran insurgency, that involvement may reflect Cuba's leadership role and, specifically, its influence on the Soviet Union. Cuba is not a Soviet proxy but a valued ally, not a puppet but a vanguard.

The security concerns of the United States and its allies are not less significant if this analysis is correct, but it suggests that the answer to Central America's problems lies, first, inside each of those countries. Second, to the extent that the conflict has indeed become internationalized, there is more to discuss in Havana than in Moscow. It has been U.S. government policy, however, not to engage the Cuban government on this subject.

Support for Revolutionary States

The Soviet Union and Cuba

Soviet support for the Cuban government has been extensive and deep but not free of difficulties or costs. The Cuban revolution could not have survived in power, nor could it have conducted the ambitious foreign policy worthy of a major power, without Soviet support. The highlights of this vast subject can be summarized. Beginning in the early 1960s, the Soviet Union began to supply weapons to Cuba free of charge. That policy has continued. A substantial modernization program was launched in the aftermath of the Angolan war (1975–76) and accelerated after the Horn of Africa war (1977–78). After a brief pause, the Soviet-Cuban response to the Reagan administration (whose first secretary of state, Alexander Haig, threatened to "go to the source") was to accelerate the rate of weapons deliveries so that what was planned for the entire 1981–85 period was delivered within two years. Note, however, that the build-up had been planned; the effect of the Reagan administration's position was not to create it but to accelerate it. Cuba has never joined the Warsaw Pact nor is there a formal Soviet military commitment to the defense of Cuba. On the contrary, Cuba's military doctrine is to be prepared to fight alone to defend the homeland. Several thousand Soviet military personnel have been in Cuba for many years (with normal rotation), advising and coordinating with the Cuban armed forces.

Soviet economic subsidies also date from the early 1960s. However, the spectacularly generous Soviet support for Cuba dates from their 1976 agreement, as Cuba's participation in the Angolan war was coming to a successful end. As the price prevailing in the world market fell, the Soviets increased markedly their price for Cuban sugar, thereby raising dramatically the Soviet contribution to Cuba and changing its character. Through the price system, the Soviets also subsidized Cuban nickel exports and Cuban petroleum imports. Subsidies through the price system work as grants; they bear no interest and the principal is not repaid. The extant Cuban commercial debt to the Soviet Union is but a small fraction of the real, though difficult to measure, Soviet aid to Cuba in weapons and through the price system.

In the early 1980s, however, the Soviets cut back by shifting the nature of their aid. Prices paid by Cuba for its imports from the USSR continued to rise; prices paid by the Soviets for Cuban sugar fell from 1980 to 1981. Cuba's terms of trade have deteriorated. The increased Cuban trade deficit was covered by Soviet loans, repayable and bearing interest. That is still, of course, a Soviet support for the Cuban economy but different in kind from the experience of 1976 to 1980.

The Soviet Union also supports Cuban economic development projects. Ordinarily these are commercial contracts, bearing low rates of interest. When the Soviets finance a project for export promotion, Cuba repays with the products instead of cash. The Soviets also provide thousands of scholarships for study in the Soviet Union. Thousands of Soviet technicians work in Cuba.

Notwithstanding these close relations, Cuba has been an unruly ally. The Soviet Union imposed economic sanctions on Cuba in early 1968 in the wake of sharp disputes between the two governments over a host of issues, including their relations with Communist parties and revolutionary movements, Soviet commerce with Cuba's enemy governments in Latin America, Soviet links with some who wished to overthrow Fidel Castro's leadership or at a minimum change his government's policies, and the very terms of the bilateral relationship. The Soviet Union coerced Cuba into backing down, and thereby established the framework of hegemony that governs Cuban-Soviet relations. Within that hegemonic framework, however, Cuba has retained much autonomy provided it does not challenge nor oppose major Soviet foreign policy interests and policies.

Even after bilateral relations have improved, the Cuban government's behavior often surprises the Soviets. For example, evidence has mounted that the decisions to send Cuban troops to Angola in 1975 were made not in Moscow but in Havana, from design to implementation. Mention has been made, of course, of Cuba's leadership role with regard to revolutions in Central America. The Cuban-Soviet relationship rests on Soviet support for Cuban boldness—but Cuban boldness is very much its own.

The Soviet Union and Grenada

Soviet relations with Grenada deserve examination not only because Grenada is a case of a consolidated revolutionary state that failed and was overthrown by U.S. and English Caribbean forces, but also because there is a wealth of documentation on it.

The record reveals an apparent contradiction: the Soviet Union had little interest in Grenada, and yet it supplied Grenada with massive shipments of weapons. Thus it appears that the Soviet operational response to a definition of a country's "low significance" is neither to stay away nor to deprive it of assistance. Instead, the USSR still supplies many weapons, although these are mostly old, and there are sharper limits on economic aid. Although a country may matter little to the USSR, it may still get a significant amount of military support.

U.S. government officials often argue that these weapons deliveries were "far in excess of Grenadan defense needs." Considering that the United States had threatened Grenada militarily since 1981 (extensive August 1981 eastern Caribbean air and naval maneuvers aimed at "Amber and the Amberdines"), that Grenada was invaded by U.S. and English Caribbean forces, and that its government was overthrown in October 1983, this argument is a little silly. Nonetheless, there was certainly a disproportion between Soviet interests and Soviet actions.

The Soviet Union responded slowly to Grenada's revolution. In July 1983, three months before the Grenadan revolu-

tion committed suicide, the Grenadan ambassador to the Soviet Union, Richard Jacobs, wrote his superiors that the Soviets are "very careful, and for us sometimes maddingly slow, in
making up their minds about who [sic] to support. They have
decided to support us for two main reasons. Cuba has strongly
championed our cause," and the Soviets had become impressed with the Grenadan revolution's internal development.
This statement is significant for three reasons. First, it
confirms Soviet caution; second, it confirms the Cuban leadership role; and third, it confirms that the Soviets knew so little
about Grenada that they would become so impressed by its
internal processes just on the eve of self-destruction.

Grenada, in turn, relied on Cuba as a transshipment point
for all assistance from Communist countries and even for private advice on how to negotiate with the Soviets. The Grenadan ambassador to the Soviet Union, who had also served as
ambassador to Cuba, warned his comrades near the end of
1982 that "we have to work on the Soviets for some considerable time before we reach the stage of relationship that, for
example, we have with the Cubans." He added that "the
Caribbean—as they [the Soviets] repeatedly state . . . is very
distant from them. It is, quite frankly, not one of their priority
areas."

Beyond weapons and some other military aid, the Soviets
had some economic and technical collaboration agreements
with the Grenadans but, for example, refused to finance
Grenada's showcase project, the building of a new international airport. The Cubans worked hard on it; financing came
from various sources other than the USSR. The airport was
designed for civilian use. To be sure, an airport is an airport,
and that one could have been used for military purposes in
emergencies, but there is no evidence of a plan to use Grenada
as a link in a transnational military chain.

There is also no evidence that Grenada was subverting its
immediate English Caribbean neighbors. Although the New
Jewel Movement had political relations with kindred political
parties, as is common in many countries, the Grenadan government was careful to work with the neighboring govern-

ments. The latter's fears were about what might happen in the future, not about the past. However, Grenada's government actively and materially supported revolutionary movements farther away from the homeland—as near as El Salvador and as far as Namibia. This suggests a shrewd strategy—though it failed in the end—to limit revolutionary fervor to distant lands only.

There has been some speculation that the coup led by Finance Minister Bernard Coard and General Hudson Austin that overthrew Prime Minister Maurice Bishop was instigated by the Soviets and opposed by the Cubans. Cuban opposition to Bishop's overthrow is clear. Soviet views are very unclear. The Soviets knew Coard better; Coard was more ideologically orthodox from their perspective; Bishop held back from the Soviets secrets in which they were interested, and the Soviets knew it. However, there is no evidence that the Soviets knew about the anti-Bishop coup or that they did anything about it. In fact, the Soviets seemed to have been grossly uninformed about internal Grenadan events. There were, as a result, Soviet-Cuban differences in behavior at the moment of Bishop's overthrow. The Cubans condemned the coup; the Soviets did not, remaining aloof. The Cubans fought and many died for the Grenadan revolution; the Soviets did not. The end of the Grenadan revolution, like its early weeks in power, found Cuba in the thick of things but the Soviet Union rather remote.

In short, the most significant point about the Soviet relationship to Grenada is at odds with most conventional wisdom. No, the Soviets were not particularly interested in Grenada. But, yes, they were deeply committed to supplying revolutionary Grenada with a spectacular military arsenal. Grenada's main significance for understanding Soviet policy in Third World settings is this peculiar mixture of aloofness and resource commitment: get involved even if it does not matter.

The Soviet Union and Nicaragua

Soviet-Nicaraguan relations were established in October 1979, three months after Somoza's overthrow, in contrast to

Cuba's immediate establishment of relations and the beginning of its assistance in July. Soviet economic and technical aid was modest through 1980. Soviet economic aid to Nicaragua amounted to $76 million from 1979 through early 1982, about half the level of either Mexican or U.S. aid to Nicaragua. Nicaragua also got some economic assistance from Czechoslovakia, East Germany, and Bulgaria in this early period.

Soviet economic aid to Nicaragua increased after Daniel Ortega's trip to the Soviet Union in May 1982. Agreements were signed on hydroelectric engineering, communications, geological prospecting, agriculture, personnel training, public health, and other sectors. Soviet concessionary development credits included support for installing a floating dock on Nicaragua's Pacific coast and for building a ground station to connect with the Intersputnik system. These projects may also have military value. By 1983 Soviet economic aid to Nicaragua rose to $30 million in donations and $96 million in lines of credit and loans.

Including funds disbursed as well as those pledged for future years, the total commitments of the Soviet Union and its allies made to Nicaragua between 1979 and 1983 are impressive. According to U.S. academics Theodore Schwab and Harold Sims (using only official Nicaraguan, Cuban, and Soviet sources), during the five years the Soviet Union committed $443.7 million; Cuba, $286 million; Bulgaria, $232.5 million; the German Democratic Republic, $103.25 million; Czechoslovakia, $75 million; the Democratic People's Republic of Korea, $31 million; and Hungary, $5 million, for a total of $1176.45 million. There is no evidence of Polish or Romanian aid; Yugoslavia had committed $40 million. Still, in 1984 Nicaragua retained diplomatic and technical aid relations with the Republic of China (Taiwan), carried over from Somoza's years.

In February 1984 Nicaragua signed its first formal agreement with the Council for Mutual Economic Assistance (CMEA). The first joint Nicaragua–CMEA Intergovernmental Commission met in September 1984. Nicaragua attended the CMEA annual meeting in Havana a month later as an observer (along with Angola, Afghanistan, South Yemen, Laos, Mozambique, Ethiopia, and Mexico). In short, since 1982 the commitments to Nicaragua from the Soviet Union, Cuba, and their allies have risen sharply. There is little evidence of a resource constraint. They seem willing and able to support Nicaragua.

The build-up of the Sandinista armed forces began in advance of efforts to overthrow the regime. The International Institute for Strategic Studies reported the arrival in Nicaragua of twenty-five Soviet T-55 main battle tanks in 1981—before the U.S. government began, in December 1981, its support for the anti-Sandinista forces seeking to overthrow the Sandinista regime. (The anti-Sandinista forces are commonly called the *contras,* though they prefer to be called freedom fighters.) Nicaragua had also received East German and Bulgarian military and internal security aid and training. Although Sandinista reflections on the Cuban experience would have led them, in prudence, to anticipate efforts to overthrow them, the record shows that the beginning of militarization in Nicaragua was not caused by external aggression. The subsequent build-up of the Sandinista armed forces, however, is a more understandable response to the U.S.–backed anti-Sandinista forces.

The U.S. government reported in March 1985 that Nicaragua had 340 tanks and armored vehicles, 70 long-range howitzers and rocket launchers, and 30 helicopters. Although the tanks are mostly older Soviet models, the helicopters, suitable to the warfare the Sandinista regime faces, include some of the best Soviet equipment. The U.S. government also reported some 7,500 Cuban personnel in Nicaragua, of whom 3,000 were listed as military and internal security personnel. The Nicaraguan armed forces have become Central America's most formidable military establishment.

Cuba and Nicaragua

According to Cuban sources alone, there were in 1983 approximately 4,000 Cubans in Nicaragua, of whom half were teachers and approximately 500 were health personnel. There were several hundred construction workers and a smaller group in agriculture. Cuba reported only 200 regular military personnel in Nicaragua. A comparison between what the U.S. alleges and Cuba admits suggests a fair match on the numbers of Cuban civilians in Nicaragua and on the fact of a Cuban military role in Nicaragua but a large difference on the numbers of regular Cuban military personnel in Nicaragua. Past experience suggests it is likely that a large proportion of Cuban civilians in Nicaragua are trained also as military reservists, and would fight as Cuban construction workers did in Grenada. In early 1985, Nicaragua's President Daniel Ortega spoke of about 800 Cuban military personnel in Nicaragua.

Cuban aid to Nicaragua is substantial in both effort and effect. For example, Cuba's education program in Nicaragua is its largest anywhere. From 1979 to 1984, 250,000 Nicaraguans (of a total population of 2.6 million) were taught by Cubans. In 1984 another 5,000 Nicaraguans were studying on scholarship in Cuba. Cuba also supplied approximately a third of the total number of health personnel in Nicaragua. The tone of Sandinista leaders indicated that their relations with Cuba were excellent and, as in the Grenadan case, better than their relations with the Soviets.

With the glaring exception of support for Salvadoran revolutionaries, Cuban political advice to the Sandinista leadership has been moderate. President Fidel Castro and other Cuban leaders have counseled caution in internal and international affairs. They have not pressed for rapid socialization of the means of production. In 1979–80 they welcomed good U.S.–Nicaraguan relations. They have encouraged the Sandinistas to cultivate good relations with Western Europe, Canada, and Japan. Cuba has publicly supported negotiations between Nicaragua and its neighbors and between Nicaragua and the United States. Cuba has offered to withdraw its military and, if necessary, other personnel from Nicaragua as part of a settlement. Cuba has supported from the outset the multilateral negotiations efforts of the Contadora Group countries (Colombia, Mexico, Panama, and Venezuela).

However, within Cuba there is a debate on the wisdom of

the Contadora process and on the nature of the Sandinista regime. That debate parallels discussions in other countries. Some within Cuba believe that the Sandinista regime is merely reformist, that it just wants to hang on to power, and that it will make any deals that allow this. Six years after revolutionary victory, they point out that half of the means of production are still privately owned, that the Roman Catholic church is still vigorously and publicly criticizing the regime, that the labor movement is not yet unified and centrally controlled, that opposition parties have a full voice and vote in the national parliament where they control a third of the seats, and that the country's main newspaper is virulently antiregime. Others within Cuba argue that the Sandinistas have been prudent, that they needed time, and in due course that there would be a full transition to socialism. Cuba's official position is that Nicaragua has a revolutionary government committed to socialist transformation.

The debate in Cuba about the Contadora process focuses on what might happen in El Salvador. The Contadora process calls for the suspension of external support to parties in internal conflict but, in particular, would cut off support for those seeking to overthrow any of the region's governments. Cuban opponents of the Contadora process do not wish to abandon the Salvadoran revolution. Cuban supporters of the Contadora process believe that the Salvadoran revolution can continue without external support whereas the Salvadoran government would be much weakened without it. Cuba's official position is to support the Contadora process.

From the perspective of the United States and its allies, Cuba is the more troublesome supporter of revolution. However, Cuba has generally behaved with moderation in its support for Nicaragua. In contrast, accelerated Soviet weapons deliveries to Nicaragua alarmed other Central American countries, some South American countries, and the United States. The prospects for U.S. military action in Nicaragua appear best in response to this Soviet-Nicaraguan relationship. The path to negotiations on this question leads to Moscow as well as Havana. But with regard to Nicaragua, unlike with regard to Cuba, the U.S. government has not yet been willing to breach the ideological prohibitions embedded in the Monroe Doctrine framework and alive and vibrant in the thinking and the mood of the Reagan administration.

Soviet Relations with Mexico and South America

In the 1980s the Soviet Union had diplomatic relations with Mexico and all South American countries except Paraguay and Chile, where they were interrupted by the 1973 military coup. The Soviet diplomatic isolation that had marked the Cold War in Latin America ended around 1970. The Soviet Union was an active and important diplomatic partner of Latin America's major states. Of particular concern to the United States has been the Soviet's longstanding use of their embassy in Mexico to coordinate some Soviet intelligence activities in the Western Hemisphere, including the United States. Mexico has long prided itself, however, on its good relations with the Soviets; it has curbed Soviet activities only by exception. Mexico and the Soviet Union emphasize their political relations; their economic relations have not developed much. Mexico and the USSR value their relations to promote Mexican independence from the United States.

Soviet trade with Latin America has expanded. Soviet trade data indicate a tenfold increase of Latin American exports to the Soviet Union from 1970 to 1982, reaching the level of $3.2 billion. That was, however, just over 4 percent of Latin America's exports. Soviet data also show that Soviet–Latin American trade expanded only modestly until 1979. The first large jump occurred in 1980, thanks to the dramatic increase in Argentine grain exports to the Soviet Union. In the early 1980s, Soviet trade expanded, principally with Argentina and Brazil. Nonetheless, Latin American imports from the Soviet Union remain very modest and, consequently, there is a massive Soviet trade deficit with Latin America. In the best of years in the 1970s, Soviet exports to Latin America amounted to a third of Soviet imports from Latin America. As Soviet purchases from Argentina and Brazil increased, Soviet exports to the region amounted only to approximately 10 percent of the level of Soviet imports. As the Soviets told the Argentines in 1985 at a formal meeting to discuss their relations, "there must be a balanced trade."

Soviet diplomatic and trade relations with South American countries have not been much affected by the nature of South American political regimes. For example, the Soviets reestablished diplomatic relations with Brazil under democratic rule in 1961. Relations continued after the 1964 military coup. Trade prospered; military-ruled Brazil was the Soviet Union's main Latin American trade partner for much of the 1970s. The leading Soviet Latinamericanist, Anatolii Glinkin, in 1985, attributed this trend to "Brazil's tendency to discard the heritage of anti-communist prejudices." The same, of course, might be said for the Soviet willingness to deal with right wing authoritarian regimes. Glinkin noted with satisfaction that Brazilian-Soviet trade in the early 1980s was the most dynamic component of Brazilian foreign trade although, of course, from a low base line.

The real star in Soviet–Latin American trade is Argentina. When the Carter administration imposed a grain embargo on the Soviet Union in 1980 in response to the Soviet intervention in Afghanistan, Argentina greatly increased its grain exports to the Soviet Union, helping thereby to render U.S. policy ineffective. Although the Soviet Union plays a negligible role in Argentine imports, the Soviet market is of central importance for Argentine economic growth. Since 1980 Argentina has sent no less than 20 percent of its exports to the Soviet Union, almost twice what it has exported to the United States. Argentine exports to the Soviet Union have exceeded Argentine exports to the United States since the mid-1970s. The excellent Soviet-Argentine trade relations have endured through civilian and military regimes.

During the 1982 South Atlantic war, the Soviet Union and Cuba gave as much political support to Argentina as did any other country. That was not much in real terms, but Argentina was bereft of allies at that time of need. Moreover, the Soviet Union sold Argentina enough heavy water in early 1981 to meet its nuclear energy needs for two years. That was, in part, a response to earlier U.S. efforts to curtail Argentine access to industrial-scale heavy water technology and to bring Argentina under the full-scope safeguards of the International Atomic Energy Agency, which Argentina has not accepted. In 1983 the United States, too, sold heavy water to Argentina.

Argentina has also had excellent trade relations with Cuba since the early 1970s. These, too, have continued through civilian and military regimes. Argentina has given trade credits to Cuba. Cuba supported Argentina politically during the South Atlantic war.

Cuban policy has evolved toward the Soviet position, dealing with South American countries regardless of their internal political regime. Cuban policy toward South America has moderated, in contrast to its active support for revolutionary movements to overthrow South American governments, democratic or authoritarian, throughout the 1960s. Both Cuba and the Soviet Union now distinguish sharply between their formal state-to-state relations with South America and Mexico, on the one hand, and their "revolutionary conduct" in Central America.

Since the early 1970s, there has been only one instance when Cuba has gone back on a pledge to a Latin American government to conduct normal state-to-state relations and not to support those who seek to overthrow it—Colombia, 1980–81. Although the Cuban military relationship with the antigovernment Colombian M-19 was complex and uneasy, it did exist. Colombia again broke its diplomatic relations with Cuba in 1981. The Soviet Union stuck to its policy, however. In 1982 Anatolii Olshani reported with satisfaction on the quadrupling of Colombia–CMEA trade from 1970 to 1980; trade increased 50 percent in 1978–80 just as Cuba and Colombia moved to a break.

The only South American country to import weapons and other military equipment from the Soviet Union is Peru. According to the U.S. government, the Soviet Union has sold Peru $1.6 billion worth of military equipment (including tanks, combat aircraft, nonstrategic missiles, and helicopters) and other supplies and services since 1973. Approximately 3,000 Peruvian military personnel have been trained in the Soviet Union; approximately 150 Soviet military personnel in Peru provide continuing training and maintenance services.

In return, the Soviets have gotten very little beyond economic benefits. Their main gain has been logistics support for the approximately 200 Soviet fishing ships operating off the Pacific coast of South America and the use of Lima as Aeroflot's modest South American headquarters. The Soviets were unable to prevent the Peruvian armed forces' drift away from the left throughout the 1970s; they were helpless in the face of the presidential election of Fernando Belaunde in 1980 and were uninfluential in Alan Garcia's presidential election in 1985. Most Soviet military equipment is irrelevant in the Peruvian military's fight against the Shining Path guerrillas (*Sendero Luminoso*). The Soviets do not support these guerrillas and have published statements arguing that the guerrillas' position is "clearly wrong."

Soviet military relations with Peru are a shining tribute to the imperfect link between military sales and political influence—a point most arms merchants know. The Peruvian arms market has been good for the Soviets; Soviet political gains have been negligible.

Conclusions

Latin America, except for Cuba, still has relatively low priority in Soviet foreign policy. Soviet policy toward Latin America has threatened vital U.S. security interests only with regard to Cuba. That threat has been effectively contained through the gradual development of a security regime that has limited severely, though not ended, Cuba's military value to the Soviet Union. Nonetheless, those security understandings have not covered other aspects of Cuban behavior that are incompatible with U.S. and allied interests. The United States and its allies legitimately have been concerned over Cuban support for revolutionary movements seeking to overthrow established governments. They are also concerned over the projection of Cuban military power in the Third World, though especially in Africa. And they are more recently concerned about the possible effect of Cuban and Soviet capabilities in the Gulf of Mexico and the Caribbean that might impair the resupply of Western Europe in the event of conventional war.

U.S. policy, in turn, has been handicapped by the Reagan administration's unwillingness to negotiate with Cuba over these issues. The unwillingness persists in part because the administration does not believe Cuba has a legitimate role to play and in part because it does not believe that Cuba has enough autonomy from the Soviets to negotiate on its own. Whatever one's stand on the question of the legitimacy of Cuban involvement, it is a fact—and so is the substantial degree of Cuban foreign policy autonomy within the framework of Soviet hegemony.

At the other end, Soviet relations and, more recently, Cuban relations with Mexico and South America pose little discernible threat to U.S. and allied interests. Soviet military relations with Peru may burden the Peruvian economy unnecessarily but demonstrate as well the inefficacy of Soviet influence. Soviet trade relations with Argentina help it to honor its international debt obligations to the West. Soviet diplomatic relations with Latin America have required their foreign ministries to become more sophisticated in their international activities.

There is a specter haunting the Western Hemisphere. It is the specter of U.S. panic over Soviet and Cuban activities that might lead to war. The focus is Nicaragua. It is the one and only country which has breached (without the U.S. consent that has come to apply in the case of Cuba) the ideological barriers first identified in the Monroe Doctrine that still grip U.S. thinking and feelings about what the United States chooses to permit in Latin American politics. This possible panic in the United States is not a historical aberration—nor is it wholly irrational.

The Sandinista and Cuban governments bear a major responsibility for the deterioration of their relations with the United States. The deterioration was partly a result of their military support for the Salvadoran revolution in 1980 even though the Carter administration had warned them clearly about the consequences. The Sandinista decision to build up their military establishment with Soviet support, in anticipation of U.S. aggression, had the consequence of feeding U.S. fears of the worst scenarios. The acceleration of Soviet military deliveries in the 1980s, in response to the threat that had then developed to continued Sandinista rule, has not been accompanied with enough Soviet reassurances to the United States about the limits of Soviet engagement. Curiously, with regard to Nicaragua, the Cuban government's behavior after 1981 has been fairly moderate.

Nonetheless, Nicaragua in the mid-1980s did not present to the United States or to its neighbors a security threat that could not be swiftly crushed by the United States. On the contrary, such a potential threat is easily deterred by U.S. policy and force posture, without necessary recourse to support for irregular forces, and can be further contained through available negotiating processes. Panic need not lead to war, nor is war inevitable.

The result of these trends, on balance, has been that the Soviet Union by the late 1980s had become a significant actor in the Western Hemisphere. It had developed a substantial network of diplomatic and trade relations. It had consolidated the Cuban revolution and was assisting in the consolidation of the Nicaraguan revolution. It had revitalized its revolutionary image through these means. It changed its earlier views concerning the prospects of revolution in northern Central America. The Soviets came to support the efforts to overthrow the governments of El Salvador and Guatemala and backed the changes of the Communist parties of those countries away from the peaceful road toward the armed struggle in the early 1980s. The Soviets have successfully pressed most of their CMEA allies into undertaking joint efforts to back both Cuba and Nicaragua and, to some degree, the revolutionary movements in Central America. The regular deployments of Soviet naval task forces to the Caribbean, the strengthening of Cuban and Nicaraguan military capabilities, the modest but persistent Soviet military presence in Cuba, and the use of Cuba for

sophisticated intelligence activities have required the redeployment of substantial U.S. military assets to the Caribbean–
Central American area at the expense of U.S. forces whose
mission had been the defense of Europe and East Asia. In
short, the Soviet Union and Cuba have had ideological, diplomatic, and political accomplishments in the Western Hemisphere since the 1970s.

They have also had important setbacks. The appeal of the
Cuban and the Nicaraguan revolutions, pervasive in 1960 and
1980 respectively, has been sharply curtailed. The Grenadan
revolution committed suicide, and burial was provided by a
reassertive, albeit uninformed, U.S. and English Caribbean
invasion. The Soviet Union and Cuba have had to accept U.S.
strategic supremacy in the Americas and even further limits on
the deployment of conventional Soviet forces in Cuba. Neither
the Cuban nor the Nicaraguan economies has performed satis-
factorily for their governments, or for the Soviets and Eastern
Europeans. The Soviet Union has remained unable to persuade the South Americans and the Mexicans to buy much
from it. Both Soviet and Cuban political influence outside of
Nicaragua have been remarkably modest, despite decades of
exertion, without prospects of greater successes.

No single policy of the United States and its allies can address all Soviet and Cuban policies. But it would be appropriate to focus on the components of Soviet and Cuban policies
identified in this chapter and to address them separately and
directly. The main cost to the United States and its allies,
which has already occurred, is the diversion of military resources. Paradoxically, this would only be worsened, not improved, if the United States were to emphasize military strategies. The central goal of U.S. military policy in Central
America and the Caribbean should be to return to an "economy of force" posture to enable the redeployment of military
resources back to Europe and East Asia. This goal can be
achieved at least cost through negotiations that limit strategic,
conventional, and unconventional military activities by all relevant parties. The United States should be cautious as well to
adopt policies that might seem successful in the short run but

at greater longer-run costs. For example, one long-run effect of the overthrow of Salvador Allende in Chile was to strengthen those who argued that only armed revolution was the path to power for Communists.

"Many of our own major mistakes, indeed, in this hemisphere," argued Assistant Secretary of State for Inter-American Affairs Adolph Berle in 1939, "have been due more to the fear of European domination than to any desire to increase the area of our territory" or, he added, to protect U.S. investments. Substitute "Soviet" for "European" and the roots of U.S. policy in Latin America are longstanding. In 1961, the same Adolph Berle forgot his own advice and played a major role in the failed Bay of Pigs *(Playa Giron)* invasion of Cuba. The main threat to U.S. interests in the hemisphere is to forget, again and again, what the major mistakes of U.S. policy have been.

4

The Soviet-American
Rivalry in Asia

DONALD S. ZAGORIA

Introduction

Although Europe remains the critical region of super-power rivalry, and the Middle East, the most dangerous, it can be plausibly argued, as it was by John Erickson in the February 1981 *Asian Affairs,* that "the Soviet leadership sees the strategic center of gravity moving slowly but inexorably in the direction of East Asia, the source of a potentially critical challenge to Soviet power and prestige."

Indeed, in the late 1980s and 1990s, Moscow faces the prospect of a fundamental shift in the Asian balance of power through a tacit Sino-American security relationship, significant Japanese rearmament, the probability of a successfully

DONALD S. ZAGORIA is the author of books and numerous articles reflecting his special interest in Soviet foreign policy and in the politics and international relations of East Asia. Dr. Zagoria has served as consultant for the Department of State and the National Security Council, as well as for educational and professional organizations. He is a professor of government at Hunter College and at the Graduate Center of the City University of New York. He is also a fellow at the Research Institute on International Change at Columbia University.

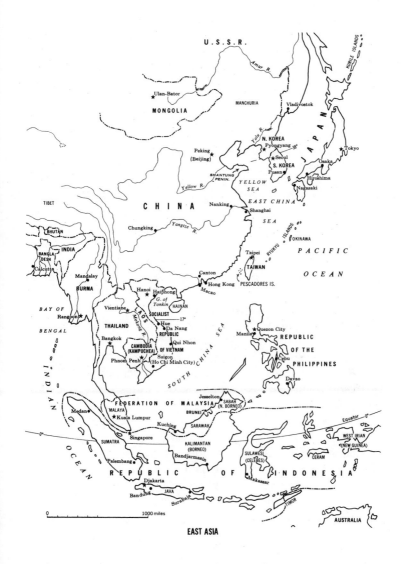

EAST ASIA

modernizing China that will remain a permanent adversary, and a more assertive United States at the head of an informal security coalition including China, Japan, South Korea, the Association of Southeast Asian Nations (ASEAN) countries, and the Australia New Zealand United States Council (ANZUS).

In no other region of the world is there such a gap between Soviet military power and Soviet political influence. Moreover, the longer-range trends are against the Soviets. By the year 2000, Japan is likely to be the second greatest industrial power in the world, China may have a gross national product (GNP) of close to $1 trillion, and the emerging Pacific community of free market economies may be closer to reality.

The Soviets clearly recognize these adverse trends. As recent commentaries in the Soviet press point out, Japan already has the fourth largest fleet in terms of tonnage and is eighth in overall military spending. It could quickly become a nuclear power. Moreover, "any special relationship with the United States may prove to be illusory . . . Tokyo is following its own program." At the same time, the United States and Japan also have "far reaching plans for South Korea," which is to become "the third member of a Far Eastern NATO."

Even more alarming for the Soviet Union is the growing prospect of a Sino-Japanese entente, a phenomenon that, as Erickson points out, is "fraught with serious strategic consequences" and brings "added defense problems in northeast Asia as well as along the inner Asian frontier lines." *Red Star,* commenting on the 1985 visit to China by the deputy chief of the Japan Defense Agency, reported that China seems to have an "active approach" to the expansion of military ties between the two countries as well as a "positive approach" to the U.S.–Japanese security treaty. Nor is China complaining about the growing U.S. military presence in Asia or the build-up of Japanese military potential.

At the same time, as the Soviets have also noted, Chinese relations with the United States are intensifying. U.S. Defense Secretary Caspar Weinberger, Navy Secretary John F. Lehman, Chief of Staff John W. Vessey, and Air Force Chief of Staff Charles A. Gabriel all visited China in the early 1980s; the

Chinese minister of defense has visited Washington; President Ronald Reagan went to China in 1984; China's President Li Xiannian visited Washington in 1985; and Vice President George Bush paid a return visit to China in the fall of 1985.

What makes these trends in Sino-American and Sino-Japanese relations even more alarming for the Soviets is the fact that despite growth in trade and cultural exchanges, Sino-Soviet political relations have reached something of a plateau. In 1985 one of Moscow's shrewdest political observers, Alexander Bovin, conceded that "internally [the Chinese] are not yet ready to develop better relations with the USSR on so broad a basis. The causes of this may be varied, but the fact itself is indisputable." Bovin went on to complain that Beijing "supports the American policy of militarizing Japan" and also favors the deployment of new American weapons in Western Europe. He concluded that Sino-Soviet relations were "full of contradictions."

But if the Soviets understand the nature of their Pacific dilemma, there are as yet few signs that they understand their own role in helping to bring it about. Despite Mikhail Gorbachev's new "smile" diplomacy, the Soviets continue to increase their own formidable military power in the region; they show no signs of substantially thinning out their forces on the Chinese border or of returning the disputed northern territories to Japan; they remain determined to consolidate their power in Afghanistan; they continue to support Vietnam's occupation of Kampuchea; and they show no willingness to make concessions on any of the outstanding issues. Moreover, they are hinting privately about their dissatisfaction with the existing adverse "correlation of forces" in Asia and their determination to alter that balance.

Under these circumstances, it would be naive to expect that there can be any substantial accommodation between the Soviet Union and the United States in Asia. On the contrary, the United States is building up its own military power in the region. The U.S. Seventh Fleet has been equipped with Tomahawk cruise missiles, some of them nuclear-capable; the *Carl Vinson*, a nuclear-powered attack carrier, and the *New Jersey*, a battleship retrofitted with cruise missiles, have been added to the U.S. Pacific Fleet; two additional squadrons of F-16s are based on Japanese territory; and a second battleship group, led by the U.S.S. *Missouri,* has greatly increased American surface strength.

Moreover, the Soviets will have to contend with the Japanese fleet as well. The Japanese navy, though it needs to be modernized, is the fourth largest and is "one of the best maintained and trained fleets in the world," according to Japanese diplomat Hisahiko Okazaki. Some 80 percent of that fleet is operational at all times. In view of the much lower estimated operational rate of the Soviet Pacific Fleet, the addition of the Japanese fleet to the U.S. Seventh Fleet is not at all insignificant.

But if the Soviets have their problems in the Pacific, the Western position is far from secure. The continuing growth of Soviet military power, the growing economic "cold war" between the United States and Japan, the developing crisis in the Philippines, the unpredictability of North Korea and potential instability in South Korea, the uncertainty about China's policies after Deng Xiaoping, and many other challenges will have to be surmounted.

This chapter will first offer some general observations on the serious internal and external problems facing the Soviets in the coming years. If this chapter's assessment of the gravity of these problems is correct, these problems are bound to condition Soviet foreign policy in the years ahead both in Asia and elsewhere. An examination of the superpower rivalry in Asia will follow in some detail, with particular emphasis on the "weak links" in the Western position in Asia. Finally, the chapter will conclude with some observations on how to cope with Soviet power in Asia, including some thoughts on possibilities for reducing regional tensions.

The Global Setting

Strategic Weapons

The late 1980s and 1990s are not likely to be a promising period for the Soviet Union in its drive to become an effective challenger to the United States in the global arena. The trends in the strategic competition which previously favored Moscow are changing. A series of U.S. strategic modernization programs—the MX, perhaps the "Midgetman," the new, more accurate Trident submarine-launched ballistic missiles, the revived B-1 bomber, the advanced technology (Stealth) bomber, and Pershing II, as well as ground-, sea-, and air-launched cruise missiles, will soon enhance the American nuclear arsenal. Moreover, as Arnold Horelick pointed out in 1985 in *Foreign Affairs:*

Superior U.S. technology in such areas as sensors, computers, computer programming, signal processing and exotic kill mechanisms being harnessed in connection with President Reagan's Strategic Defense Initiative is bound to increase Soviet anxiety about the possible shape of the strategic balance in the years ahead.

Domestic Issues

The Soviet Union faces severe economic and social stagnation at home. Some Soviet intellectuals have been warning that, if present trends are not soon reversed, the "Polish disease," disaffection within the working class, could spread to the Soviet Union. Soviet leader Mikhail Gorbachev has implied that the Soviet Union, unless it improves its technology and economic productivity, may not be able to maintain its present strategic position in competition with the West. In a brutally frank report delivered on December 10, 1984, three months before he became general secretary of the Soviet Communist party, Gorbachev attributed the "slowdown of growth in the late 1970s and early 1980s" to the "stagnant retention" of "outmoded production relations." He warned that the ills of the system were of "truly tremendous scale" and that it would be a "titanic task" in terms of innovation and complexity to deal with them. What was at stake, he concluded, was nothing less than the need to make sure that the Soviet Union could "enter the new millenium worthily, as a great and flourishing power." And, in an unusually candid admission, he conceded that because of Soviet economic failures, the West was winning not only the economic and technological race, but the ideological competition as well.

On June 11, 1985, Gorbachev continued his dire warning. He said that "urgent measures" were required to improve the economy because he could not cut social programs or reduce defense expenditures in the face of the "imperialist threat." He may yet be forced to do one or the other.

Soviet Foreign Relations

Declining trends in the strategic competition and severe economic difficulties at home are not Gorbachev's only problems. The Soviet Union is still bogged down in Afghanistan, and it faces a possible insurrection in Poland. Elsewhere in Eastern Europe, its economically hard-pressed satellites want greater independence and increased trade with the West. Some of them want to experiment with Chinese- and Hungarian-type economic reforms. A harshly worded *Pravda* article in June 1985 reacted to all of this by warning of the dangers of "revisionism" and even of "Russophobia."

In the Far East, the Soviet Union is increasingly "odd man out." In Europe, despite clumsy Soviet efforts to split the North Atlantic Treaty Organization (NATO) and to prevent the deployment of the Pershing IIs and cruise missiles, the Western alliance is still firmly intact, and the missile deployment has proceeded on schedule. In the Persian Gulf, Iran's revolutionary regime has severed natural gas deliveries to the Soviet Union; greatly increased its trade with Pakistan and Turkey, two American allies; and continued to broadcast revolutionary Islamic propaganda to Moscow's predominantly Muslim southern republics. The other major power in the Persian Gulf, Iraq, has been establishing closer economic relations with the West.

In the Third World more broadly, Moscow faces armed insurgents in almost all of its desperately poor client states; there is almost universal condemnation of the Soviets for their policies in Afghanistan and Kampuchea; and many less developed countries increasingly recognize the limits of Soviet economic assistance and are looking more and more to the West for aid, credit, technology, and know-how. In the meantime, the American economy continued to recover, and President Reagan launched the most sustained U.S. military build-up in postwar history.

Implications for Soviet Policy toward Asia

None of this means that Gorbachev is going to opt out of the international competition with the United States. The Soviets continue to add to their already huge military arsenal, and Gorbachev will almost certainly try to exploit differences within the Western alliance and to improve relations with China. Soviet media continue to stress Western Europe's adherence to the spirit of detente and the opportunities this presents for Soviet diplomacy. But the problems Gorbachev faces are formidable and deep-rooted; they cannot be solved quickly. It could take a decade or more just to begin a turnaround in the ailing Soviet economy, particularly since Gorbachev seems to have ruled out Chinese- or Hungarian-type market reforms as too risky. Consolidating the fragile Soviet empire in an era of economic austerity will be an equally long-term and uncertain process. All of this means that Gorbachev needs a long period of calm in relations with the United States while he concentrates on internal and imperial problems.

The need for "breathing space" is precisely what Soviet Foreign Minister Eduard Shevardnadze hinted at in a speech to the Helsinki Conference in July 1985. In an unusual linkage between Moscow's internal and foreign policy, Shevardnadze said that "the foreign policy of any state is inseparably linked to its internal affairs" and that in order to implement its vast internal plans to improve the economy, "the Soviet Union needs a durable peace. . . ."

But the more important point for the purposes of this chapter is that the Soviet Union may now be entering a period when, for its own reasons, it will require a period of calm in relations with the West. In such a mood, it may not want to stir up tension with the United States in Asia or in any other region. This is not a guarantee of peace and stability in Asia, but it is an encouraging element in the overall picture and one that could be exploited by an alert adversary to help reduce tensions.

The Soviet Stake in Asia

Although Europe remains the region of key concern to the Soviet Union, the USSR has vital security interests at stake in East Asia. Geography, geopolitics, and economics all ensure the immensity of this stake.

In geographic terms, the Soviet Union, although generally regarded as a European power, is actually, next to China, the second largest Asian power. One-third of its vast territory lies east of Irkutsk in East Asian Siberia. Moreover, large stretches of Soviet Siberia border on China and Mongolia; the Soviet Pacific coastline is close to Japan, Korea, and China; and, as a result of the Russian conquest of much of Central Asia in the nineteenth century, 50 million people, or approximately 20 percent of the Soviet population, are Asians.

Geopolitics is another critical factor in shaping Soviet policy in East Asia. The Soviet presence in the region and status as a world power are inseparable from Moscow's global strategic competition with the United States. Yet the United States, by dint of its naval and air power, its bases, its alliance system, and its economic and cultural influence, remains the strongest power in the Pacific. The Soviets are determined to weaken that U.S. alliance system, to contain China while improving relations with it, and to project their own power and influence in this important region. Moscow's acquisition of new bases in Vietnam in the late 1970s represents an important strategic gain; it is perhaps the most significant strategic change in the Pacific during the past decade. These new naval and air bases will enable the Russians to project their power more readily into the Persian Gulf and the Indian Ocean.

A third factor that shapes Soviet policy in the Asia-Pacific region is economic. In the remaining decades of the twentieth century, and far into the twenty-first, Moscow will seek to develop Siberia, a region that contains a large proportion of potential Soviet mineral wealth, energy resources, and precious metals. The development of these Siberian resources will become increasingly important toward the latter part of the 1980s when the Soviet Union may be facing an energy crunch.

Fears and Uncertainties behind Soviet Policies

Finally, Soviet policy in Asia is shaped by certain fears and insecurities—some of them rooted in reality, others in paranoia; some inherited from the past, others rooted in recent developments.

(1) There is the fear of having to fight on two fronts if it comes to a general war. The Soviets still vividly remember what might have happened in World War II if Japan had joined Germany and attacked Russia in 1941 instead of turning south against China and Southeast Asia and then against Pearl Harbor. Under these circumstances, the Soviet Union would almost certainly have been defeated. As late as the battle of Stalingrad, the Soviets kept large forces on the Siberian front to guard against such a danger.

(2) There is the fear that one day a strong, irredentist China may claim back the territories grabbed from a weak Manchu empire by czarist Russia in the middle of the nineteenth century. The Soviets surely cannot forget what Mao Tse-tung told the Japanese Socialists in 1964 when he was sympathizing with their demands for a return of the Kuriles—that China had not yet presented *its* bill to the Soviets for *its* lost territories.

(3) There is a sensitivity about the vast borderlands with China. Is a powerful China likely to be reconciled to the Soviet domination of Mongolia? The Kazakhstan/Sinkiang frontier will also remain sensitive because of minority races on both sides of the border.

(4) There is the fear of a powerful Japan, already the third largest industrial power in the world, a country with whom the Soviets have an unpleasant history and an intractable territorial dispute.

(5) There is concern about the geopolitical vulnerability of

Siberia, a region that is sparsely populated, a long distance from European Russia, with long, overland lines of communication that are vulnerable to interdiction; and it is a region that will be very difficult to develop.

(6) There is uncertainty about the loyalty of approximately 40 million Muslims in Soviet Central Asia at a time of an Islamic awakening on the Soviet Union's southern border.

An Asian Overview

By and large, Soviet policy in East Asia has been a spectacular failure. The reasons for this failure are varied. Some have to do with the success of American policies; others, with the heavy-handedness of Soviet diplomacy; and still others, with the extraordinary economic dynamism of the region itself. A brief overview of the region will demonstrate that the basic trends are—with some notable exceptions to be discussed later—extremely encouraging for the West and quite unfavorable for the Soviet Union.

(1) The Asia-Pacific region is one of extraordinary economic dynamism. The Pacific economies have displayed the greatest resilience and the highest rates of growth in the world. The economic output of the Pacific region as a whole now equals more than two-thirds of total U.S. GNP. U.S. trade with East Asia, which only a decade before was $42 billion, was $170 billion in 1984 and accounts for almost 30 percent of our total world trade. U.S. direct investment in the Pacific is now conservatively estimated at more than $30 billion.

(2) Not unrelated to its economic dynamism, the Asia-Pacific region is now, with the notable exception of Kampuchea, basically at peace. Peace and prosperity are interrelated. Without peace, the region would not have enjoyed such economic prosperity. Without economic prosperity, the region would almost certainly have been more unstable.

(3) Despite serious trade frictions, the U.S.–Japanese strategic alliance remains strong. Under Prime Minister Yasuhiro Nakasone, Japan has changed from a passive to an active ally. There are joint planning, joint basing, and joint training exer-

cises. Japan is expanding aid to key countries throughout the world, some of them—Turkey, Egypt, Pakistan—threatened by instability, not just traditional Japanese trading partners. Japan is taking responsibility for the defense of its sea lanes. Public opinion in Japan is more favorable to the Western alliance than ever before. There has, in fact, been a sea change in Japanese attitudes toward the alliance with the United States. Japanese public opinion polls bear this out. Even the Japanese Socialist party, the largest opposition party, is trying to break away from its earlier position of "unarmed neutrality."

(4) China has been engaged since 1978 on a historically significant reform and modernization program comparable to Japan's Meiji Restoration in the nineteenth century. If it continues to be as successful as it has been since 1978, China, by the early twenty-first century, will have a GNP approximately equal to that of the Soviet Union today. China's experiment with market reforms is bound to have an enormous impact on the Third World, on Eastern Europe, and on the Soviet Union. It has already had an impact on North Korea, which has recently instituted a new tax program designed to attract foreign investment. So long as China is absorbed with domestic modernization, it will have a continuing stake in peace and stability in Asia and in expanding its economic and other cooperative ties with the West—even as it simultaneously seeks to reduce tensions with the Soviet Union. In foreign policy, China now shares with the West an interest in containing Soviet power, in a strong U.S.–Japanese alliance, in improving relations with South Korea while restraining North Korea, in forcing Vietnam out of Kampuchea while improving relations with ASEAN, and in removing the Soviet Union from Afghanistan while shoring up Pakistan. Over the longer run, while China will certainly not be anyone's "card," it will remain—by reasons of geography, history, and national interest—a massive barrier to the spread of Soviet power in the Pacific and a deterrent to Soviet adventurism elsewhere.

(5) Yet another piece of good news is the developing dialogue between North and South Korea. At this writing, eco-

nomic and Red Cross talks have begun. The North is even suggesting a summit meeting. All of this portends a significant change in North Korean policy that is partly attributable to economic difficulties at home, partly to China's encouragement, and partly to the vitality of South Korea, which now has a GNP more than four or five times that of North Korea's.

(6) In Southeast Asia, since the fall of Saigon ten years ago, the dominoes have not fallen but banded together in a unified ASEAN, one of the world's most successful regional organizations.

(7) More broadly speaking, communism as an ideology and moral force and as a model for development has, with the single exception of the Philippines, lost much of its appeal. China's open questioning of Marxism, the enormous successes of free market systems, and the economic weaknesses of Communist countries from the Soviet Union to Vietnam and North Korea have put communism on the historical defensive.

(8) Also, despite its substantial military build-up in the Pacific, the Soviet Union has failed to convert its military power into political advantage and is unlikely to do so. In fact, it is pursuing counter productive policies in the Asia-Pacific region, and retreat from these policies will be difficult. Among illustrations of the situation are: the Soviet invasion of Afghanistan and the indications that the Soviets will remain; the Soviet-supported Vietnamese invasion of Kampuchea; the Soviet military build-up on the northern islands that are disputed with Japan; the enormous Soviet build-up on the Chinese border, including its forces in Outer Mongolia; and the crude handling of Asian sensibilities. All of this has contributed to a new strategic consensus which has developed since 1978 in the Asia-Pacific region.

(9) In the Pacific, as elsewhere, there has been in recent years a substantial resurgence of American military power.

(10) Then, too, in the Far East, as in no other region of the world, the East-East conflict plays a major role in helping to maintain a favorable balance of power. In Asia today, with the sole exception of the Korean peninsula, which still remains

divided along East-West lines, the most serious and bitter confrontations are those between contiguous Communist states: Russia against China, China against Vietnam, and Vietnam against Communist insurgents supported by China in Kampuchea. All the Asian Communist states are finding that their most active and dangerous adversaries are not faraway Western powers but neighboring Communist states with whom they share disputed and heavily armed borders and a historical record of conflict going back several centuries—a record undiminished by a supposedly common ideology. These East-East conflicts are likely to last. They are deeply rooted in history and geography. These divisions among the Communist states contribute to a new balance of power in East Asia that is more favorable to the West than anyone could have imagined ten or fifteen years ago.

(11) Finally, and not least important, there is growing in the West a recognition of the strategic interdependence of Europe, Asia, and the United States. The Soviet deployment of medium-range ballistic missiles, the SS-20s, has highlighted this interdependence. Japan and China have manifested a clear interest in preventing any redeployment of the SS-20s from Europe to Asia. The West has an equally clear stake in ensuring that any Soviet-Chinese detente does not lead to a transfer of Soviet forces from the Siberian border to Europe.

In sum, for the West, the Asia-Pacific region is extremely encouraging. The region is prosperous and generally peaceful, relatively stable, and basically pro-Western. The overall balance of power in the region favors the West. For the Soviet Union, the region must look quite disturbing.

Moscow's Future Prospects

This generally favorable situation for the West in Asia could change, but if such adverse changes were to take place, they would more likely come about not as a result of Soviet actions, but through bad management of the Western alliance, or political or economic instability in key countries, to name two of the possibilities. Before turning to some of these possibilities, a

brief review of Soviet relations with the various countries in
the region will expose Moscow's weak political position.

The USSR and China

With regard to China, the Soviets are well aware that here
is a long-range adversary. The clash between the USSR and
China is an old-fashioned contest between two huge land empires with potentially unstable buffer zones lying across their
long common frontiers. As a Eurasian empire, the USSR has
a special concern about China because it has not and cannot
fully assimilate its own Central Asian peoples. The long-range
"China threat" is made even more serious in Soviet eyes by the
American strategy of trying to tie down Soviet power in Asia
in order to weaken Soviet capabilities elsewhere.

Moreover, there are conflicting geopolitical interests between the USSR and China in Mongolia, Indochina, and
southern Asia; there is an unsolved border conflict; there are
deep-seated mutual suspicions and fears on both sides; and
eventually China will modernize its armed forces, particularly
its nuclear forces. It will then pose a real threat to Soviet
security.

To be sure, a tactical detente is now in being, and it will
probably continue. It is in the interests of both countries so
long as both need to concentrate on internal economic problems, but this detente will almost certainly be limited. Over the
long run, Russia knows that a more powerful China will be a
more dangerous China.

In trying to assess the future prospects for Sino-Soviet relations, it is useful to divide the obstacles to normalization into
two sets of problems. First, there are the intractable geopolitical issues. Second, there are the bilateral issues that are somewhat more susceptible to compromise because they do not
involve third parties.

Geopolitical Problems. China's geopolitical demands on the
Soviet Union are well known. The Chinese insist that the Soviets pressure the Vietnamese to pull their troops out of Kampu-

chea and that the Soviets themselves pull out of Afghanistan and remove their forces from Outer Mongolia. It is quite unlikely that there will be progress on any of these particular demands in the foreseeable future. The Soviets do not have the leverage necessary to force Vietnam out of Kampuchea, and they are unlikely to exercise great pressure. The Soviet acquisition of naval and air bases in Vietnam has greatly increased Soviet power projection throughout the Western Pacific, and Moscow is not likely to risk the loss of those bases for what is yet a will-o'-the-wisp in Beijing. A unilateral Soviet withdrawal from Afghanistan would, under present circumstances, lead to the collapse of Moscow's client government in Kabul and its replacement by an anti-Communist and anti-Soviet government. A negotiated withdrawal still seems very unlikely despite the recent flurry of talks at the United Nations and elsewhere. Almost certainly, the Soviets will not withdraw their troops from Outer Mongolia, a buffer country of great strategic importance and one which the Chinese have laid claim to in the past.

Bilateral Issues. In contrast to the issues involving "third countries," the bilateral issues between Moscow and Beijing are theoretically more susceptible to compromise. The most critical of these issues—and the one that has proven difficult to resolve in more than a decade of negotiations—is the border dispute and the related presence of large numbers of Soviet troops in forward positions along the border. Throughout the past decade or more, the Chinese have insisted that the Soviets withdraw their troops from "disputed areas" of the border as a precondition to resolution of the border conflict. They have also insisted that the Soviets formally acknowledge that the treaties signed between czarist Russia and a weak Manchu dynasty in the nineteenth century were "unequal treaties." The Soviets, on the other hand, have refused to concede that there are any "disputed areas," and they insist that the Chinese recognize the legality of the nineteenth century treaties.

Given the political will in both countries, it is not difficult to imagine a number of compromises that could resolve the issue. The Soviets could unilaterally pull back some of their troops from the border as a gesture of good will. The Chinese could drop their unrealistic demands for the Soviets to recognize that the nineteenth century treaties were "unequal," demands that seem largely intended for psychological warfare purposes in any case. Such concessions could be followed by a thinning out of forces on both sides of the border and the signing of a variety of "confidence-building measures." These measures could set the stage for a breakthrough on the border conflict, and, ultimately, the Soviets and the Chinese could sign some type of nonaggression pact or "friendship treaty" similar to what the Soviets have been offering Beijing in recent years.

Constraints on Concessions from Soviets

The obstacles to progress on these issues are substantial. First, the troop deployments along the border are such that the Soviets, who are forward-deployed, would have to do most of the withdrawing. It must be assumed that conservative leaders in the Politburo, supported by the military, will oppose such a move. The trans-Siberian railroad runs very close to the Chinese border, and it will be argued that Soviet troops need to be forward-deployed in order to protect that vulnerable railroad. It will also be argued that unilateral Soviet pullbacks from the border will be interpreted by the Chinese as a sign of weakness. Even more important, it will be impossible for the Soviets to dismantle the huge military infrastructure they have built on the border, including depots, airfields, underground silos, and barracks. It will be impossible for Moscow to pull back from some of the disputed areas, particularly the one on the very environs of Khabarovak. Then, too, in the years ahead the strategic importance of Siberia is bound to grow as the Soviets seek to develop its vast natural resources and to build up its labor force. This will be an argument not for reducing but for strengthening Soviet forces in Siberia.

There will be strong arguments for modernizing and

strengthening the Soviet forces opposite China in response to the planned increases in the American navy, the closer security cooperation between the United States and Japan, the increases in Japan's defense spending, and the still present threat of a Chinese-American-Japanese "united front" against the USSR. Finally, the Soviets will almost certainly not pull their troops out of Outer Mongolia, and it is these troops, only 200 miles from Beijing, that the Chinese are most concerned about.

Thus, in a country where "worst case" scenarios are common, where a belief in large—if not excessive—amounts of military power is deeply rooted in national history and psychology, where the leader is heavily dependent on the marshals for consolidating his power base, it seems unlikely that there will be significant Soviet concessions to China on the question of Soviet forces in Siberia.

Obstacles to Progress from the Chinese

On the Chinese side, there are equally important constraints on flexibility. Why should the Chinese drop their insistence on a significant Soviet pullback from the border? Tensions along the border have already been reduced. What more could the Chinese realistically hope to gain? Even if there were progress toward "confidence-building measures" and a "nonaggression pact," is this really in China's interest at this time? Success in such negotiations would run the risk of profoundly disturbing China's newly acquired "friends" in the United States, Europe, and Japan, many of whom would point to any Sino-Soviet "deal" on the border as an indication that China could not be trusted as a long-term opponent of Soviet expansionism. This could jeopardize China's access to Western technology at a time when the Reagan administration has lifted some restrictions on such technology transfers to Beijing.

To sum up, a modest improvement in Sino-Soviet relations, limited to increases in trade and exchanges and to reductions in tensions, is not going to alter certain key facts in the strategic triangle.

(1) The Soviet Union and the People's Republic of China will remain potential enemies, and China will have less to fear and more to gain from a United States that is hostile to the Soviet Union than from the Soviet Union itself.

(2) The Soviet Union will continue to maintain one quarter of its army and one quarter of its nuclear forces opposite China.

(3) China will seek to maneuver within the strategic triangle in order to improve its position within it, but the Chinese will not be able to afford "equidistance" between the superpowers. On the crucial matters affecting the balance of power in Asia, China and the U.S. will continue to have parallel interests.

The USSR and Japan

Japan, too, is almost certain to be a long-range Soviet adversary. Soviet relations with Japan are now at one of their lowest points in the entire postwar period and not likely to improve substantially. There are a number of reasons for this.

First, there is an enormous suspicion of the Soviet Union in Japan, a suspicion nourished by nineteenth century rivalry over Korea and Manchuria, the Russo-Japanese war of 1904, fighting on the Manchuria-Mongolian border in the 1930s, and the entry of the Soviet Union into Manchuria and Korea during the last days of World War II when the Soviets captured tens of thousands of Japanese soldiers and confined many of them to prison camps. Quite recently, one of Japan's popular books was titled *Why Do We Hate Russians?*

Second, Japanese trade with the Soviet Union has declined substantially in recent years and is unlikely to increase much in the future. As a result of the energy glut and easier access to other sources of oil in China, Canada, Indonesia, and elsewhere, Japanese businessmen and the Japanese government are losing interest in Siberian development. Japanese trade with China has been expanding much more rapidly than trade with the Soviet Union, and this pattern is likely to continue.

Third, the territorial dispute between the two countries will be extraordinarily difficult either to resolve or to put aside. No elected Japanese prime minister could make concessions on the issue. Even the Japanese Communist party (JCP) wants the four Kurile islands back; indeed, the JCP claims Sakhalin as well. This is a good barometer of Japanese public opinion on this issue.

On the other hand, the Soviets are equally intransigent. Despite repeated Western speculation, no Soviet government is likely to make any concessions on the islands. There are a variety of reasons for Soviet intransigence. The Soviets have a territorial domino complex, and they fear that returning territory acquired from Japan after World War II will stimulate the claims of other nations whose territory the USSR also acquired at the same time. But the most important consideration from the Soviet point of view has to do with the strategic importance of the northern islands.

The disputed islands and Hokkaido, the northern island of Japan, command one of the key straits leading from the Sea of Japan to the Pacific. A hostile power in command of these straits could block the sea lanes of communication between Vladivostok, Moscow's main naval base in the Pacific, and Petrapavlovsk, an important submarine base for the Soviet Pacific Fleet. During recent years, and especially since the late 1970s, the Soviets have been developing a Sea of Okhotsk–Sea of Japan–Maritime Province complex that could be used as an "ocean bastion" in which the Soviets could submerge their strategic submarines without having to worry about their being tracked by the American Seventh Fleet. The disputed northern islands have become an important link in this complex.

The Soviet Union and Korea

A dramatic breakthrough for the Soviets on the Korean peninsula seems equally implausible. The visit by Kim Il-Sung to Moscow in May 1984, his first in seventeen years, has produced a new warming trend in Soviet–North Korean relations. There has been increased diplomatic contact in the past year,

and the Soviets have evidently begun to sell MiG-23s to Pyongyang, a break with their past policy of withholding modern
aircraft from North Korea. There have also been Soviet naval
visits to North Korean ports.

Still, suspicions between the two countries run deep. The
Soviets can hardly view Kim as a satisfactory vehicle for expanding their own influence on the Korean peninsula. To
begin with, North Korea under Kim has generally been much
closer during the past three decades to China than to the
USSR. Second, Kim has, at least until quite recently, opposed
Soviet policy in Afghanistan and Kampuchea. He continues to
provide a residence in Pyongyang for Prince Norodom Siha-
nouk, the nominal leader of the anti-Vietnamese resistance in
Kampuchea, a man whom Soviet media routinely describe as
a "hireling of the imperialists." Third, in the past Kim has
publicly accused the Soviet Union of "dominationism" and of
efforts to exploit the North Korean economy. Fourth, during
the past several decades Kim has developed into something of
a state religion his philosophy of *chu'che,* or self-reliance, and,
although he has not been able to live up to this philosophy to
the extent that he has preached it, it symbolizes his determination not to become dependent on the Soviets. And despite
what probably have been considerable Soviet pressures for
North Korea to provide the USSR with military facilities and
to join the Soviet-sponsored Council for Mutual Economic
Assistance (COMECON), Kim has so far resisted such pressure. Finally, Kim is a "hot potato" who has frequently involved Moscow in unwanted confrontations with the United
States.

Kim is equally suspicious of Moscow. His distrust of the
Soviets stems from a number of deeply rooted considerations.
First, he does not need to be reminded how close the Soviets
came to incorporating North Korea into the Soviet Union
during the period from 1945 to 1950. Kim knows only too well
how the Soviets use their military and economic advisers, their
troops, and their Secret police to infiltrate governments which
they intend to dominate. That is why he has allowed only a few
such Soviet advisers in North Korea during the past thirty

years. It can be assumed that all of those still remaining are under strict surveillance. Moreover, Kim has seen the fate of a number of the USSR's neighbors from Eastern Europe to Outer Mongolia to Afghanistan. And he knows about the "Brezhnev Doctrine" by which the Soviets have arrogated to themselves the right to intervene in the internal affairs of any "socialist state" that defies Moscow. For such reasons alone, he would keep his distance from the Soviet Union.

Second, Kim saw for himself during the Korean War that Moscow would not risk war with the United States in order to salvage North Korea. Even at a time when American troops were marching toward North Korea's Tumen River border with the USSR, the Soviets gave no indication that they were prepared to intervene in the war. It was only the Chinese intervention that saved Kim Il-Sung's regime from being toppled by the Americans.

South Korea is tied to the United States and is likely to remain so as long as Korea is divided and surrounded by two giant Communist states. Taiwan continues to be economically dependent on the United States and is extremely unlikely to make any moves toward warming relations with Moscow.

The Soviet Union and Southeast Asia

In Southeast Asia, the ASEAN countries (the Philippines, Indonesia, Singapore, Thailand, Malaysia, and Brunei) are all quasi-authoritarian, capitalist, anti-Communist states, and so the Soviets start with a great handicap there. Any kind of communism is regarded by those governments with suspicion, for internal security reasons if for no other. Furthermore, the Vietnamese invasion of Kampuchea has greatly alarmed all of the non-Communist states of Southeast Asia, particularly ASEAN's "hard-line" states, Thailand and Singapore. Thailand, because it has now lost its Kampuchean buffer to its traditional Vietnamese enemy, is determined to get the Vietnamese out of Kampuchea. Because Thailand shares this interest with Beijing, it has moved perceptibly closer to the Chinese. This "pro-Chinese" position of Thailand worries some of the other ASEAN members, but since Thailand is the "front line" state, and since all of ASEAN prizes unity above all else, the Thais in effect hold a veto over ASEAN strategy on the Kampuchean problem. The Thais will almost certainly continue to oppose the Vietnamese occupation by subsidizing and supporting the resistance inside Kampuchea.

Moreover, the Soviet invasion of Afghanistan greatly stiffened ASEAN, and, at recent meetings of the United Nations and other international groupings, a successful ASEAN strategy has been to link the Soviet invasion of Afghanistan with the Vietnamese invasion of Kampuchea. As a result, the ASEAN countries have developed a community of interests with many of the Islamic countries. This has led to a considerable weakening of Soviet influence in the "nonaligned" movement.

For the Soviets, the one big bright spot in the Pacific is their alliance with Vietnam and Vietnam's two client states, Laos and Kampuchea. However, it should not be supposed that this Soviet-Vietnamese alliance is easy on either of the partners. There are many signs of strain. The Vietnamese are proud nationalists; they fought a thirty-year war against the French and the Americans, and they are not likely to surrender their independence to the Soviets.

Challenges for the West

While the basic outlook for the West in the Pacific is extremely positive, there are a number of serious problems and challenges. Some of these problems are related to Soviet policies but others, perhaps the most important, are not. It will be useful to examine some of the more serious potential challenges to Western interests in the Pacific.

(1) Although the United States maintains naval and air superiority over the Soviet Union in the Pacific, the margin of this superiority has been decreasing. In the fifteen years or so prior to 1980, the tonnage of the Soviet Pacific Fleet was more than doubled while that of the U.S. Seventh Fleet was reduced by one-third. The Soviet submarine force is the largest in the world, and the Soviets are currently producing or testing seven different classes of submarines. The trend in major sur-

face warship programs has been toward larger, more techno-
logically sophisticated ships. Substantial numbers of Backfire
bombers now represent a considerable threat to the U.S. Seventh Fleet. At the same time, the Soviets, by deploying more
than 100 SS-20 intermediate-range nuclear missiles in Siberia
pose a serious threat to the entire American base structure in
the region. In addition, the Soviets continue to maintain fifty
divisions of troops opposite China. The danger of this impressive Soviet military power in the Pacific is not so much that it
is likely to be used in overt military activity. Opportunities for
the use of Soviet forces in Asia will probably remain limited.
Rather the dangers are that growing Soviet military power
could encourage the Soviets to use coercive diplomacy against
their adversaries; it could also encourage a drift toward political neutralism in Asia.

(2) There remains the possibility of a backlash against the
"open-door" policy in China that could lead to a substantial
reorientation of Chinese domestic and foreign policy. The
Chinese, although so far successful in implementing their ambitious reforms, are running into very major problems including equality, inflation, and corruption. Future post-Deng leadership may seek to curtail ties to the West and to revert to a
more traditional, Soviet-style centralized economic system. If
this were to be accompanied by continuing U.S.–Chinese frictions over Taiwan and a steady improvement in Sino-Soviet
relations, it could have an adverse effect on the overall balance
of power in Asia.

(3) North Korea is pursuing a double-track policy which is
still fraught with uncertainty. On one hand, it has entered into
a dialogue with South Korea for the first time in a decade. On
the other hand, it has purchased advanced fighter planes from
the Soviet Union, deployed U.S.–made helicopters smuggled
into the country, and increased its menacing forward deployment near the demilitarized zone.

(4) South Korea enjoys a precarious stability. It remains to
be seen whether power will be transferred peacefully in 1988
or whether there will be a new and familiar cycle leading to
unrest and crackdown.

(5) Vietnam shows no sign of removing its 180,000 troops

from Kampuchea or of negotiating a political solution there that would be acceptable to China or to ASEAN.

(6) Antinuclear sentiment is rising in the South Pacific. A Labor government in New Zealand is committed to banning from its ports all nuclear-powered and nuclear-armed ships, and this is imposing serious strains on ANZUS, one of the oldest U.S. alliances.

Finally, there are three "weak links" in the present pro-Western balance of power in the region that seem the most serious of all. They have to do with the U.S.–Japanese trade rivalry, the emerging crisis in the Philippines, and the growing Soviet pressure on Pakistan. These problems will now be considered in somewhat more detail.

U.S.–Japanese Trade

Perhaps the greatest single threat to the American position in the Asia-Pacific region is not the Soviet Union but the emerging economic cold war between the United States and Japan. A growing number of U.S., Japanese, and Asian leaders share a nightmare—that of the U.S. and Japan sinking into a bitter trade war, with the U.S. setting up walls to keep Japanese goods out, while the Japanese, embittered, are gradually pushed out of the U.S. orbit.

From 1980 through 1984, U.S. trade deficits reached unprecedented proportions, and projections show further dramatic deteriorations are likely in the future. These huge U.S. trade deficits have produced several ominous consequences: increased protectionist sentiment in the United States; the demands of powerful constituencies in the United States for greater "reciprocity" in American-Japanese economic relations; growing Japanese resentments over American pressure to open and liberalize the Japanese economy.

What is most alarming is that many influential figures on both sides of the Pacific are escalating their rhetoric and putting most of the blame on the other side. Many Japanese are beginning to view the U.S. as a helpless giant, unable to compete economically and unable to pursue a clear course politically. Many Americans, on the other hand, focus on the need for a removal of many of Japan's nontariff barriers such as the government's complex system for setting standards and certifying products that can be sold in the country.

Whatever the causes of the trade deficit, and they are obviously multiple, there is evidence of rising frustration in the United States. In July 1985, the widely read *New York Times Magazine* featured a highly opinionated, one-sided attack on Japan by journalist Theodore White under the inflammatory title "The Danger from Japan." According to White, the Japanese are engaged "in one of history's most brilliant commercial offensives, as they go about dismantling American industry." White put virtually all of the blame for the trade problems on the Japanese and ended by ominously reminding the readers of "the course that ran from Pearl Harbor to the deck of the U.S.S. *Missouri* in Tokyo Bay just 40 years ago." That such a simplistic analysis could be featured on the front cover of the *New York Times Magazine* is indicative of the public mood in the U.S. A more knowledgeable but equally frustrated observer, Jeffrey E. Garten, vice president of Shearson Lehman Brothers, claimed that in 1984 American imports of Japanese products accounted for almost all of Japan's national growth and that it was "time to call in some chips." Meanwhile, there was a variety of protectionist legislation being readied in the American Congress.

Pessimists believe that the macroeconomic trends will make U.S.–Japanese economic relations difficult to improve. According to New Zealand's Minister of Finance Robert D. Muldoon in the summer 1983 *Foreign Affairs,* it was only the U.S. recovery and the successful rescheduling of the largest debtor countries that averted "for the time being at least, the very real danger of a collapse into global depression, financial crises and wholesale disruption of world trade flows." Other capable analysts such as Robert Gilpin believe that the advanced industrial countries are headed for a period of slower growth and that this will make it more difficult to deal with the U.S. deficit in trade with Japan. Gilpin concluded in a March 1985 paper for the Center for Strategic and International Studies that there are three major obstacles to a return to the rapid growth decades of the postwar era. These are the decline of American leadership, the powerful tendency of national economies to resist necessary adjustment, and the increased tendency of governments to place domestic priorities above international ones.

On the other hand, three Hudson Institute analysts are more optimistic. Their plausible analysis argues that trade disputes between the two allies are likely to be ameliorated during the second half of the 1980s by the relatively buoyant economic environment that the authors believe is likely to prevail in both countries. They also insist that the enormous benefits of U.S.–Japanese cooperation, including larger markets for both countries, cheaper sources of supply, higher growth rates, a stronger Western alliance, and an emerging concept of a Pacific community, so clearly outweigh the more visible costs of bilateral economic frictions that the competitive aspects of the relationship will be kept within limits.

Other optimists such as Robert Hormats, formerly U.S. assistant secretary of state for economic affairs, say that Japanese efforts to open markets combined with U.S. efforts to reduce the federal budget deficit will bring the problem within manageable proportions.

Danger in the Philippines

In addition to the threat now posed to the U.S.–Japan alliance, there is an emerging crisis in the Philippines that is one of the most serious problems we face in the region.

(1) In the past several years, the Philippines has been experiencing a combined political and economic crisis, while Communist-led guerrillas continue to grow in strength. Since the August 1983 assassination of former Senator Benigno Aquino, the credibility of the Marcos government has been greatly reduced among broad sectors of the Philippines population. There is what social scientists would call a growing crisis of legitimacy.

(2) On the economic front, there is a flight of capital, a

substantial decline in manufacturing output, a declining GNP, an unemployment rate of 35 percent, an inflation of 50 percent in 1984. There is an inability to service a $25 billion foreign debt. There is a serious deterioration in some rural areas, particularly sugar and coconut regions hurt by falling commodity prices. The government is saddled with a number of industrial "white elephants" as a result of what has been called "crony capitalism."

(3) Meanwhile, the insurgency grows. According to Acting Chief of Staff Fidel Ramos, the Communist-led New People's Army (NPA) now operates in practically all seventy-three provinces. It mounts unit-size attacks of 50 to 300, and the NPA itself, according to Ramos, is just the tip of the iceberg. A much larger organization conducts propaganda and raises money. In some areas, the NPA collects taxes, and village chiefs do not sleep in the villages at night. The NPA is threatening to extend the insurgency to urban areas, including Manila.

(4) The bloated and top-heavy Philippine army has lost much of its spirit and discipline and is badly in need of reform to prevent abuses, but President Ferdinand Marcos is reluctant to reform an army he increasingly needs for support. There is a moderate opposition, but it lacks an acknowledged leader who can unify it.

(5) Optimists can point to the new reform movement among the junior officers in the army who are determined to get rid of incompetent and corrupt senior officers and to end the abuses of military power. At this writing, a key question is what will happen in the elections Marcos has scheduled for 1986. Will the elections be fair? Is it likely that Marcos will allow the opposition to come to power? An election process that seems tarnished will probably contribute to Marcos's unpopularity and feed the forces of radicalism. Pessimists point to the division within the army; to the difficulties of ensuring free and fair elections; to divisions within the moderate opposition; and to many other obstacles to a smooth post-Marcos transition.

Revolution and/or radicalization in the Philippines could have many adverse effects on the security of East Asia and on the balance of power in the region.

The impact on U.S. attitudes would be deep. As Larry Niksch has pointed out, the post-Vietnam doubts about the political viability of the non-Communist states of East Asia would pose the question: if a country with half a century of American tutelage and backing could not develop viable political institutions, how can U.S. support for other Southeast Asian governments have positive results? Questions could arise about the future of ASEAN. There would be increasing penetration of the region by the Soviet Union. The Soviets have shown a low-key but growing interest in the Philippines. The loss to the United States of Subic and Clark military bases would be seen as a big plus for the Soviet Union and Vietnam and as an enormous blow to American credibility.

The Soviet Threat to Pakistan

The building Soviet pressure on Pakistan and the potential breakup of Pakistan as a result of external and internal pressures represent a third serious challenge to Western interests in Asia.

When Pakistani President General Mohammed Zia ul-Haq went to Moscow in March 1985 to attend Konstantin Chernenko's funeral, the new Soviet leadership bluntly warned him to cut off Pakistani aid to Afghan insurgents or face a new Soviet campaign to goad the disgruntled Baluch minority into breaking away from the Pakistani state. According to one informed analyst, Mohammed Ayoob, writing in the summer 1985 *Foreign Policy,* Pakistan's military leadership has led the country into peril by sharply restricting internal political activity and by neglecting the grievances of ethnic minorities. "Together, internal divisions and external pressures are pushing Pakistan to the point at which other Third World countries, such as Cyprus, Lebanon and Pakistan itself in 1971, have fallen apart."

Pakistan's ethnic problems stem largely from the continuing struggle of its three smaller provinces, Baluchistan, the Northwest Frontier Province, and Sind, to resist the domination of the far more populous Punjab. The Sind has become a hotbed of separatist feeling since the execution of its favorite son, Zulfikar Ali Bhutto, in 1979. The province's small towns and rural areas erupted in late 1983, and reports suggest that much of the Sindhi countryside, the most economically depressed part of the country, continues to seethe with resentment. A radical populist movement, the Sindhi Awami Tehrik (Sindhi Peoples Movement), blending peasant radicalism and Sindhi nationalism, has become extremely powerful.

Baluchistan has been remarkably passive in recent years. According to one Baluch leader, the reason is that the Baluch are husbanding their resources and waiting for the external environment to become favorable before striking Pakistan a deathblow.

In the Northwest Frontier Province, 3 million Afghan refugees have streamed into the province, and they are heavily armed. The Pushtun people of the province sympathize with their displaced Afghan cousins, but the Pakistani Pushtuns resent the new competition they now face for grazing land and jobs. Moreover, some leading local politicians demand autonomy for the province and favor negotiations with Kabul to find a political solution to the Afghanistan problem.

Zia continues to search, so far without success, for a formula to legitimize his authoritarian rule. In 1983 he unveiled a plan for an "Islamic" Pakistan with no political parties, but this triggered new antiregime outbursts. The opposition political parties, now virtually outlawed, boycotted the referendum on Islamization. Meanwhile, the Soviet Union has so far refrained from stepping up its support to Pakistani dissidents and separatists in Baluchistan and other areas, presumably because it still hopes to force Zia into accommodation with its client state in Kabul. But if Zia refuses such accommodation, the Soviets may yet escalate support to provincial dissidents.

In sum, although the overall picture in Asia is exceedingly positive, there are a variety of problems and challenges. The United States certainly cannot take Asia for granted. The Soviet military build-up in the Pacific, problems of political instability, and continuing Soviet opportunism will pose a number of difficult issues.

Coping with Soviet Power in the Pacific

The problem of coping with Soviet power in Asia can be discussed under four headings: the need to balance Soviet power; the importance of maintaining an effective security coalition; the importance of dealing with the "weak links"; and, finally, the desirability of some limited cooperation with the Soviet Union to manage and prevent crises and to reduce tensions.

Balancing Soviet Power

As already indicated, during the past decade or more, the Soviets have made impressive efforts to build up their military power in the Asia-Pacific region. Between 35 and 45 percent of Moscow's ICBM forces and ballistic missile firing submarines and more than 30 percent of its strategic bombers are now deployed east of the Urals. The Soviets have begun to deploy in the Far East a substantial number of SS-20 intermediate-range nuclear missiles which are capable of covering the entire East Asian archipelago from positions in Siberia. The Soviets are modernizing and expanding their Pacific fleet which is now the largest of their four fleets. They have acquired significant support facilities for this fleet in South Yemen, Ethiopia, and Vietnam. Moreover, the Soviet Union has a large naval construction program underway that, according to *Jane's Fighting Ships* will provide "formidable reinforcement." That program includes at least eight classes of surface ships and seven types of submarines. The Soviet submarine force is already the largest in the world. The Soviet naval aircraft program has kept pace with the ship building program and more than 100 Backfire bombers are now in service with Soviet Naval Aviation. In addition, approximately 325 long- and medium-range aircraft, some of them now stationed in Vietnam, are tasked for reconnaissance and antisubmarine warfare against U.S. Navy ships. Also, the Soviet Union is adding to the already large number of antiship cruise missiles deployed throughout the Soviet fleet.

Whatever the intentions of this huge Soviet military build-up in the Pacific, the very fact of its existence poses severe challenges to the United States and its allies. As the world's largest trading nation and head of a global maritime alliance, the United States has a vital interest in command of the Pacific. Its present strategy in the Pacific is based on a forward deployment of ground and air forces and a substantial naval presence. To carry out this forward strategy, maritime superiority is indispensable. There may be differences among U.S. military strategists on what kind of forward strategy and force projection capabilities best serve U.S. interests, but all schools accept the need for such naval superiority.

Although the United States still maintains naval superiority in the Pacific, the margin of that superiority is declining. Both the quantity and quality of Soviet surface ships, submarines, and naval aviation are increasing. The Senate Armed Services Committee heard testimony in 1984 from the commander in chief of the Atlantic Command that in the mid-1980s U.S. naval forces continue to be "stretched so thin that very little surge capability exists for rapid responses to additional crises."

It has been estimated that approximately 80 percent of the U.S. sealift fleet would be needed to support a continuing military presence in the Persian Gulf. The commander in chief of the Pacific Command testified in 1985 that, moreover, "the Pacific and Indian Ocean basins present a different military challenge than any other theater" because "the vast distances influence everything we do" and because our facilities and our allies are widely spread over islands and around the littoral.

There is also the chronic problem of credibility. Although the Reagan administration's military build-up has gone a long way toward dispelling doubts among American allies as to American reliability in case of crises, such doubts continue to exist. Recent polls among Japanese indicate a basic lack of confidence that the United States would honor its commitments under the security treaty signed by the two countries in 1960. The *New York Times* reported on August 6, 1985, that "suspicions that the United States may be a muscle bound giant set in during the hostage crisis in Iran five years ago, and they have not been dispelled by American immobility during more recent episodes."

To meet the Soviet military challenge in the Pacific and elsewhere, the United States is engaged in a long overdue effort to build a 600-ship navy that includes a level of 15 deployed aircraft carriers by 1990. Deployable naval vessels reached 545 in 1985. It will be necessary to sustain these programs in the face of rising U.S. public criticisms of allegedly excessive defense spending. This will not be an easy task in a nation where public moods on defense are highly volatile. It will also be important for Japan to continue the quantitative and qualitative improvements of its fleet and to sustain the higher level of cooperation with the U.S. fleet that has developed in recent years.

Finally, more thought needs to be given to the role in Pacific defense of other interested parties, including South Korea, Australia, the ASEAN states, France, Britain, and China. It is possible, for example, to imagine cooperative efforts between the United States and a number of Pacific countries on air defense and intelligence gathering. Japan could play a key role in guarding the exits from the Sea of Japan and thereby greatly complicate Soviet defense planning. So long as the Soviet Union continues to build up its military power in the Pacific at such an impressive rate, the need for greater efforts and greater burden-sharing on the part of the Western alliance will remain.

The Pacific Coalition

Building and maintaining an effective coalition to contain Soviet power is the second challenge facing the United States in the Pacific. At a time when relative U.S. economic and military power is declining, when Soviet military power is growing, and when nuclear stalemate reduces the credibility of extended deterrence, the U.S. needs the help of its allies more than ever before. Robert Komer, in *Maritime Strategy or Coalition Defense,* concludes:

Indeed, the single greatest remaining U.S. strategic advantage over the USSR is that we are blessed with many rich allies while the Soviets have only a handful of poor ones. Most of theirs are a strain on the Soviet exchequer whereas most of ours pay their own way. They also fear their own forced allies while we fear *for* ours.

The U.S. has to maintain the Pacific coalition in the face of substantial Soviet efforts to break it up and in spite of equally substantial divergences of interest among the members of this coalition. It can be expected that Soviet efforts to intimidate Japan will grow to the extent that Japan increases its security cooperation with the United States and adds to its own military forces. Efforts to intimidate may be coupled with efforts to woo. Similar tactics will be employed against China.

The United States will be faced also with the need to try to reconcile divergent perspectives and interests among its Pacific partners. The conflict with New Zealand over port calls of U.S. nuclear warships is an example of the difficulties such a task presents. Dealing too harshly with New Zealand runs the risk of jeopardizing the ANZUS alliance. Dealing too leniently runs the risk of encouraging other American allies in the region to follow in New Zealand's path.

Other contradictions abound. The United States requires Japanese naval assistance in keeping open the Pacific sea lanes of communication; yet other Asian allies are extremely wary of the Japanese. Similarly, the United States intends to help China defend itself against the Soviet Union, but other Asian countries are fearful that the United States may go too far in developing China's military power. It will be the continuing task of American diplomacy to be sensitive to these differences and to prevent them from disrupting the security coalition.

Weak Links

Plugging the "weak links" in the U.S. position in the Pacific will also be difficult. There will be no easy or quick solutions to the U.S.–Japanese trade competition, to the crisis in the Philippines, or to Pakistan's ethnic rivalries. Nor can anyone be sure that China's new "open door" will remain as open in the post-Deng era as it has been since 1980. Dealing with these issues will require great skill and patience.

The United States has adopted a sensible course of action toward the building crisis in the Philippines. It has begun to insist on military, economic, and political reform in the Philippines and to link progress in these areas with the levels of American military and economic assistance. It has made clear to President Marcos that it expects free elections in the future, and it has not hesitated to broaden its contacts with the moderate opposition. But no one can be certain of a smooth post-Marcos succession. There will always remain the danger of a military coup or even of civil war.

Under these circumstances, the United States can only continue to press Marcos to turn over power peacefully and democratically and to hope that a post-Marcos government, after receiving a democratic mandate, can more effectively deal with the insurgency. If Marcos does pass on power peacefully, the United States and its allies should be prepared to inject massive amounts of economic assistance into the Philippines.

With regard to the U.S.–Japanese trade issue, one can only hope that Japanese efforts to open domestic markets and American efforts to lower the budgetary deficit, accompanied by continuing economic progress in both countries and a declining dollar, will gradually defuse the present inflammatory situation. It is encouraging that, despite the trade issue, the overwhelming majority of Americans and Japanese continue to regard the other country as friendly. In a recent survey of 1,569 adult Americans, 88 percent viewed relations with Japan as friendly, with 23 percent describing them as very friendly. Similarly, a solid majority of 1,428 Japanese adults surveyed, 73 percent, described ties between the two countries as amicable. The task for American and Japanese leaders is to make sure that these overwhelmingly positive attitudes do not erode in the years ahead as a result of continuing trade frictions.

In contrast to the first two or three years of the Reagan administration, when U.S. relations with China were erratic and tense, these relations have now become much more stable. This relationship should be able to weather minor changes in China's "open door" policy. Technology transfer from the

United States to China has grown rapidly in the past two years. Scientific, educational, and cultural exchanges have proliferated. Some thirteen American companies are collaborating with the Chinese in the search for oil. Trade has increased rapidly. The United States is now exploring ways of assisting the Chinese in upgrading their antitank and antiair defense as well as their capacity to wage antisubmarine warfare.

Given the Soviet military build-up in Siberia, the long and disputed border between Russia and China, the continuing geopolitical competition between the two countries in Korea, Indochina, and Southern Asia, and the past history of relations, it seems likely that China will continue to regard the Soviet Union as its main enemy and to welcome U.S. efforts to balance Soviet power, particularly in Asia. A stable and cooperative Sino-American relationship is as much in China's interest as it is in America's.

In Pakistan, as in the Philippines, there will be no quick or easy solutions to the problems of potential political instability. The United States should continue to increase military assistance to Pakistan as a token of support against Soviet efforts to intimidate, but it also should encourage President Zia to give greater autonomy to the provinces in order to defuse ethnic unrest. The United States should also seek to enlist India's efforts in defusing Soviet pressure on Pakistan. It surely could not be in India's interests for Pakistan to be dismembered again.

Cooperation with the Soviet Union

Finally, there is the problem of dealing with the Soviet Union directly as an Asian power. It is time to engage the Soviets in some dialogue on Asian security issues. The basic relationship between the U.S. and the Soviet Union in Asia will continue to be a competitive one. But we have a common interest in avoiding nuclear proliferation and in damping down regional conflicts that could lead to superpower confrontation.

It cannot be reasonably denied that the Soviet Union, while

an adversary, is also an Asian power with some legitimate interests in the region. In Asia, the United States and the Soviet Union share some limited but significant common interests. Neither wants a new Korean war. Neither wants incidents at sea that could lead to confrontation. Neither wants to see the proliferation of nuclear weapons to non-nuclear states. Neither wants to see the conflict in Kampuchea escalated. In sum, the Soviet Union is as concerned as the United States about the dangers of confrontation and escalation and the threat of war.

In the early months after his assumption of power, Soviet leader Mikhail Gorbachev offered to undertake a wide-ranging discussion of Asian security issues with interested Asian powers. It is time for the United States, *after* very careful consultation with its Asian allies and friends, to explore some aspects of this offer.

The Korean peninsula may be the place to begin. In the past, Moscow has been extremely prudent in the Korean peninsula. Until quite recently it had refused to sell advanced fighter planes to North Korea, and, on a number of occasions in the 1960s and 1970s, it made clear its disapproval of provocative North Korean actions against the United States and South Korea. The Soviet Union does not want a new Korean war. The Soviets cannot afford to let Pyongyang win or lose a new Korean war. A North Korean loss in a new war would have profound political and psychological consequences among the Soviet Union's other allies and treaty partners. A North Korean victory would run the risk of a Soviet-American military confrontation on Soviet borders, end whatever chances there are for improving Soviet-American relations, carry the risk of Chinese intervention, and lead to great pressure within Japan for Japanese remilitarization, all of which would be severely detrimental to Soviet interests.

The Soviets have probably warned Kim Il-Sung privately that the price of increased military and economic assistance is greater obeisance to Soviet foreign policy positions. There are signs that these warnings have been relatively successful. This warming trend in Soviet–North Korean relations comes at a time when both Moscow and Pyongyang want to improve relations with the West. Pyongyang, for its part, is losing the economic and diplomatic race with South Korea, and, if present trends continue, there will also come a time when it will fall behind in the military competition as well. At the same time, China has been acting as an intermediary between Pyongyang and Washington. Even more recently, a direct North-South Korean dialogue has begun. There have been Red Cross and economic talks, negotiations for an interparliamentary meeting, and even some talk of a summit meeting.

In sum, the present moment is the most propitious time since the early 1970s for a reduction of tension in the Korean peninsula. But South Korea remains wary. While the North makes overtures, it also continues to build up its military capabilities near the border. It is, in fact, unlikely that the direct dialogue between the two Koreas will go very far without substantial encouragement from the Great Powers.

The United States, *after* careful consultation with Japan, China, and South Korea, could begin to probe the Soviets on the Korean issue. The Soviets, if they so choose, could lend their weight to a substantial reduction of tensions in Korea by improving their relations with South Korea as the U.S. improved its relations with North Korea. If the two superpowers could lend their respective weights to an easing of tensions on the Korean peninsula, this in itself would have an extremely beneficial impact on their relationship more generally.

To sum up, if the West wants to reduce tensions with the Soviet Union in East Asia, it will have to adopt a policy that combines the important but limited insights of both "hawks" and "doves." On the one hand, it must continue to build up its strength to balance Soviet power. On the other, it must seek, whenever common interests dictate, to probe for ways to reduce tensions.

5

East-West Tensions
in Africa

DAVID E. ALBRIGHT

T he 1980s have witnessed a visible decline in the overall
importance of East-West rivalry in the affairs of Africa.
Indeed, such problems as mounting political instability on the
continent, the poor economic performance of many states, the
widespread failure of food production to keep pace with population growth, and a major debt crisis have made East-West
tensions there pale in significance. Nonetheless, friction between East and West persists in Africa, and there is substantial
potential for it to increase in severity and consequences for the
West in general and the United States in particular in the years
ahead.

DAVID E. ALBRIGHT is professor of national security affairs, Air
War College, Maxwell Air Force Base. He has lectured extensively at
military and academic institutions and the State Department's Foreign Service Institute, and served as an editor of *Problems of Communism* with the United States Information Agency. Dr. Albright has
published widely on issues of foreign and defense policy and comparative politics, with an emphasis on the Communist states and a concentration on Africa. The views expressed in his chapter are his own
and do not necessarily reflect those of the U.S. government.

AFRICA

Both East and West have contributed to the discord and conflict that exist between them on the continent in the 1980s, but the fundamental reasons for the tensions lie on the East's side. Specifically, the friction stems from a combination of two circumstances: the USSR has global aspirations that it seeks to further in Africa, and Moscow regards East-West competition there as essentially a zero-sum game, in which gains for one side inevitably entail losses for the other side. To be sure, ideological considerations still play some role; however, they have become decidedly secondary as an influence.

Another factor greatly exacerbates the tensions that flow from these root causes. In pursuing its ends in Africa, the USSR has come to rely heavily upon military instruments. These include not only its own but also those of its allies. Although military instruments have always figured in the Soviet approach to the continent since the USSR first emerged as a major actor there in the mid-1950s, they have assumed much greater prominence in that approach since the early 1970s.

This chapter will discuss in some depth the nature of these sources of East-West tensions in Africa and will look at their precise ramifications in three specific regions—North Africa, the Horn, and Southern Africa. These areas have generated most of the difficulties between East and West on the continent in the 1980s.

Basic Origins of Tensions

Of the fundamental reasons for East-West tensions in Africa in the 1980s, the USSR's drive for global power status must be judged the key one. The significance of the rest derives in large measure from their links to it.

Global Power Ambitions

Major Soviet contacts with Africa began in the mid-1950s with the USSR's establishment of close ties with Egypt, but Moscow did not come to look upon the continent as a proving ground for Soviet global power status until after the Soviet launching of an Intercontinental Ballistic Missile (ICBM) in late 1957. In the wake of that development, Nikita Khrushchev declared that the USSR had emerged as a global power. As the USSR quickly discovered, however, global power status is not something that the international community simply confers on a country. It must be achieved and sustained by the nation itself. To acquire it and keep it, moreover, requires that a state demonstrate its power to reach into even the remotest corners of the world and affect events there. Thus, Africa became an arena in which Moscow sought to show that the USSR deserved recognition as a global power.

Soviet Dedication to Goal. At the outset, the USSR actually did not have much of a presence in Africa and played little role in the affairs of the continent. Indeed, the setbacks that the Soviets suffered in trying to alter this situation quickly—for example, in the Congo, Guinea, and Algeria—contributed to Moscow's decision in the mid-1960s to soft-pedal its global power claims. Yet the Soviet commitment to validating these claims in Africa and elsewhere around the world did not waver. By the early 1970s, the USSR had made sufficient progress toward accomplishing this goal that it again voiced its pretensions openly. Andrei Gromyko, then foreign minister, told the Twenty-fourth Congress of the Communist Party of the Soviet Union (CPSU) in April 1971 that "today there is no question of any significance which can be decided without the Soviet Union or in opposition to it."

The ensuing years have brought abundant evidence of the continuing resolve of Soviet leaders to use Africa as a locale for substantiating their contentions that the USSR qualifies as a global power. Moscow has labored assiduously to build up its links with the continent. By the mid-1980s the USSR had succeeded in setting up embassies in all but a handful of African states, the most important of which was South Africa. It had also concluded formal treaties of friendship and cooperation with six African countries, although two of these countries, Egypt and Somalia, had subsequently renounced the accords after the documents had entered into force. As of late 1983 the USSR had signed agreements on economic and technical cooperation with 35 African states, and it had promised to construct more than 500 industrial, agricultural, and other projects on the continent. Its specific economic undertakings include helping Nigeria to build an iron and steel complex at Ajaokuta and assisting Morocco to develop phosphate deposits at Meskala. The Nigerian enterprise, when completed, will constitute the largest such facility in Africa, and the Moroccan phosphate scheme involves Soviet credit and trade arrangements expected to amount to $10 billion by the end of the twentieth century. By the early 1980s, about 20,000 Soviet economic technicians were working in Africa. During 1980–82, the USSR's trade turnover with countries on the continent had reached an average of $3 billion a year. Over the period from 1973 to 1982, Moscow provided arms to twenty-five different African states plus several "national liberation" movements, mostly in Southern Africa. Moscow during these years constituted the sole source of weapons and equipment for three states and the primary source for another thirteen states. By the early 1980s, nearly 9,000 Soviet military technicians were functioning as advisers in African countries.

In addition, the USSR has striven to enlarge its physical presence in Africa. Besides the new elements of presence connected with Moscow's burgeoning ties with the continent, there has been a substantial increase in Soviet military forces in the waters around Africa. In 1964 the USSR had deployed Soviet naval units in the Mediterranean Sea, near the shores of North Africa, for the first time on a permanent basis. The size of this squadron peaked in the early and mid-1970s at about fifty ships at any given juncture, but as of the mid-1980s the squadron still consisted of an average of eight to ten submarines, twelve to fourteen surface combatants, ten to twelve auxiliaries, and four to six intelligence-collection vessels a day. By the mid-1980s, the continuing naval presence that the USSR had established in 1969 in the Indian Ocean off the east coast of Africa had grown to an average of two or three submarines, eight surface combatants, two amphibious ships, and twelve support vessels at any single moment. In 1970, the USSR instituted a naval patrol in the eastern Atlantic along the west coast of Africa, and the size of this patrol averaged six to eight vessels a day in the mid-1980s.

Finally, Moscow has insisted on having a say in the continent's affairs. Perhaps the most dramatic illustrations have had to do with African crises. During the Angolan civil war of 1975–76, the USSR collaborated with Cuba and the German Democratic Republic to install the Popular Movement for the Liberation of Angola in power in Luanda. Although Soviet contributions to this undertaking lay largely in the realm of logistics, they were vital to its success and hence decisive in the outcome of the war. The same was true of the conflict between Ethiopia and Somalia in the Ogaden in 1977–78. A massive supply of Soviet arms, estimated to have amounted to about $1 billion in value, enabled Cuban and Ethiopian troops to turn the tide of battle in favor of Ethiopia. But there have been many other instances as well. For example, Moscow has prodded Egypt and the other Arab states of North Africa to endorse the convening of an international conference on the Arab-Israeli problem at which the USSR would serve as cochair.

Former Soviet Foreign Minister Gromyko underscored the import of all these strands of policy in June 1983 in a report that he made to the USSR Supreme Soviet. He observed: "The Soviet Union's international ties with states representing a broad political spectrum testify . . . to realization of the fact that practically not a single serious question of world politics can be solved—nor is in fact solved—without its participation. That is as it should be."

Anti-Western Thrust. The determination of Soviet leaders to fashion a relationship with Africa that will bolster the USSR's claims to global power status does not in itself, of course, threaten Western interests. What renders that determination troubling from the Western standpoint is Moscow's strategy for bringing about the relationship that it desires. This strategy has varied in nature over the years, but a common element has run through its different formulations. The USSR has consistently attempted to exploit and even heighten anti-Western sentiments in Africa. A brief review of the major phases in the evolution of the Soviet strategy will reinforce the point.

From the late 1950s until the mid-1960s, Moscow believed that, with the collapse of colonialism in Africa, there were good prospects in at least portions of the continent for revolutionary changes that would drive a permanent wedge between the states there and the West, and it tried to associate the USSR with the forces that it felt would effect such changes. The character of these efforts altered somewhat over the period. At first, Moscow regarded Africa's new postcolonial rulers as capable of launching initial "progressive" reforms but unprepared to carry out "genuinely socialist" changes; nevertheless, the Soviets foresaw that the revolutionary process, once set in motion by the present rulers, would quickly bring to the fore orthodox Communists dedicated to the total restructuring of their societies. When Communist parties failed to form in most African countries and those that did exist remained weak in influence, Moscow revised its position. It persuaded itself that radical African leaders like Kwame Nkrumah of Ghana, Modibo Keita of Mali, Gamal Abdel Nasser of Egypt, and Ahmed Ben Bella of Algeria had long-range revolutionary potential. That is, these leaders might, like Fidel Castro in Cuba, embrace Marxism-Leninism and move to implement it in their states. In the course of doing so, they would set up Communist parties to consolidate their new orders.

From the mid-1960s until the end of the 1970s, Moscow no longer held out hopes for Communist revolutions in Africa in the foreseeable future, but it did perceive possibilities for building long-term structural relationships with African countries attempting to decrease the local role of the West. Although Soviet leaders put a diversity of states in this group, they paid the most attention to those which they classified as "socialist-oriented." That was particularly true in the latter part of the 1970s, with the emergence of a substantial number of self-proclaimed Marxist-Leninist governments in sub-Saharan Africa.

The long-term structural relationship that Moscow originally had in mind was an international economic division of labor. That is, the USSR would furnish the financing, technical advice, and equipment for economic projects that would produce goods for the Soviet market when completed. However, developments in the 1970s triggered a modification in Soviet thinking on this matter. The mounting problems that the Soviet economy was experiencing reduced the chances that the USSR would be able to forge a meaningful international economic division of labor with African countries. At the same time, the rising number of avowedly Marxist-Leninist regimes on the continent suggested to Moscow another kind of structural relationship that it might foster—joint collaboration with radical African governments in constructing institutions that would permit these governments to entrench themselves in power. This would entail cooperation in building a party apparatus, in creating or bolstering intelligence and security services, in training military personnel, and the like. By the late 1970s, the USSR was devoting the bulk of its energies to establishing this sort of structural relationship.

In the 1980s Moscow has, at least in most cases, abandoned efforts to fashion long-term structural relationships with African states; yet it has continued to rely primarily on frictions between the West on the one hand and ruling and nonruling African political forces on the other as a basis for enhancing Soviet presence and influence on the continent. Several considerations brought about the rethinking on long-term structural ties with Africa. To begin with, Soviet leaders concluded that the condition of the USSR's economy at present precluded the creation of an international economic division of labor with the continent. As for the notion of collaborating with radical African governments in institution-building, Moscow now judged that the great bulk of African countries were going to pass through a "capitalist" stage of development, and it anticipated that such a circumstance would inevitably keep the number of "socialist-oriented" states relatively low for the indefinite future. Furthermore, even the self-professed Marxist-Leninist governments in "socialist-oriented" countries had, in Soviet eyes, displayed a tendency to vacillate in their foreign policies, so the prospects for long-range cooperation between the USSR and any "socialist-oriented" governments were at best somewhat cloudy.

Despite its disillusionment with undertakings to establish long-term structural links with African states, Moscow has perceived that harmony does not exist between various African political elements and the West. In fact, Soviet analysis has contended, even many non-"socialist-oriented" forces display a substantial degree of antagonism toward the West. Some, for example, speak out for "national-capitalist" development and against "dependent-capitalist" development based on close economic ties with the West. Others deplore the encroachment of Western ideas of modernization on Islamic traditions and call for a return to Islamic fundamentalism. Such attitudes, Moscow has maintained, offer openings for the USSR further to improve its position on the continent.

As Soviet leaders have been aware, of course, opportunities of this sort derive from limited convergences of interests; thus, the opportunities can disappear fairly rapidly if interests overall diverge significantly. Therefore, to minimize the adverse effects that specific instances of such divergence might have, Moscow has opted to expand and diversify its contacts in Africa. The more extensive Soviet relations with the continent, it has calculated, the less important any individual ones become.

The USSR's attempts to manifest global power attributes in the African context, then, do have a distinctly anti-Western thrust to them. This thrust makes it difficult for the West to draw a clear line between what constitute legitimate Soviet pursuits on the continent and what do not. The consequence is that all Soviet undertakings in Africa tend to take on an illegitimate air from the Western perspective.

Zero-Sum Game Mentality

Moscow's inclination to see its fortunes in Africa as inversely related to those of the West in general and the United States in particular heightens the anti-Western aspect of the USSR's efforts to function as a global power on the continent. Thus, it contributes significantly to Western concerns about the Soviet push for global power status in Africa.

This propensity to view East-West rivalry in Africa in terms of a zero-sum game runs deep among the Soviet elite. Signs of it appear constantly in Soviet commentaries about the continent. A remark in late 1978 by Anatolii Gromyko, the director of the African Institute of the USSR Academy of Sciences and the son of then Foreign Minister Gromyko, affords a good illustration. "After the collapse of the Portuguese colonial empire and especially after the Angolan events," he said, "the U.S. government drastically stepped up its diplomatic, political and ideological activities in Africa in an attempt to prop up its waning prestige and weaken the growing influence of the USSR and other countries of the socialist community."

Even when Soviet analysts have conceded a long-range role to the West in Africa, they have done so by and large on grounds that the USSR and its allies lack the means to replace the West in these contexts in the near future. The principal example comes from the economic sphere. For many years, Soviet writers have counseled even the more radical "socialist-oriented" states of the continent to work out "a system of regulation" that would "grant sufficient advantages to [Western] foreign investors to attract them." Such advice, however, has typically been accompanied by anticipation of an eventual decline of the direct Western economic impact on Africa. This would result from "a long-term [Soviet and African] strategy" for "industrialization of the former colonies and semicolonies according to fundamentally different principles of social and international economic relations than those inherent in capitalism."

During the late 1970s and early 1980s, it is true, a school of thought emerged within the Soviet hierarchy that represents a departure from the traditional outlook on the nature of East-West competition in Africa and other portions of the Third World. It holds that some Third World issues loom so large that they require "global" attention. That is, they constitute problems upon which East and West can work together to the benefit of all parties. The African economic situation seems to qualify as one such problem in the eyes of the supporters of this perspective.

Nevertheless, the adherents of this school of thought have not had much visible effect on the USSR's policy toward Africa. The single possible exception of note relates to Southern Africa. During 1984, Soviet representatives began to argue —to some degree in print and much more extensively in private conversations with Americans—that neither superpower has "vital" interests in Southern Africa. Rather, these representatives contended, both have "legitimate" interests. Implicitly, this formulation asserted that it was possible to reconcile the interests of the two in the region. Even in this case, however, the evidence of the influence of the "globalist" viewpoint was not absolutely clear-cut, for the innovation in the Soviet approach came at a time when Moscow perceived that the USSR's position in Southern Africa might well be eroding.

The belief of most of the Soviet elite that East-West relations with Africa constitute a zero-sum game probably derives in a specific sense from the Marxist-Leninist tenet about the basic hostility of "capitalism" and "imperialism" toward "socialist" forces, but it is important to remember that a zero-sum game mentality is not unique to the champions of Marxism-Leninism. The rulers of Nazi Germany and Japan in the 1930s and 1940s evinced it in their policies in Europe and Pacific Asia respectively. Even the leaders of the United States and Great Britain have exhibited it at times across the twentieth century—for instance, during the confrontation with fascism in Europe in the 1940s.

The Ideological Element

When the USSR first established itself as a significant actor on the African scene in the mid-1950s, traditional Marxist-Leninist perspectives greatly affected its behavior on the continent. Hence, ideology had a lot to do with the tensions that prevailed between East and West during the early years of their competition in Africa. By the 1980s, however, Moscow had discarded many of these Marxist-Leninist notions as a basis for approaching the continent. As a result, ideology per se has become a fairly minor generator of East-West tensions.

To delineate the extent of the changes that have taken place in this regard, it is useful to focus on four key questions that Moscow addresses in shaping its policy toward Africa. These are: What is the nature of the enemy on the continent? Who are the objective opponents of this enemy? With whom of these opponents should the USSR try to ally itself? On what foundation should it attempt to effect an alliance?

Nature of the Enemy. In accordance with longstanding Marxist-Leninist doctrine, Moscow in the 1950s held that "imperialism" constituted the main enemy in Africa of all international "socialist" forces, headed by the USSR. "Imperialism" Moscow defined as the West in general and the United States and the colonial powers of Western Europe in particular. Soviet analysts did acknowledge that certain local "feudal" and "reactionary" elements on the continent might qualify as enemies too because of close ties with "imperialism," but they regarded these as decidedly secondary in significance. In keeping with Marxist-Leninist thinking about "imperialism," Moscow also viewed the West as a permanent, implacable foe. Temporary compromise with the West might be possible on specific matters; however, its fundamental hostility would not alter.

The passing years have witnessed little modification in this Soviet conception of the enemy in Africa. As mentioned earlier, a strand of opinion that stresses the possibility of working productively with the West to deal with issues of overriding "global" consequence did develop among the Soviet elite in the late 1970s and early 1980s. Yet even the proponents of this outlook have not questioned the perception that the West has a long-term, underlying antagonism toward the USSR. Moreover, their influence on Soviet policy toward the continent has been quite limited.

Opponents of the Enemy. In the mid-1950s, Moscow's identification of the adversaries of the West in Africa followed orthodox Marxist-Leninist lines. These adversaries consisted of two essential groups. One was composed of representatives of the working class and peasantry who demanded an end to "imperialist" domination of their countries and a total restructuring of their societies. At the forefront of these stood the committed Marxist-Leninist parties and individuals of the continent. The second group was comprised of "national bourgeois" elements. They wanted their countries to be independent of "imperialism," but they balked at the idea of a "socialist" transformation of their societies.

Over subsequent years, however, Moscow discerned many other kinds of opponents of the West in Africa, none of which existed in classical Marxist-Leninist teachings. In the early 1960s, Soviet analysts discovered "national democrats" on the continent. As Soviet observers portrayed them, these elements issued from "national bourgeois" circles, but they did not seek merely to free their countries from "imperialist" political domination. Rather, they proposed to launch their countries on a "noncapitalist" path. From the Soviet standpoint, their conceptions of such a path had a variety of deficiencies, not the least of which was a vision of the path as a distinctively African form of socialism. Nevertheless, their general stance on the subject clearly set them apart from the traditional "national bourgeoisie." By the 1970s, Soviet commentators were employing the label "socialist-oriented" to refer to organizations and persons of this type, but Soviet spokesmen continued to see such elements as part of the African scene even in the 1980s.

Not long after Moscow acknowledged the presence of "national democrats" among the adversaries of the West in Africa, it expanded the list of foes again by including "revolutionary democrats" on it. These elements, in Soviet judgment, had a lot in common with "national democrats" yet differed from them in a key respect—that is, they depicted their versions of "socialism" as adaptations of Marxism-Leninism to African conditions and called for a radical revamping of their societies. Until the mid-1960s, indeed, Soviet leaders hoped that these "revolutionary democrats" might even effect a transition to Communist rule in their states in the not too distant future.

Although such Soviet hopes had vanished by the late 1960s, Soviet analysts persisted in regarding "revolutionary democrats" as a distinct African force at odds with the West.

In the 1970s Moscow divided African "revolutionary democrats" into two categories and began to treat them as separate types of opponents of the West. One group conformed to past definitions of "revolutionary democrats," while the other group had attributes of a somewhat higher order of revolutionary. Specifically, the latter group's representatives professed to be committed Marxist-Leninists and operated through "vanguard" parties in pursuing their ends. According to Soviet assessments, such people lacked a good understanding of Marxism-Leninism at present, and the "vanguard" parties through which they functioned fell considerably short of Communist parties. Nevertheless, Soviet observers deemed that the group possessed features that distinguished it from other "revolutionary democrats." This two-tier Soviet perception of "revolutionary democrats" still prevails in the 1980s.

The late 1970s and early 1980s yielded further additions to Moscow's roster of African adversaries of the West. The first and foremost of these was the "national capitalists." In the Soviet perspective such elements favored development of their countries along "capitalist" lines, but they rejected "dependent-capitalist" development, or development in which the West played a large role. Thus, they wanted to strengthen both the political and economic independence of their states, even though they preferred the "capitalist" road instead of the "socialist" road. In this sense, they differed from the straightforward "national bourgeoisie" of the continent.

Islamic fundamentalists constituted the other noteworthy addition. From the Soviet viewpoint, to be sure, the religious commitment of these elements was a sign of the backwardness of their outlook in certain regards; yet their dedication to Islam had positive aspects as well in Soviet eyes. Islam was an all-embracing way of life and not just a religion, and that way of life faced challenges from modernization, secularization, and Westernization in all African societies in which Islam existed. To those who wished to preserve the way of life in its pure form, all of these threats seemed to emanate from the West. Consequently, Islamic fundamentalists evinced a strong dislike of the West.

Choice of Allies. Moscow's decisions in the 1950s about whom in Africa to court as allies against the West reflected hallowed Marxist-Leninist criteria. As principal allies, the USSR looked to the Marxist-Leninist parties and individuals of the continent. Soviet analysts conceded the present weakness of the Marxist-Leninist forces there, but the analysts asserted that with the impending demise of colonialism in Africa the ranks and influence of these forces were going to grow rapidly. At the same time, in light of the current lack of strength and impact of the continent's Marxist-Leninist forces, the USSR turned to the African "national bourgeoisie" as a secondary ally. Not only did this group dominate the opposition to the West on the continent, Soviet commentators pointed out, but it also was assuming the leadership of the newly independent states that were blossoming forth there.

During the ensuing years, however, traditional Marxist-Leninist criteria figured less and less in Moscow's judgments about desirable allies in Africa against the West. Two factors contributed heavily to this decline. Orthodox Marxist-Leninist forces on the continent remained small in numbers and marginal in influence. In Soviet eyes, this situation did not make these forces worthless as allies across the long haul; nonetheless, it did render dubious their utility as primary allies for the indefinite future. Marxism-Leninism also offered little practical guidance on how to evaluate many of the proliferating adversaries of the West that Soviet observers perceived in Africa, for these elements did not conform to existing Marxist-Leninist categories.

A short rundown of the major shifts in the USSR's view of its main potential African allies against the West and the apparent grounds upon which it singled out these elements will suffice to illustrate the decreasing relevance of Marxism-Leninism to such matters. At the outset of the 1960s, Moscow defined ruling "national democrats" in states like Guinea,

Ghana, and Mali as its chief targets to woo as allies. These governing forces, it contended, not only professed to want to launch their countries on a "noncapitalist" path but actually had the authority to take such a step. Moreover, they displayed an inclination to allow local Marxist-Leninists to play a role in the affairs of their countries.

Later in the 1960s, Moscow focused its attention on ruling "revolutionary democrats" in states like the United Arab Republic (Egypt), Algeria, Ghana, and Mali. These leaders, from the Soviet perspective, could well become converts to Marxism-Leninism. They equated their versions of "socialism" with Marxism-Leninism, and they showed a willingness to undertake major internal reforms within their countries.

By the latter part of the 1960s, Moscow had designated all rulers of "socialist orientation"—those of Tanzania as well as those of Algeria and Guinea—to be the principal objects of its courtship as allies. It now discounted the possibility that "revolutionary democrats" might accept Marxism-Leninism as a guide for their policies, but it held that the commitment to "socialism" on their part and on the part of other "socialist-oriented" leaders offered solid ground for mutual cooperation between them and the USSR. In the 1970s, as self-proclaimed Marxist-Leninists assumed power in states like the Congo, Angola, and Mozambique and set up "vanguard" parties there, Moscow paid greater heed to these "socialist-oriented" rulers than to others on the continent, for their outlooks seemed to have the most in common with that of the USSR. Nevertheless, Moscow did not revise its notion of chief potential allies to exclude other governing elements of "socialist orientation" on the continent.

At the beginning of the 1980s, Moscow broadened its conception of the main African targets for Soviet wooing to encompass "national-capitalist" leaders in states like Nigeria as well as "socialist-oriented" leaders. It had concluded by this juncture that most African countries were going to pass through a phase of "capitalist" development, and such a prospect, as Moscow was quick to point out, meant that "socialist-oriented" rulers probably would constitute a minority on the continent for a long time to come. This likelihood, in turn, suggested a need to search for allies among "capitalist-oriented" leaders. According to Soviet analysis, the desire of "national-capitalist" rulers to preclude economic development that would increase the dependence of their countries on the West provided them with good reason to be interested in working with the USSR in certain respects.

Basis of Cooperation. Moscow's thinking in the mid-1950s about the foundation upon which the USSR could build an anti-Western front with those whom Moscow had pinpointed as desirable allies in Africa derived entirely from classical Marxist-Leninist prescriptions. With the Marxist-Leninists of the continent, Soviet leaders held, the USSR would try to collaborate to bring about a transition to Communist rule there; with the "national bourgeoisie," and especially the governing elements of new states, it would seek to cooperate in the realm of foreign policy, specifically on a program of peaceful coexistence of countries with different social systems and a rapid abolition of colonialism.

But this situation altered drastically across the following years. The most striking evidence comes from the bases upon which the USSR approached the forces that it identified as its key potential allies on the continent. These had little in common with Marxist-Leninist precepts on how to construct alliances with non-Western "anti-imperialist" elements that did not qualify as Marxist-Leninists.

At the beginning of the 1960s, Moscow proposed to work with Africa's "national-democratic" rulers not just on foreign policy questions of mutual concern but also in the reshaping in a "noncapitalist" fashion of the societies that these leaders governed. A similar agenda underlay Soviet courtship of "revolutionary-democratic" rulers on the continent later in the decade, but Moscow in this case actually hoped to induce such leaders to embrace Marxism-Leninism and to introduce "genuine socialism" in their countries.

By the late 1960s, when the USSR fixed upon all rulers of "socialist orientation" as its logical primary allies, Moscow no longer anticipated that any portion of this group might join the ranks of committed Marxist-Leninists; nevertheless, it still discerned grounds for cooperation with them that extended beyond foreign policy. It maintained that their "socialist orientation" on internal matters opened up a possibility for the USSR to effect an international economic division of labor with their countries. Over subsequent years, Soviet faith in the USSR's ability to establish such an international division of labor gradually waned, but with the emergence of several avowedly Marxist-Leninist governments on the continent in the 1970s, Moscow did perceive an alternative basis for cooperation in the domestic arena with at least these governments. This involved the need of the governments to set up and bolster organizations that would help them implant themselves firmly in their local soil.

At the outset of the 1980s, when the Soviet definition of potential main allies in Africa broadened to include "national-capitalist" rulers there, Moscow asserted that these leaders had reason to desire to work closely with the USSR or issues of internal as well as external import. Specifically, they wanted to pursue "capitalist" development in their states that would have a minimum amount of strings to Western "capitalism."

In sum, then, the relevance of Marxism-Leninism to the way in which the USSR behaves in Africa in the 1980s lies essentially in the nature of the enemy that Moscow posits on the continent and the characteristics that it attributes to this enemy. Here Marxism-Leninism ties in with both the anti-Western thrust of the USSR's efforts to demonstrate global power status in Africa and the Soviet perception of East-West competition there as a zero-sum game.

On matters connected with the forming of alliances on the continent against the West, Marxism-Leninism has virtually no bearing. It does not determine what forces in Africa Moscow considers suitable allies, and it does not affect how the USSR goes about trying to forge alliances with these forces.

This diminished role of ideology with respect to the choice of potential allies and the approach to building alliances with them does not, it is true, enjoy universal support within the

Soviet hierarchy. Indeed, there have been signs that some members of the Soviet elite would prefer the USSR to devote greater energies than it does to the fostering and nourishing of traditional Marxist-Leninist parties in Africa. Yet these elements apparently constitute only a small minority of the elite, and they certainly do not exert visible influence on Soviet policy toward the continent in the 1980s.

An Intensifying Factor

Since early in the 1970s, a factor less fundamental than the foregoing three has contributed to East-West tensions in Africa. The USSR has emphasized military instruments in pursuit of its ends on the continent.

Moscow's Revised View of Military Means

Soviet use of military instruments in Africa dates from the initial days of major Soviet involvement on the continent in the mid-1950s. Indeed, a willingness to supply arms to Egypt accounted for the USSR's first big success in its efforts to establish relations with Africa.

Nevertheless, Moscow for many years tended to think of military instruments as merely supplemental to political and especially economic instruments. From the late 1950s, Soviet officials touted highly the USSR's ability to furnish economic aid to the states of the continent, and Soviet spokesmen attributed this ability to the USSR's model of development and specifically to the superiority of its socialist system. Although Russia had lagged behind the West in economic and technological terms at the time of the Great October Revolution in 1917, Russia's embrace of socialism, they argued, had permitted it to close the gap in a relatively short time. Now, they maintained, the USSR was on the verge of surpassing the West in these realms.

The pattern of Soviet assistance to African countries during these years conformed to such a perspective. Between 1955 and 1964, the states of sub-Saharan Africa received $490 million in economic commitments and $170 million in military deliveries from the USSR. To the countries of North Africa other than Egypt, Moscow extended $250 million in economic credits and furnished nearly $200 million in arms and equipment. The USSR committed $1 billion in economic aid and delivered approximately the same amount of military goods to Egypt.

As the 1960s progressed, however, it became increasingly apparent that the heady optimism of previous years about the speed at which the USSR would overtake and pass the West in economic performance had been misplaced. Thus Moscow felt compelled to downplay the Soviet model. Nonetheless, its belief in the efficacy of economic instruments as the key tools for achieving Soviet goals in Africa did not fade. It decided simply to take a different tack in economic activities. That is, it would henceforth offer economic aid to countries on the continent not essentially to try to curry political favor with them but rather to attempt to work out an international economic division of labor with them. In Soviet eyes, such a division of labor, as noted earlier, would lay the foundation for long-term cooperation of a mutually beneficial sort and, not incidentally, loosen the "imperialist fetters" that bound these countries.

The Soviet switch to a stress on military instruments is hard to pinpoint exactly, but indications of the change accumulated as the 1970s advanced. One telltale sign was the USSR's growing disposition to project its own military power even to the remote areas of Africa. Its behavior during the civil war in Angola in 1975–76 and the conflict between Ethiopia and Somalia in the Ogaden in 1977–78 constituted the leading examples.

Even more revealing, however, was the shift in the balance between the economic and military components of Soviet aid to African states. During the years 1965 to 1974, countries in sub-Saharan Africa garnered $380 million in Soviet economic credits, while Soviet arms deliveries to them totaled $240 million. Across the same period, the states of North Africa obtained $740 million in Soviet economic commitments and nearly $2.9 billion in Soviet deliveries of weapons and equipment. About $2.4 billion of the latter figure went to Egypt alone. From 1975 through 1979, the countries in sub-Saharan Africa got Soviet economic credits valued at only $335 million, but Soviet military deliveries to them shot up to more than $3.1 billion. Moscow's economic commitments to the states of North Africa over the same years rose to almost $2.4 billion; yet its deliveries of weapons and equipment to them exceeded $6.5 billion.

Although in the 1980s the USSR has attempted to reduce the weight of military instruments in its dealings with Africa, they have still remained the predominant element in its approach to the continent. During the period 1980 to 1984, the USSR preferred nearly $2.1 billion in economic assistance to the countries of sub-Saharan Africa, while its arms deliveries to them reached more than $5.9 billion. In the case of the North African countries, Moscow extended about $650 million in economic commitments and delivered almost $7.9 billion in weapons and equipment to them.

An eminent Soviet scholar in 1979 capsulized Moscow's basic rationale for the shift in emphasis. He observed: "We cannot match the U.S.A. in industry or agriculture, but we can overtake you in military power."

Effect on the West

Increased Soviet reliance on military means to further the USSR's purposes in Africa has aroused considerable concern in Western capitals. As Western leaders see things, it heightens the already severe instability of the continent, it enhances the chances of East-West military confrontation there, and it has adverse consequences for the West from a strategic standpoint.

Impact on Africa's Stability. According to Western assessments, the ready availability of Soviet arms and equipment works to destabilize the continent in two ways. First, it spurs Africans to pour scarce resources into excessive military buildups. Certainly, there can be no doubt that a major "militarization" of the continent has taken place since the early 1970s. At the end of the 1960s, only 40 percent of the states there devoted 2 percent or more of their gross national products to military expenditures, but by 1982 that figure had jumped to 80 percent. Whereas just two states allocated 5 percent or more of their gross national products to military outlays in the late 1960s, fourteen states did so by 1982. Arms imports provide equally telling evidence. From 1961 to 1971, African states received only about $4 billion in weapons and equipment from abroad, but during the period from 1978 to 1982 —half as many years—they obtained $31.5 billion worth of military deliveries from outside suppliers.

Second, easy access to Soviet arms encourages Africans to resort to force to resolve their grievances and conflicts. In Western perspective, such a stimulus is especially deleterious because of the tremendous proliferation of grievances and conflicts on the continent since the early 1970s.

Within African countries, mass popular movements have virtually disappeared, and ruling groups almost everywhere enjoy only limited social and political bases. Nevertheless, these ruling groups typically couch their particularistic interests in terms of "the national interest." As a consequence, they have prompted challenges from other groups with no less valid claims to reflect "the national interest." The inevitable result has been growing political fragmentation and rising political strife in domestic affairs.

Such circumstances have been exacerbated by the widespread lack of political institutions to aggregate interests and to channel political competition along constructive lines, by the fragility of most of the institutions that do exist, and by the pronounced cultural and ethnic differences in many states. In Namibia and South Africa, continued rule by whites over populations with large black majorities has provided an additional complication.

The economic problems that African countries have experienced have also created new sources of friction and discontent. About half of the African states recorded negative average rates of real growth of gross domestic product per capita in the 1970s and early 1980s. Even a larger proportion of them had average rates of increase in food production that fell short of average rates of population growth. Many countries, particularly those that produced no oil, faced a consistent worsening of their balance of payments situations in the 1970s and early 1980s, and a large number of them ran deficits during many years. To some extent, they succeeded in offsetting these losses through development assistance, but they had to sharply increase their borrowing abroad as well. This policy left them with external debts that they could not manage to service, let alone repay. Thus, most have had to reschedule their debt payments to commercial and/or multilateral lenders. All of these things together have made it exceedingly hard for governments on the continent even to maintain past standards of living in their countries, to say nothing of meeting the rising expectations of their peoples.

In the interstate realm, many disagreements stemming from precolonial and colonial days have turned into severe disputes. Libya, for example, has adamantly insisted on annexing portions of northern Chad and has actively sought to assert domination of at least the Muslim elements of the country's population. Rivalry over the Ogaden, furthermore, has sent traditional animosities between the ruling groups of Somalia and Ethiopia soaring.

Besides these historically rooted difficulties, there have emerged others of more contemporary origin. In the 1980s, for instance, Nigeria has antagonized not only its immediate neighbors but even countries like Ghana by closing its borders and expelling huge numbers of illegal immigrants to ease local unemployment and economic hardships for its own citizens.

East-West Military Confrontation. To the West, Moscow's reduced inhibitions about the direct military involvement of the USSR in Africa increase the danger of an East-West military clash on the continent. Although many African states have spent large amounts of money since the early 1970s to improve their military prowess, most of the countries of the continent remain exceedingly weak in military terms. In fact, a small but well-trained, well-equipped, and disciplined force could pose a major threat to the vast majority of them, particularly those in sub-Saharan Africa. To fend off a Soviet or Soviet-backed military operation, therefore, the great bulk of African states would probably require Western military assistance of some kind. The extension of such aid by the West, however, would inevitably risk an enlargement of the conflict.

As is widely recognized, of course, the USSR still faces significant limitations on its capabilities to function militarily in Africa. Perhaps the most critical limitation relates to the rapid deployment of men and equipment to the continent. Soviet sea lift capacities, to be sure, are impressive, especially in light of the USSR's possession of the world's largest merchant marine fleet; yet transport by sea from Soviet shores entails a lot of time. By the mid-1980s, the USSR had built up a fleet of about 600 military transport aircraft for carrying out quick deployments, and it could theoretically mobilize a large share of these in support of an undertaking in Africa. Nevertheless, the most advanced models in this fleet could fly only within a radius of 1,500 to 2,000 miles from Soviet bases without refueling—a distance that would put them well shy of many parts of Africa. Because the USSR also lacked in-flight refueling capabilities, it was thus dependent on access to en route refueling facilities to move men and equipment from Soviet bases to areas as remote as much of Africa. Aircraft with longer-range capabilities were under development, but they were not expected to make up a meaningful portion of the transport fleet before the early 1990s. Such considerations have continued to act as a brake on Soviet military activities on the continent.

Nevertheless, in the eyes of at least many Western observers, certain policies that Moscow has adopted have tended to offset the handicaps under which it labors in trying to project Soviet military power to Africa. The most important of these have to do with constraints on the USSR's ability to deploy men and equipment swiftly to the continent.

As mentioned previously, the USSR now maintains substantial naval forces in the waters around Africa on a permanent basis. These forces can reach the littoral states of the continent in fairly short order.

Soviet leaders help sustain the presence of Cuban combat troops in Africa. Relations between Havana and Moscow, it should be underscored, are complex, and Cuba plainly has interests and objectives on the continent distinct from those of the USSR. Yet Cuban military units could not operate for an extended period there without Soviet arms and logistical backup. Moreover, Fidel Castro seems to regard Cuban military activities in Africa as a means of rendering Moscow receptive to Cuban requests for additional economic and military aid. Consequently, the two Communist states perceive mutual benefits in working hand in hand on the continent.

By the mid-1980s, it is true, only two African states, Angola and Ethiopia, had proved willing to accept Cuban combat troops on a long-term basis, and the sizes of both contingents had dropped from peaks of 36,000 men in Angola in the mid-1970s and 12,000 in Ethiopia in the late 1970s to an estimated 30,000 soldiers in Angola and 2,500 in Ethiopia. But the significance of these deployments exceeded their geographic scope and their precise numbers. They meant that if a need arose, Cuba could dispatch forces to other nearby venues in sufficient quantities to have a good chance of influencing a situation in a manner that Havana and Moscow wished. There was some precedence for the use of deployed Cuban troops in this fashion. During the period in 1977 when Soviet-Ethiopian relations had become close, a substantial group of Cuban soldiers had gone from Angola to Ethiopia to assist the Ethiopians in fighting Somalia.

The USSR also seeks access to facilities in Africa that might simplify a rapid transfer of troops and/or military equipment to remote places on the continent. Over the years it has had both successes and reversals in such efforts, but in the mid-1980s it could apparently employ the port and airfield at Luanda, Angola, the naval installations in the Dahlak Islands and the airport at Asmara, Ethiopia, the harbor at Conakry,

Guinea, and perhaps ports and airfields in Libya for this purpose if it chose to do so.

Finally, Moscow supplies some African countries with arms well beyond their requirements for defense, and the excess stocks in effect constitute pre-positioned arsenals upon which the USSR conceivably could draw as long as it had the concurrence of the local governments to which it has delivered the weapons and equipment. Libya affords the classic case in point. By the mid-1980s, the USSR had sold Libya more than $15 billion in arms, about $10 billion of which it had already turned over to Libyan authorities. Among the items were 2,-800 tanks and about 450 combat aircraft, including both MiG-23s and MiG-25s. Much of this inventory of weapons and equipment, however, remained unused and in storage.

Strategic Ramifications. In Western and particularly U.S. appraisals, Moscow's heightened emphasis on military instruments to pursue its goals in Africa creates a mounting Soviet challenge to Western strategic interests related to the continent. Such a judgment rests upon two sorts of evidence.

To begin with, the expansion since the early 1970s of the USSR's naval presence in waters surrounding Africa—especially in waters off its west and east coasts—has meant a major growth of Soviet naval forces adjacent to areas of strategic consequence to the West. The USSR's West Africa patrol carries on its activities near states like Nigeria that produce large quantities of oil consumed by the West. Moscow's Indian Ocean squadron operates in close proximity to the Strait of Bab el-Mandeb and astride the sea lanes leading from the Persian Gulf down around the Cape of Good Hope. The Strait of Bab el-Mandeb constitutes an excellent point for choking off traffic between the Mediterranean Sea and the Indian Ocean. Since the 1970s, to be sure, the importance of transit from one of these bodies of water to another via the Suez Canal and the Red Sea has declined because the Canal cannot accommodate giant oil tankers; nevertheless, the route continues to be significant to the West for both military and commercial reasons. Along the Indian Ocean sea lanes going down to the Cape of Good Hope pass the Persian Gulf oil destined for the United States and Western Europe. Although the portion of total U.S. oil imports coming from the Persian Gulf had fallen to less than 10 percent by the mid-1980s, the share for Western Europe still stood at almost 50 percent.

Second, increased Soviet access to facilities in Africa for military purposes has improved the USSR's capabilities to counter Western military forces seeking to protect Western strategic interests connected with the continent. At the harbor in Luanda, the USSR has installed a floating drydock with a capacity of 8,500 tons. This can handle most major Soviet naval combatants. The USSR has also moved a similar floating drydock to the Dahlak Islands. This and floating piers, helipads, fuel and water storage, a submarine tender, and other repair ships give the USSR the ability to provide maintenance and supply there for Soviet naval combatants operating in the Indian Ocean and the Red Sea. Use of the airfield in Luanda permits Moscow to deploy BEAR long-range maritime reconnaissance planes to Angola for missions over the South Atlantic. Similarly, the Soviets can send Il-38/MAY antisubmarine warfare and maritime reconnaissance planes out of airfields at Asmara and in Libya to reconnoiter Western naval units in the Red Sea or the Mediterranean Sea.

Arguments persist among Western observers about whether the USSR had broad strategic ends in mind when it enlarged its naval presence around Africa and sought additional access to facilities on the continent for its military forces. Yet there is virtually universal agreement that the objective impact of such steps has been to aggravate the Soviet strategic threat to the West.

Key Areas of Contention

These general causes of East-West tensions in Africa manifest themselves in concrete situations, of course, and the situations themselves lend precision to the tensions. Moreover, one set of circumstances differs from another. Therefore, it is imperative to examine specific tensions that exist between East and West in varying contexts on the continent. The discussion here will concentrate on the three regions where tension levels have been the highest in the 1980s—North Africa, the Horn, and Southern Africa.

North Africa

Perhaps the most critical source of East-West stress in North Africa in the 1980s lies in the legacy of concerted Soviet efforts to exploit anticolonialism and the Arab-Israeli conflict in order to minimize Western influence in the area. These efforts originated in the mid-1950s, but they intensified considerably in the latter part of the 1960s. At that juncture, Moscow assigned the "southern rimlands" of the USSR a ranking behind only Europe and East Asia on its list of geopolitical priorities. The "southern rimlands" consist of those countries forming a broad arc to the south of Soviet borders, from South Asia in the east around to North Africa in the west.

Anti-Western Activities. Over the years, Soviet undertakings against the West in the region have assumed many forms. Moscow entered into an arms relationship with Gamal Abdel Nasser of Egypt in the mid-1950s that enabled him to nationalize the Suez Canal, and the USSR subsequently became Egypt's primary supplier of weapons and equipment until the mid-1970s. By then, the total of Soviet military aid to Cairo had reached about $4 billion. Across the twenty-year period, the USSR replenished Egyptian arms stocks after each of the Arab state's three major wars with Israel (in 1956, 1967, and 1973). At the peak of the military collaboration, in the early 1970s, Moscow even dispatched about 10,000 air defense personnel to Egypt to expand and operate the country's air defense system.

In the mid-1950s, the USSR agreed to finance Cairo's big Aswan Dam project, and for a decade or so thereafter the USSR strove to replace the West as Egypt's principal aid donor. Although Soviet faith in the long-term viability of such an objective faded in the 1970s, Moscow by the late 1970s had extended about $1.5 billion in economic credits to Cairo.

After Algeria obtained its independence from France in 1962, the USSR rushed to offer military assistance to the new state, and Moscow has been Algeria's main source of arms ever since. By the mid-1980s, Soviet leaders had promised the Algerian government nearly $5.4 billion worth of weapons and equipment and had already delivered items valued at more than $5 billion. In addition, the USSR had about 1,000 military advisers in the country. About half of these worked in Algerian academies, schools, and training centers, and the remainder were in equipment repair installations and individual combat units.

Prior to the ouster of Ahmed Ben Bella in 1965, Moscow entertained some hopes that Algeria might soon embark on a Communist path, and the USSR did all possible to encourage such a development, including the proffer of economic aid. Although Ben Bella's overthrow dashed Soviet hopes in this regard, the USSR still devoted considerable resources over ensuing years to reducing the economic role of the West in Algeria. By the mid-1980s, these Soviet commitments had amounted to well over $1 billion. Furthermore, Soviet economic technicians in the state numbered about 6,000.

In the 1970s, after Mu'ammar al-Qadhafi had taken power in Tripoli, the USSR moved to establish itself as Libya's chief arms supplier. By the mid-1980s, as pointed out earlier, Soviet military sales to Libya had topped $15 billion, and weapons and equipment worth about $10 billion had actually arrived in the country.

Similarly, Moscow has sought to weaken the West's economic position in Libya. Although the USSR has not provided any economic credits to the Qadhafi government, it has pledged to help with a number of Libyan projects of an economic nature that the Libyans propose to finance themselves. These have included a 300-megawatt nuclear power plant, an atomic research center, a 600-kilometer gas pipeline from Brega to Misuratah, a 5 million–ton iron and steel plant, a unified power grid, oil and uranium exploration, and preparation of a development plan for the gas industry through the year 2000. By the mid-1980s, projected Soviet inputs to all such undertakings were running at several billions of dollars.

Soviet efforts to fan general opposition to the West in the region have been even more extensive than the USSR's commitments of its own tangible assets to curtail Western influence there. In countless public and private forums and in an incessant media barrage, Soviet leaders have depicted the West and particularly the United States as anti-Arab and pro-Israel. At the same time, they have held up the USSR as the prime defender of the Arab cause on the international scene. Moscow has also repeatedly lauded anti-Western activities of the local governments and people. These have ranged from Tunisia's 1961 takeover of the naval base at Bizerte from the French to Libya's efforts in the 1980s to keep the United States out of the Gulf of Sirte, which Libya claims as part of its territorial waters.

Such a record makes Western states highly suspicious of all Soviet behavior in the area. Indeed, they have a propensity to look for signs of a grand design behind everything that the USSR does there.

Other Causes of Tension. The more proximate causes of East-West tensions in North Africa in the 1980s are relatively few in number. This situation reflects a simple reality. Both East and West enjoy solid enough positions in the region that little happening there at present or likely to happen there in the foreseeable future would drastically alter the existing balance between the two, and both sides appear to recognize this fact, even though neither may be entirely happy with the status quo.

Two aspects of the Soviet approach to North Africa do, however, have a potential from the Western standpoint to lead to major upheavals and hence do promote East-West friction. They are the USSR's courtship of Libya and the Soviet attitude toward Islamic fundamentalists in the region.

Moscow's relationship with the Qadhafi regime in Libya has been far from smooth since the early 1970s. Although the USSR has supported Qadhafi's anti-Westernism, it clearly has reservations about him and some of his policies. In 1983, for instance, Soviet leaders refused to yield to strong pressures from Tripoli for conclusion of a mutual treaty of friendship and cooperation. They did announce a "preliminary agreement" with Libyan representatives to contract such a treaty, but they have conspicuously avoided any follow-up actions. Qadhafi, for his part, has not hesitated to take the USSR to task for what he deems to be its excessive caution. He was particularly incensed, for example, at Moscow's failure to respond militarily to Israel's invasion of Lebanon in 1982.

Nevertheless, Moscow has deemed it essential to stay on as good terms as possible with Libya in light of Egypt's rapprochement with the United States and Israel in the 1970s and Algeria's remoteness from the primary arena of Arab-Israeli conflict. For this purpose, the USSR has relied heavily on arms sales to Qadhafi.

From the Western standpoint the Soviet policy of furnishing Qadhafi all the arms for which he can pay has had highly unwelcome consequences. Access to virtually unlimited quantities of weapons and equipment has given Qadhafi the capacity to cut a far wider swath on the international scene than is normally possible for the leader of a state with a population of roughly 3.5 million, and he has availed himself freely of it. He has meddled in the internal affairs of African countries as diverse as Uganda, Sudan, Egypt, Ethiopia, Tunisia, Chad, and Morocco. Thus he represents a substantial challenge to the stability of not only North Africa but other portions of the continent as well, although Western observers disagree on precisely how large a threat he poses.

As for Moscow's attitude toward the region's Islamic fundamentalists, there is evidence that Soviet agents have had contacts with and otherwise encouraged the activities of such groups in countries with which the USSR has had poor relations at the governmental level. Egypt under Anwar Sadat and Sudan under Gaafar Nimeiri afford the primary illustrations. Islamic fundamentalists constitute a growing problem in all of the countries of North Africa except Libya, and that problem has reached significant proportions in Tunisia, Egypt, and the Sudan—all states with which the West has maintained fairly close relations since the 1970s. The rise to power of Islamic fundamentalist forces in these countries could yield major set-backs for the West, just as it did in the case of Iran.

The Horn

East-West tensions in the Horn in the 1980s derive in large measure from persisting Soviet attempts to establish hegemony over the region. The USSR's push to make itself the dominant power in the Horn dates only from the latter half of the 1970s. Prior to that time, Soviet leaders had concentrated simply on acquiring a meaningful role in the area.

In the late 1950s, Moscow flirted briefly with Haile Selassie after the United States, Ethiopia's primary international ally, provoked the Emperor's ire by endorsing the unification of British Somaliland and the United Nations Trust Territory of Somalia (administered by Italy) as an independent state. But these overtures produced few practical results, and Moscow soon directed its attention elsewhere. Although it paid some heed to the rebels fighting Ethiopian rule in Eritrea, it focused on the government of the new state of Somalia in its drive to gain a foothold in the region.

During the 1960s and early 1970s, the USSR fashioned growing links with Somalia, particularly after the military coup that brought Mohamed Siad Barre to power in Mogadishu in October 1969. By the mid-1970s Moscow had offered more than $150 billion in economic credits to the Somali govern-ment and had delivered well over $300 million worth of arms to it. Moreover, some 3,600 Soviet advisers, of whom 1,200 to 1,400 were military personnel, were working in the country. Of perhaps greatest significance, the USSR had persuaded Mogadishu to let it set up a naval complex at Berbera, on the Gulf of Aden, and fly naval reconnaissance missions over the Indian Ocean from airfields in Somalia. At that juncture, the Berbera complex comprised a deep-water port, housing for about 1,500 persons, a communications facility, storage facili-ties for an estimated 175,000 barrels of fuel, an airfield eventu-ally to have 13,000 to 15,000 feet of surfaced runway, and a facility for handling and storage of tactical missiles.

Hegemonic Pursuits. However, with the collapse of Haile Selassie's rule in Addis Ababa and the emergence of an increasingly radicalized military government in Ethiopia, Moscow saw a chance to broaden its position in the Horn. Not only did it woo the new authorities in Ethiopia, but it also promoted a scheme for a federation of Marxist states around the eastern end of the Red Sea. In Soviet calculations, such a federation would embrace Somalia, Ethiopia, and the People's Democratic Republic of Yemen and have the USSR as its international guarantor. Resolution of the prevailing conflicts over the status of Eritrea and the Ogaden would take place within this overall framework through the granting of autonomy to the two areas within an Ethiopian state.

Eventually, to be sure, the plan foundered in the face of the animosities between the Mogadishu and Addis Ababa governments, and Soviet leaders in 1977 had to side with one country or the other. Confronted with this choice, they picked Ethiopia.

Nevertheless, Moscow has by no means abandoned efforts to draw all the major states in the region together under a Soviet protective umbrella. Its policy toward Somalia during the first half of the 1980s is indicative. At times, the USSR endeavored to prevail upon Mogadishu to end the close cooperation with the United States that Siad Barre had instituted in the wake of Somalia's rout in the Ogaden by Ethiopian military forces supplied by the USSR and spearheaded by Cuban troops. On other occasions, Moscow lent support to the Somali opposition's undertakings to topple Siad Barre. Neither of these tacks by the mid-1980s had produced a Somali government favorable to a *pax Sovietica* in the region, but Moscow clearly retained hopes that such a government would emerge over the long run.

The USSR's actions to try to restore a substantial degree of Soviet influence in Somalia, it is worth underscoring, have gone ahead despite strains of various kinds between Moscow and the government of Mengistu Haile Mariam in Ethiopia. Although Mengistu in 1984 finally formed the "vanguard" party that Soviet officials had long urged upon him, he still has not convinced Moscow that he will allow it to supersede the military in the political life of the state. By the mid-1980s, Soviet economic aid to Ethiopia since the late 1970s had exceeded $300 million, but Mengistu has nonetheless criticized the USSR for its lack of generosity in this sphere. Perhaps most serious, Mengistu has fumed at Moscow for its inability or unwillingness to help him quell the rebellions that have raged in many parts of Ethiopia in the 1980s, most notably in Eritrea and Tigre.

In Western, and especially U.S., perceptions, the Horn has major strategic importance. Parts of it form the southern side of the Strait of Bab el-Mandeb, a critical choke point on the route between the Mediterranean Sea and the Indian Ocean through the Suez Canal and the Red Sea; other portions of it stretch a substantial distance along the Red Sea littoral. Because of the Horn's situation near the sea lanes extending from the Persian Gulf down to the Cape of Good Hope, the region could serve as a convenient launching pad for efforts to sever these sea lanes. Finally, since the late 1970s at least, the United States has come to regard use of facilities in the Horn as necessary for the mounting of a strong Western defense of the Persian Gulf in the event of a crisis there.

In such a light, Soviet maneuvers to entrench the USSR as the key outside patron of the Horn inevitably raise alarm in the West. Whatever Moscow's ultimate purpose in trying to create a hegemonic relationship with the region might be, its success in doing so would have objective consequences highly adverse to the West.

Military Aid to Ethiopia. A secondary source of East-West stress in the Horn in the 1980s is the Soviet military assistance program for Ethiopia. That program, which by the mid-1980s entailed arms transfers approaching $3 billion in value, has had much the effect on authorities in Addis Ababa that the less extensive but still large Soviet military aid program for Somalia in the 1960s and 1970s had on the Mogadishu government. Specifically, military backing from the USSR emboldened Siad Barre to seek to oust the Ethiopian army from the

Ogaden in 1977–78, and it has encouraged Mengistu to attempt to overturn Siad Barre in the 1980s. Not only has Addis Ababa supported the opposition to Siad Barre militarily, but in 1982 units of the Ethiopian army even participated directly in an invasion of Somalia by the Somali opposition designed to cut the main highway joining the two parts of the country and to spark an uprising against Siad Barre.

As a result of Ethiopia's activities against Siad Barre, Western powers like the United States and Italy have felt compelled to raise the level of military assistance that they provide to Somalia. Washington, for example, doubled its military aid program to Mogadishu between the outset of the 1980s and the middle of the decade, from about $20 million a year to roughly $40 million a year.

However, the United States especially has taken such a step with more than a few misgivings. It recognizes that Siad Barre's determination to bring all Somali-speaking areas, including the Ogaden, under Mogadishu's rule has not flagged, and it does not want to unsettle the region further by inadvertently seeming to endorse Siad Barre's ambitions. For this reason, it has attempted to confine the military assistance to spheres strictly defensive in nature. Yet it would much prefer not to have to run risks of this sort at all.

Southern Africa

Two factors contribute about equally to East-West tensions in Southern Africa in the 1980s. First, the history of the USSR's involvement in the region since the 1960s prompts the West to conclude that Soviet leaders want violent upheavals rather than peaceful, evolutionary change in Namibia and South Africa. Second, Moscow endeavors to portray the West, and particularly the United States, as a partisan of the white minority government in South Africa and the USSR as an ardent champion of "black liberation" throughout Southern Africa.

Soviet Preference for Violent Revolution. Since the early 1960s, the USSR and its allies have served as arms suppliers for most of the guerrilla movements that have emerged in Southern Africa. The list of recipients of Soviet weapons and equipment has at various times included the Popular Movement for the Liberation of Angola, the Zimbabwe African People's Union, the Front for the Liberation of Mozambique, the South-West African People's Organization of Namibia, and the African National Congress of South Africa. During the 1970s, the USSR and its allies even became the primary source of arms for the Zimbabwe African People's Union, the South-West African People's Organization, and the African National Congress, and they have continued to perform this function for the last two groups in the 1980s.

At the outset, such support for movements dedicated to altering the existing orders in their countries through the use of force plainly reflected a dual calculation on Moscow's part. Soviet leaders contended that black majority rule, which the USSR had long endorsed as a moral imperative, would only come about in Southern Africa through armed struggles, for the white minority rulers in most of the countries there firmly rejected the notion of relinquishing their authority. At the same time, Moscow held that the deep hostility of the region's white minority governments toward the USSR left little way for it to strengthen its weak position there except through association with black elements opposed to these governments. Until the mid-1970s, only the black leaders of Zambia evinced any willingness at all to have dealings with the USSR, and even they adopted a correct but not cordial posture.

Developments in the region since the mid-1970s have bolstered these Soviet judgments in certain respects and shaken them in others. For instance, Moscow unquestionably believes that armed struggle had a decisive impact on the collapse of Portuguese colonial rule in Angola and Mozambique and on the transfer of power to blacks in Zimbabwe, but it is not sure that armed struggle will prove so crucial in the demise of white minority rule in Namibia and South Africa. Since the early 1980s, it has conceded that internal forces other than those committed to armed struggle may play significant roles in shaping the future of South Africa at least, and since the spring of 1985, it has even been tacitly admitted that apartheid might end in South Africa through shifts in the attitudes of whites.

With respect to improvement of the Soviet position in the region, Moscow credits armed struggle with producing Marxist governments in Angola and Mozambique with which the USSR could forge strong ties. However, it sees the outcome of armed struggle in Zimbabwe as quite different. Although the new government there professes to be Marxist, control of it rests with a long-time rival of the Zimbabwe African People's Union (ZAPU), the Zimbabwe African National Union (ZANU), and even as late as the mid-1980s Moscow had not managed to overcome the legacy of hostility toward the USSR that previous Soviet backing of ZAPU had left among adherents of ZANU. As Soviet leaders are well aware, furthermore, the peaceful transfer of power in states like Botswana and Lesotho did not prevent the USSR from setting up productive relations with their black-ruled governments during the late 1970s and early 1980s.

Nonetheless, in most Western estimates, Moscow clings to a preference for transitions of authority through armed struggle in Namibia and South Africa. According to Western analyses, from Moscow's vantage point such transitions would give Marxists or other radical elements disposed to enter into close cooperation with the USSR the best chance to have a major influence in the new governments. Thus, transitions of this kind would afford the USSR maximum opportunity to enhance its position in the two countries. Western observers grant that in the 1980s Moscow has recognized—in the wake of South African military attacks on Angola, Mozambique, Lesotho, and Botswana for allegedly harboring Namibian and South African opposition elements—that intensified armed struggles in Namibia and South Africa could pose dangers to Soviet interests elsewhere in Southern Africa. As Soviet leaders see things, the increased involvement of the USSR in the region has given it a considerable stake in the fortunes of the governments in Angola and Mozambique, and heightened conflict in Namibia and South Africa could spill over into these neighboring states and threaten the already tenuous hold that their governments maintain on power. A desire to limit such a possibility may even have helped inspire Soviet protestations to the United States in the mid-1980s that both superpowers have "legitimate" interests in Southern Africa, although neither has "vital" interests there. However, in most Western assessments, Moscow has shown no sign as yet of forsaking its basic preference for a resolution by force of the disputes in Namibia and South Africa.

The West regards this preference as tantamount to fostering turmoil throughout Southern Africa. Western observers point to the formidable military capabilities of the South African government, and they suggest that the past behavior of this government attests to its willingness to employ these capabilities to the fullest extent if it feels sufficiently threatened. Such a policy would entail not only harsh repressive measures internally but also efforts to strike at what the South African government deemed to be external backers of its local opposition. These efforts could involve increased military incursions into neighboring states and/or stepped-up military support for political challengers of the existing governments there.

Regional turmoil, in turn, would probably have two highly negative consequences from the Western standpoint. It would obviously cause serious disruption of normal activities and perhaps even major loss of life in the countries of Southern Africa, and it could well impede Western access to the minerals of the region. The Western powers depend heavily upon Southern Africa for imports of chromium, platinum, manganese, and vanadium, four minerals of key importance to modern industry. Thus, keeping the supplies of these minerals flowing is of substantial concern to the Western states. That is especially true because the USSR constitutes the primary alternative source of platinum and vanadium and one of the few significant alternative sources of manganese. General chaos in Southern Africa, however, could greatly hamper the mining and transportation to market of the minerals. Indeed, in the eyes of Western leaders, this possibility constitutes the principal threat to uninterrupted supplies of the minerals for the West. By the mid-1980s, most Western analysts tended to discount the chance that exports of these minerals to the West would cease even if Marxist governments came to power in Namibia and South Africa, and to sustain that view they cited Angola's continued sale of oil to the West after the Popular Movement for the Liberation of Angola assumed control of the government in Luanda in the mid-1970s.

The Campaign to Link the West with South Africa. The USSR has expended great energies in the 1980s to convince black Africans that the United States and other Western powers are colluding with the South African government against the black majorities of Namibia and South Africa. Soviet spokesmen and media constantly reiterate this theme. At the same time, they hold up the USSR and its allies as staunch adversaries of the South African authorities.

This Soviet propaganda campaign, it is true, has not permitted the USSR to mobilize black Africans to do its bidding, but the effort has had some effects that are worrisome to the West. In Southern Africa, it has diminished the capacity of the West and particularly the United States to act as a facilitator of peaceful change. For example, it has encouraged the Pretoria government to believe that the West cannot afford to desert South Africa, for the West would thereby destroy the foundations of its position with respect to the USSR in the region. As a result, the Soviet campaign has reduced still further the already limited leverage that the West can exercise over Pretoria's policies. As for the black Africans of Southern Africa, the Soviet effort has fanned doubts about the ability of the West to serve as an honest broker between the contending forces in Namibia and South Africa. Blacks of the region have had suspicions of the West's objectivity from the outset because a number of Western states are former colonial powers and because the blacks regard the West as at least predominantly white, and the Soviet campaign has fed these suspicions.

In Africa more broadly, the Soviet propaganda effort has put in question the trustworthiness of the West. The subject of South Africa has aroused strong emotions among blacks throughout the continent, and there has been a widespread tendency among them to believe that the West could end white minority rule in South Africa if it had the will to do so. Therefore, they have been inclined to lay responsibility for the persistence of white minority control of the country at the doorstep of the West. The Soviet campaign has reinforced such an inclination and has encouraged them to perceive ulterior motives behind Western behavior in the matter. Such attitudes have complicated relations between the Western powers and African states outside Southern Africa.

Conclusion

A final issue requires brief consideration. Is it possible to ease East-West tensions in Africa, and if so, how?

In the short term, prospects for alleviating the underlying causes of East-West tensions on the continent appear exceedingly dim. The anti-Western thrust of the USSR's drive for global power status in Africa, Moscow's treatment of East-West competition on the continent as a zero-sum game, and the USSR's perceptions of the enemy in Africa all stem from deep-seated Soviet beliefs, and these are not open to easy refutation or modification. Certainly, they will probably not yield to direct Western attempts to alter them. Such efforts, in fact, could wind up being counterproductive, for they might push Moscow into a defensive, even more antagonistic, posture.

Over the long haul, Soviet beliefs that give rise to these basic sources of East-West stress in Africa could change in a way that would ameliorate East-West relations on the continent, but in all likelihood they will do so only gradually and in response to the total context in Africa and the Third World more generally, rather than in response to Western actions. The manner in which Marxism-Leninism came to play a minimal role in Moscow's identification of potential African allies and its approach to them may offer a relevant model. As the result of accumulating experiences that did not conform to the expectations engendered by some of their basic tenets about Africa, Soviet leaders began to question and eventually discarded the tenets. Because of the nature of such a process, the opportunities for the West to affect it are quite limited. Perhaps the only real way of doing so involves indirect means—by seeking to shape the character of the African situation with which the USSR has to deal.

Less fundamental causes of East-West tensions in Africa might prove somewhat easier for the West to address effectively. In light of the deficiencies of the USSR's nonmilitary capabilities, Moscow would no doubt reject suggestions from any quarter that it downplay military instruments as tools of its policy; yet it might not react so adamantly in specific circumstances if it believed that it would suffer no serious political disabilities from reducing its stress on military means. For instance, it might endorse the withdrawal of Cuban troops from Angola as long as such a withdrawal did not amount to a severe blow to its position in the African state. A continuing relationship as arms supplier to the Luanda government would probably suffice to allay any Soviet apprehensions on this score.

The West, however, need not rely solely upon persuading Soviet leaders to exercise restraint in employing military instruments in order to dampen the tensions deriving from Moscow's heavy dependence on such policy instruments in Africa. It can also seek to defuse African situations that make military instruments useful to the USSR. Successful undertakings of this sort would help to move East-West rivalry into nonmilitary spheres. To be sure, resolving African disputes and conflicts is often difficult if not impossible, but even encouragement of negotiations and dialogue between the contending parties might wind up depriving Soviet military instruments of much of their merit as tools for achieving Soviet goals on the continent.

Specific causes of East-West stress in individual regions offer perhaps the best opportunities for the West to do something positive to bring down the level of East-West friction in Africa. Possible candidates for Western initiatives in this regard include the extent of Soviet courtship of Libya, the USSR's efforts to assert itself as the dominant power in the

Horn, and Moscow's preference for political transitions through armed struggle in Namibia and South Africa.

To achieve desirable results here, however, the West will have to be conscious of certain pitfalls. First, some measures that it might adopt to alleviate specific sources of tensions in individual areas could reinforce the underlying causes of stress between East and West in Africa. For example, steps designed to alter Moscow's preference for political change in Namibia and South Africa through armed struggle could simply confirm Soviet views of East-West competition on the continent as a zero-sum game. Second, direct interaction with the USSR and its allies does not necessarily constitute the ideal way of going about easing East-West tensions in African regional contexts. Resorting to indirect means may afford the more worthwhile approach, for aspects of the African situation will probably be more susceptible to Western influence than will Soviet attitudes and policies per se.

A last word of caution is in order. Even after concerted and imaginative attempts to reduce the level of East-West tensions in Africa, the West could well find that the level remains quite high. The West must be prepared to accept that possibility and cope with its ramifications.

6

East-West Economic
Competition in the Third World

ELIZABETH KRIDL VALKENIER

Soviet economic policies in the Third World today hardly resemble the bold entry into that world that Nikita Khrushchev proclaimed in 1955. Under his leadership, the USSR set out to challenge Western predominance. Moscow was confident then that by using trade as a political weapon it could detach the less-developed countries (LDCs) from the West and redraw the economic map of the world to its own advantage.

Thirty years later the situation is quite different. The Soviets have come to value trade for its own sake and to accept the fact that the global market is dominated by the capitalist nations. They do not find that an exclusive identification with the LDCs' grievances is beneficial to themselves or resolves their

ELIZABETH KRIDL VALKENIER has written extensively on various aspects of Soviet relations with the Third World. Her publications include *The Soviet Union and the Third World: An Economic Bind,* 1983. Dr. Valkenier is a member of the faculty of the Department of Political Science at Columbia University and of the University's W. Averell Harriman Institute for Advanced Study of the Soviet Union. She has been senior scholar in official academic exchanges with Poland and the USSR.

own needs. Furthermore, they recognize that there are global problems that affect all nations and thus preclude unilateral solutions. In a word, the initial, politically motivated behavior is being altered by pragmatic, economic considerations designed to secure for the USSR a fair share of world commerce.

These changes in Soviet perceptions and policies over the past quarter century have quite radically altered the terms of East-West competition in the Third World, but the shift is not widely recognized in the West, especially in the United States. Yet an awareness of the demonstrable change is basic to any discussion of ways to manage East-West economic tensions. Hence, this chapter traces the evolution of Soviet policies from a systemic attempt at takeover to a more accommodating search for reintegration into the interdependent world economy. It argues that although the change may well be reversible, the situation in which the USSR finds itself and the way in which many Soviet experts think about domestic and international economic problems create openings for a more productive U.S.–Soviet understanding and, possibly, cooperation.

The Initial Soviet Challenge

For the first twenty years after Moscow's active entry into the Third World (i.e., from 1954 to 1975), the Soviet diplomatic offensive was supported by an equally combative rhetoric and economic policies. It would be accurate to say that economic warfare was one of the main, if not *the* main, components of the Communist challenge to Western interests in the Third World. Soviet leaders, specialists, and media represented the newly independent countries as having attained only formal, political freedom. Economic liberation was next on the agenda. The Soviet view of the situation was clearly formulated in the Communist party program adopted in 1961: the new states had "not yet broken from the world capitalist economy," and "as long as they do not put an end to their economic dependence on imperialism, they . . . will remain objects of semi-colonial exploitation." In this scenario, the program held that the LDCs were "a revolutionary force destroying imperialism."

Given its ideological convictions as well as its relative military weakness, the USSR proceeded to undermine the Western presence through a set of hostile economic policies. It offered the LDCs a socialist alternative to the capitalist ways of the West, comprised of three elements: economic assistance, a development model, and a new international economic order.

Terms of Aid

During the initial phase, Soviet aid performed an explicit political function. Basically, Soviet assistance consisted of trade loans that promoted the sale of Soviet machinery. However, these credits were offered in a manner designed to discredit the West and to facilitate "economic liberation." Moscow charged very low interest rates (about 2 percent or 2.5 percent), it offered support exclusively to the state sector, and it favored industrial projects above all others.

Naturally, Soviet propaganda extolled the distinct features of "socialist" assistance—generosity, institutional impact, and rapid modernization—to underscore the radical departures from Western practices. The circumstances under which some of the largest Soviet commitments were made also served to bring out these "systemic" claims. Moscow undertook to help with the Aswan High Dam and the Bhilai steel plant after these giant projects were turned down in Washington because of displeasure with Egypt's and India's foreign policies, as well as opposition to support of the public sector and to heavy industrial projects. Furthermore, in both cases the USSR insisted on being the sole foreign source of support until the completion of the entire project. On all levels Soviet policies were construed so as to create a public image of the USSR as the bearer of an alternate and better system of economic relations between the advanced and the developing countries.

Development Theory

Aside from introducing new terms and principles of economic assistance, the USSR also offered its own, systemic, explanation for underdevelopment. According to official statements at international forums and in scholarly monographs, backwardness was the consequence of colonial rule, and it persisted because of the survival of capitalist institutions at home and the disadvantageous exchanges with the former metropoles. The socialist development model promoted by Moscow was deceptively simple. Soviet sources held that rapid growth would result from nationalization, planning, and industrialization to curtail market forces and loosen close ties with—and dependence on—the West.

A government's political will, as measured by the expansion of the public sector, was represented as the driving force of development. In Soviet eyes, the operations of foreign business and of local private enterprise constituted a net deduction from national wealth. Hence, all that was necessary was to gain control over these sectors and to redirect their resources into constructive investment. The mere extent of public ownership was deemed enough to ensure the optimal utilization of national resources. (This was the prevailing tone of analysis, but there were some dissenting voices already in the 1960s with, for example, a discussion of the positive role of Western investment and arguments that the more backward an economy, the wider the circle of concrete problems to be solved through basic reforms that had nothing to do with either capitalism or socialism.)

The International Order

The Soviets proposed to extirpate the capitalist order from international economic relations as well. At the start of the Soviet offensive, Moscow's remedy for the malfunctioning of the international system was economic liberation of the LDCs from imperialist control by means of various domestic measures, such as import-substitution industrialization supported by Soviet assistance. By the early 1970s, as the aid-trade network expanded and became more aligned with the needs and capacities of the Soviet economy, the Soviets began to refer to their policy as promoting an alternate, socialist international division of labor (IDL). This new international economic order was asserted to be more equitable than the existing one, embodying genuine cooperation instead of exploitation.

Little specific information on how this noncapitalist IDL was to operate was ever supplied beyond general claims that specialization in industrial production, coordination in national planning, and the pooling of resources for the development of entire regions would constitute the core of the new order. The principles of planning, long-term intergovernmental treaties, production cooperation, and compensation agreements between states to establish fair prices and limit the effects of market forces were proposed as ways to improve the functioning of international trade to benefit the LDCs.

The American Reaction

Given the confrontational nature of Soviet policies, it is not at all surprising that they evoked an alarmed reaction from American political and academic figures. Soviet entry into the Third World during the height of the cold war, Moscow's avowed aim to displace the West in the former colonies, as well as the ready response of the LDCs to Soviet propaganda were seen as constituting a genuine threat. Whether one reads American commentary written in the late 1950s or a decade later, most of it tends to fall into the worst scenario category. Thus, Under Secretary of the Treasury Douglas Dillon declared in 1960 that "the Soviet economic offensive is a means of carrying the struggle against us in . . . the most vulnerable sector of the free world." Academic descriptions were no less alarmist. Some experts predicted that in a short period of time ("ten years?") the Soviet "planning commissions will have detailed blueprints to gain control of . . . the underdeveloped countries of Africa, Asia and Latin America." Even more moderate analysts concluded that "the present profile of international affairs has been strongly affected by Soviet Third World policies, and that among these policies foreign aid is without doubt most influential."

These alarmist reactions of twenty or thirty years ago resonate with a familiar ring today. Although concern with the military component of Soviet policies in the Third World is now uppermost, the specter of a Soviet economic takeover still haunts us. Some economists enroll the radical, socialist-oriented states in an expanded Council of Mutual Economic Assistance (CMEA). Many political scientists contend that a "resource-denial strategy" guides Soviet policies.

At present, one can question these assumptions and prognostications with demonstrable facts and figures. For example, despite requests from Moputu, Moscow did not admit Mozambique to CMEA. The radical LDCs have only been granted a nonvoting or observer status in the socialist common market because that relationship minimizes the bloc's economic obligations. Beyond that, the share of the USSR in the overall trade of the Third World has not risen over 2 or 3 percent in the past twenty years. (The figure stands at less than 5 percent for the Soviet bloc.) And the share of LDCs in Soviet foreign trade has remained at a constant 12 to 14 percent for over a decade. Two facts are evident: the USSR is unwilling to absorb the self-proclaimed Marxist-Leninist LDCs into the Eastern bloc economic system, nor has it been able to achieve a breakthrough on Third World markets.

Changes in Soviet Theory and Practice

Perhaps even more telling evidence against the purported Soviet drive for economic hegemony in the Third World is supplied by the veritable "revolution" that has taken place in Soviet thinking about the nature of international economics during the past ten years and the attendant departures in policy. Without doubt, the change was induced in some degree by the failure to impose the new economic patterns so boldly proclaimed at the start of the economic offensive in the late 1950s, but what is equally important about the change is that it testifies to a manifest Soviet capacity to modify or discard dysfunctional theories and policies. In other words, the Soviets are not necessarily wedded to some immutable set of Marxist-Leninist principles. Like everybody else, they are capable of learning and adapting.

Since this recent conceptual revolution is not widely known or acknowledged in the West, its substance and range are worth sketching in a volume on easing East-West tensions. Both the new Soviet understanding of the operations of international economics and the related policy shifts suggest hope for some attenuation in the relentless economic competition that the West still ascribes to Moscow on the basis of the views and policies prevailing in the USSR a generation ago.

The Single World Market

The discarding of Stalin's thesis about the division of the world economy into two hostile markets constitutes the basic reorientation. Whereas Stalin's dictum on separate socialist and capitalist markets justified the competitive use of aid-trade programs, the recent Soviet recognition of an integrated world economy has opened prospects for economic coexistence. The new theory appeared unobtrusively in 1974, without any formal renunciation of Stalin's views. Probably the most authoritative definition appeared in the new entry in the third edition of the *Great Soviet Encyclopedia,* which described the world market as "the aggregate of all national markets, seen as linked through mutual economic and trade relations [and as having] expanded in scale as social production has become increasingly internationalized."

At first, the revised theory covered only Soviet exchanges with the West, for the theory's emergence obviously was related directly to the rise in East-West trade. The LDCs were not included in the new scheme. The old normative explanations persisted in discussion of East-South trade. For example, there still were references to the Soviet goal of establishing a socialist IDL with the developing countries. Within a few years, however, the Soviet recognition of objective, universally valid economic imperatives that dictated a system-transcending interdependence came to include the Third World as well. Thus, by the late 1970s, many economists began to discuss a worldwide international division of labor without any systemic attributes.

The International Economic Order

The change in Soviet understanding of world economics was accompanied by a marked turn in policy regarding the New International Economic Order (NIEO) demanded by the Third World countries. Moscow is no longer pressing to restructure world trade by frontal attacks on Western dominance and by conjoining its interests with those of the LDCs. Telling evidence for this shift in policy comes in the Soviet bloc's statement to the Fifth United Nations Conference on Trade and Development (V UNCTAD) in 1979. It contained the unprecedented admission that it was possible to "democratize" international economic relations and to "ensure equitable and mutually profitable participation in such relations of all groups of countries and systems of property ownership," even before the "inherent defects of capitalism had been eliminated from the operations of world economy." This obtuse language announced, in effect, that the USSR accepted the existing situation and was ready to work for its improvement rather than for its replacement.

Causes of Backwardness

At the same time as the Soviets have come to acknowledge an interdependent world economy, they have also modified their explanations of what causes backwardness and what contributes to development.

Soviet experts—if not yet various official statements meant for public or international consumption—have shifted from laying the blame on external circumstances to examining domestic constraints. The emphasis now ranges from overpopulation to the persistence of traditional methods in agriculture. Discussion of the retarding social factors is no longer limited to analyzing the unjust class structure. It now extends to the deep-rooted Eastern cultural traditions (such as working habits or the use of wealth), that militate against the expectations of speedy improvements of any kind, never mind the adoption of "progressive" economic institutions, once advocated as the panacea for overcoming backwardness.

Altogether, the center of Soviet development studies has shifted in recent years from the facile attribution of backwardness to foreign domination (past and present) to an awareness of serious domestic retarding factors. As a result, many academic works, as well as some Soviet contributions to specialized international forums, no longer place all the onus on the operations of imperialism.

The New Development Model

The less systemic and more realistic appraisal of domestic conditions in Third World countries is paralleled by the emergence of a different development model. The Soviets no longer extol as the paradigm their own experience of the 1930s, rapid industrialization under conditions of autarky. They do not advise the LDCs to institute import-substitution industrialization, the nationalization of foreign assets, and strict government control of economic life. They stress instead a balanced development that begins with favoring agriculture, raw materials production, and light industry—a paradigm that makes wise use of foreign investment and leaves sufficient room for private initiative. To the extent that a Soviet model is cited, it is that of the New Economic Policy (NEP) of the 1920s when the USSR had a mixed economy with a private sector in agriculture and the services and welcomed foreign capital for industrial development.

A most encouraging aspect of the current Soviet development model is that it has abandoned many "socialist" prescriptions in favor of workable measures, no matter what their political pedigree. Gone are the days of blind faith in the efficacy of command planning and the eradication of private enterprise. The positive role of private ownership is now widely recognized. The fact that support for private entrepreneurship is recommended by many experts even for states of socialist orientation—and not merely in the service sector but also in industry and agriculture—testifies that Soviet economists have come a considerable way from identifying economic progress with noncapitalist institutions.

South-West Relations

The changed Soviet views on what causes backwardness and what contributes to development are complemented by quite a different outlook on the LDCs' relationship with the West. The 1961 party program proclaimed that the developing countries occupied a "special place" in the capitalist market, with the strong implication that they would soon shift allegiance to the socialist camp. At present, authoritative books, written by experts working for the International Department of the Central Committee and, thus, reflecting official thinking, concede that all the LDCs, including the radical states, are integrated with Western markets. Moreover, these experts say, the LDCs should adjust their expectations and development plans not to economic liberation but to the advantages offered by international trade. Here, Soviet sources no longer uniformly describe the existing international division of labor as a system of organized plunder but as one affording all components a constructive role and the benefits to be derived from comparative advantage. Although these views are diametrically opposite to those held when Soviet theory proclaimed a dual world economy, they are consistent with the adoption of a global outlook that accepts varying degrees of interdependence.

Interdependence dictates a different set of policies for the LDCs. Soviet experts advise them now to make the best of what they already have; namely, to develop their food, fuel, and raw material resources to supply the more advanced countries and to use the income thus earned to promote diversification and suitable levels of processing industry. At present, no serious Soviet expert views the production of raw materials as locking a country into a permanent dependency, but rather as giving it a welcome opportunity for capital accumulation. Nationalization of foreign property is no longer advocated as the best method for filling the national treasury. On the contrary,

Western investment is now acknowledged to be an acceptable partner in the development effort. Consequently, there have been no charges in Soviet publications and speeches that Angola is being exploited by the international oil cartel operating in Cabinda. In a related argument, Soviet specialists consider that it would be proper for Nicaragua to obtain economic assistance in equal proportions from the West, Latin America, the Soviet bloc, and the United States.

East-South Relations

Soviet economic relations with LDCs have become much more pragmatic and less politically motivated. It is instructive to consider what caused the Soviets to modify their policies. The underlying cause, obviously, was the failure of Khrushchev's offensive. It did not generate the expected trade flows, and Soviet machinery exports did not manage to capture Third World markets. Next, falling growth rates and other difficulties within the Soviet economy forced a reassessment of the USSR's capacity to pursue "socialist" (i.e., selflessly generous) policies in disregard of tangible economic benefits. Third, the oil shocks, whose effects cascaded across political frontiers, graphically demonstrated global interdependence and, moreover, enriched some aid partners with petrodollars, enabling them to withdraw from Moscow's carefully nurtured plans for long-term barter exchanges with the Soviet bloc, a basic element of the once vaunted socialist IDL.

The fate of the arrangements between the Soviet bloc and Iraq well illustrates how carefully nurtured plans for a socialist IDL went awry. The USSR and East European states had assisted Baghdad in creating a national oil company. In 1969 an additional credit of $248 million was extended, to be repaid in oil shipments. But when the barter agreement ran out in 1974, Iraq took advantage of the high prices on the world market and shifted to trading with the West. The share of CMEA in Iraqi trade fell from 28 percent in 1972 to 7.9 percent in 1975, and East Europe lost what had seemed like an assured source of fuel supply that entailed no hard currency expenditures.

The combination of economic failures, domestic constraints, and opportunities on the world market caused the USSR to switch to a policy based on comparative advantage (or "mutual advantage," as the Soviets prefer to call it). Although much of the basic institutional framework remains distinct or "socialist"—such as the state monopoly of trade, government-to-government negotiations and agreements, long-term treaties, frequent barter arrangements—many policies no longer carry a hostile political thrust. The evident practical economic motivation has modified many former systemic differences between the Western and Soviet modes of operation.

Multilateralization. The Soviet willingness to abandon strict bilateralism and introduce elements of multilateralism is among the most promising departures. At present, most of the Soviet–Third World trade is conducted in fully convertible currencies; the old clearing system obtains only with Afghanistan, Egypt, India, Pakistan, and Syria. Prices are now set in accordance with world levels, and, even though they are adopted for longer periods, trade agreements provide for annual revisions.

True, the ruble remains inconvertible. But it is evident from the writings of Soviet economists that there is much discussion on the need to make the ruble convertible so that Soviet currency can discharge fully its economic functions. The fate of this step, as that of many others, depends, of course, on the type of reforms the Soviet leadership will adopt to modernize and expand the nation's economy. Nevertheless, the adoption of partial multilateralization raises the question of succeeding steps, and many specialists consider it inadvisable to stop short with halfway measures in opening up the Soviet economy to the benefits of international trade.

Tripartite Ventures. The Soviet readiness to conclude agreements with the West for joint ventures in Third World countries is another telling departure from systemic isolationism and its attendant hostility. Trilateral cooperation has become an important and proliferating feature in the Communist bloc's overseas operations. By 1980 the foreign trade organizations of the socialist states had signed 226 such agreements with Western firms and Third World partners. East Europeans led in this innovation until about 1976; since then, Soviet involvement has risen markedly. Moscow's interest is evident in the provisions for joint cooperation in third countries (meaning the LDCs) included in the long-term economic and technological cooperation pacts the USSR has signed with major industrial powers in the late 1970s.

Profitability and Aid. There is now quite open discussion and hot pursuit of the profit motive in Moscow's dealings with the LDCs. The Soviets can be quite outspoken about the practical aims of their aid-trade programs. It is not at all unusual to read in specialized monographs that it would be "erroneous" to assert that relations between the socialist world and the developing countries are "based on the principle of socialist solidarity." A similar message is often conveyed in Soviet speeches to visiting Third World delegations who assume that the principle of selfless "socialist" assistance still obtains. At U.N. economic forums the explanations of the principle underlying Soviet policies now refer to "mutual benefits" that are ensured through the "usual commercial channels and opportunities."

The current-day distribution of Soviet aid reflects this pragmatic thrust. Whereas in the past the radical, anti-Western states received the larger share of Soviet credits, this no longer holds true. Thus, during the tenth Five-Year Plan (1975–80), Angola and Mozambique together were granted about $150 million in credits, while the conservative kingdom of Morocco received $2 billion for the development of its phosphate resources to be shipped in repayment back to the USSR. Credits to the two socialist-oriented states were increased during the next Five-Year Plan. However, Angola's largest project, the $2 billion hydroelectric power station and irrigation system on the Cuanza River, is not an exclusively Soviet operation but a multilateral venture in which Portuguese capital and a Brazilian engineering firm participate.

Frank discussion of a fair return on expenditure accompanies the dispensing of credits. In the writings of many economists, the profit motive is no longer a term for denouncing capitalist policies. It is seen either as a fair practice or as a necessary unit of accounting, a universally applicable norm that assures efficient production and effective exchanges.

As was stated by R. Andreasian, a Soviet economist specializing in the Organization of Petroleum Exporting Countries (OPEC), "Without profitability, i.e., gain, no economy can exist and develop effectively." In this context it should be noted that Soviet trade with the oil producing countries has risen perceptibly and that the increase in arms sales to those states is economically motivated (since it is an important source of hard currency). In general, Soviet arms trade is not exclusively designed to promote radical political orientation. It plays a major role in covering the deficits in Soviet commodity trade with the world market.

Aid to the Private Sector. The current interest in profit has modified the USSR's former hostility to Third World capitalists. Moscow is no longer averse to dealing with the private sector in the LDCs. In India, the Soviet Union was identified from the very start in 1955 with the promotion of state enterprises. Accordingly, some analysts interpreted the 1 billion ruble credit in May 1985 as a move to forestall too radical a change in India's economic policies under Rajiv Gandhi, in recognition of his known partiality for the private sector. But there is nothing in the text of the agreement that restricts the credit to "socialist" enterprises. On the contrary, it is explicitly stated that the "terms of credit agreement are flexible," thus making it available to the private sector. Moreover, in view of the lively Soviet interest in India's business community, evidenced by numerous invitations extended to the entrepreneurial associations and the support given to the formation of the Soviet-Indian Chamber of Commerce, it seems more than likely that the USSR seeks to sustain and revitalize its trade with India by expanding into the private sector.

Equity Investment. Pragmatic considerations are undermining aversion to other business practices formerly avoided for being synonymous with capitalism. There is now a marked interest in expanding direct investment in the Third World. Equity ownership already exists, but it has been confined to fishing companies, mixed trading firms, and joint shipping lines. Recent discussions indicate that many specialists consider it advisable to start investing in production, especially raw materials. Some economists write about outright equity; others, since it is a touchy ideological issue, prefer to speak of "long-term leases." Soviet economists G.M. Prokhorov and N. Khaldin suggest that whatever the form, the introduction of some sort of ownership rights "wherein the organizations and enterprises of one country become direct participants in production or co-owners of enterprises in the other country" is now being advocated to improve Soviet performance abroad. It is argued that what makes some form of equity attractive is that "in such cases partners have much greater opportunity to really show their interest in the creation of enterprises whose production they need most."

Policy Implications

What are the policy implications of these various changes in Soviet theory and practice? Do the deviations from the original systemic challenge toward ordinary economic pursuits make Soviet policies less of a threat and more of a legitimate form of activity, offering prospects for easing East-West tensions?

The answer depends in part on which aspect of American-Soviet competition one has in mind. In the past, economic competition clustered in three areas: economic theory, access to natural resources, and the international system—all within the overarching context of great power rivalry whose stakes far transcend these subissues. In all three areas changes indicate a significant diminution in aggressive Soviet thinking and behavior, a fact that begs for pertinent deductions and reactions from our side.

East-South Tensions

As regards the competition for the minds of the Third World—attempts to shape its economic thinking—it would be

wise to concede in the first place that the Third World has a
mind of its own, taking a bit of this from socialist practice and
then a bit of that from capitalist practice to incorporate the
borrowings into its own set of needs and beliefs. Nevertheless,
in so far as it is possible to refer to a Third World economic
philosophy, there are now clearly evident East-South fissures.
Whereas some twenty or even ten years ago one could assume
a congruity between radical Third World economics and
Marxist-Leninist theories emanating from Moscow, this is no
longer so. Disagreements arise over domestic and international issues.

The former congruence in interpreting the causes of underdevelopment no longer holds. While the *dependencia* economists continue to blame external factors and stress the stran-
gulation of the periphery by the center, Soviet specialists, as
already noted, have come to recognize the contribution of
local retarding factors and the benefits of foreign trade. Moreover, rather than let these differences pass unnoticed, Soviet
publications increasingly articulate where the disagreements
lie. For example, a 1982 monograph by B. Slavnyi argued that
the theories of the radical Third World economists were "out-
dated" because they

did not take into account the most recent trends [in international
economics] which seem to demonstrate that as the process of interna-
tionalization progresses the developing world will attain technological independence and the external factors [making for underdevelop-
ment] will cease to prevail over the domestic factors.

Revealingly, the monograph's concluding chapter summarized the arguments of various economists who reject the "ex-
tremism" of the dependency school with its contention that
interaction with the advanced capitalist states results in nothing but "plunder." Slavnyi also drew attention to Western
interpretations of the role of the multinationals as the consequence of the emergence of supra-nation-state processes and
a worldwide economic system.

Similarly, the original consensus that economic independence offered the best prospects for speedy development is no
longer there. As already noted, the Soviets now advise the

LDCs to integrate into the existing pattern of international exchanges. Indeed, they are critical of various Third World theories of self-reliance and attempts to institute South-South cooperation as creating barriers to a freer flow of trade.

The divergences that have developed in the economic thinking of East and South are evident on policy levels as well. They have undermined the ideologically motivated preference the Third World used to show for the USSR. At the IV UNCTAD in 1976, the Group of 77 stopped differentiating between the capitalist and the socialist states and granting a dispensation to the Eastern bloc. The LDCs now demand the same level of assistance from all advanced countries, i.e., 0.7 percent of their gross national product, no matter whether they once held overseas colonies or not, and no matter what their present political system—a move that is bitterly resented and loudly protested by Moscow.

Interdependence and Access to Raw Materials

The so-called Soviet drive for the control of raw materials also looks different when examined in the light of current theory and practice. There is no denying that the USSR is interested in access to raw materials. About 100 Soviet aid projects in the Third World are for prospecting and extracting natural resources; moreover, the practical turn in Soviet aid policies in the late 1960s placed emphasis on joint production abroad of resources in short supply at home or too costly to extract in Siberia.

The crux of the matter is on what terms Moscow proposes to maintain that access: through its own destabilizing imperialism or through legitimate economic means. Granted, in the past the Soviets talked of establishing a socialist IDL, but they failed to gain exclusive control in any country. In Guinea, for example, despite the early Soviet start in the mining operations, the high indebtedness of Conakry to Moscow, and the Soviet need for high-quality ore, the USSR had and still has access to less than 10 percent of the total bauxite production in that country.

At present, the evident Soviet interest in tripartite ventures suggests a willingness to cooperate, not a drive for domi- nation. If this change in Soviet conceptualization and posture was induced by weakness, then it is reasonable to assume that the same circumstances will persist in the future. After all, it is unlikely that the USSR will ever be able to overcome the West's economic predominance, based as it is on the demon- strated superiority in development and innovation.

The rise of the global outlook that recognizes interdepen- dence is even more promising for future accommodation than is the endemic Soviet weakness. One cannot claim that there is unanimity among Soviet leaders and among specialists on the degree of cooperation that the existence of a single world market enforces on both the industrial powers and the LDCs. But by and large, it is generally accepted that the global situa- tion makes isolationism untenable and dictates internationali- zation. According to N. Shmelev, writing in the January 1985 *International Affairs,* "In our day a 'closed,' autarkic economy is not only irrational and undesirable . . . but also physically impossible. . . . Evidently, the 'openness' of the Soviet national economy with regard to the external world is now on the increase." That outlook is said to represent Mikhail Gorba- chev's thinking as well. Surely, his goal to modernize the So- viet economy entails, perforce, an opening up to the benefits of world trade.

Beyond that, it is not clear what the Soviet policies regarding raw materials will be. One thing is certain, however: there is an influential and vocal group that counsels a cooperative approach. Its members argue that the growing dependence of all states on raw materials has created a world demand that in turn necessitates global regulation to assure the legitimate interests of both the producing Third World countries and the consuming industrial states, the USSR included.

Phrased thus, the argument has not yet surfaced in the for- mal statements of Soviet leaders, although since 1981 they have alluded to the constraints imposed by such global issues as the food supply and environmental problems. Nevertheless, the substantive Soviet proposals to the United Nations on commodity agreements display a marked concern for stability in pricing and deliveries. The weight of the Soviet position has shifted from denouncing the multinational corporations to seeking constructive solutions.

The USSR Seeks to Join the Existing System

The change in Soviet policies on the NIEO displays the emergence of a more cooperative approach to the international economic system. Until about the mid-1970s Moscow supported the claims that the Group of 77 pressed against the West on the assumption that the interests of the LDCs and the Socialist bloc coincided. Andrei Gromyko welcomed the declaration on NIEO, adopted in 1974, as a "progressive code of rules by which states should be guided in their economic relations." Moscow believed that through common effort the two groups would replace and reshape the existing "outmoded system" that served the interests of the West alone.

But after the IV UNCTAD in 1976 (where, as already mentioned, the LDCs lumped together the economic policies and obligations of both the capitalist and the socialist states), Moscow has switched to quite a different track. At the V UNCTAD in 1979, the Soviet bloc presented proposals that, despite the traditional sideswipes at Western policies, marked a fundamental departure. It urged "a comprehensive restructuring of *all* (emphasis added) areas of world trade" without calling for the elimination of the existing system. In that context, the bloc's statement proposed the principle of nondiscrimination (a neutral, universalistic term) instead of demanding the abolition of exploitation (a normative, political notion) as the basis for reforming the world economic order.

Thus, the outsider, who trumpeted Third World grievances and sought to refashion or at least control international economic institutions, has become a proponent of depoliticized, pragmatic policies serving the needs and capacities of all nations. Seeking ways and means to join the world market, the USSR finds that universalistic, economic arguments, not the systemic approach, are best suited to its purpose. Hence, Moscow now promotes an NIEO that will remove discriminatory trade barriers against all states, not just the various inequities affecting the LDCs. In keeping with this aim, the Soviet memorandum to the UNCTAD Board in September 1982 held that trade subordinated to political purposes "conflicts with the objective trends in the development of world economic activity." And on the eve of the VI UNCTAD in 1983, the Soviet deputy foreign trade minister stated that the USSR "always believed . . . that all trade flows are in one way or another interconnected." He proposed, therefore, that UNCTAD should establish universally observed procedures for conducting trade and that the LDC demands should be discussed in the context of a general review of all principles, rules, and norms of international trade.

Criticism of the LDCs' "local" or "parochial" plans for the NIEO is the obverse of Soviet advocacy of universal principles in international trade. Among various comments on the results of the VI UNCTAD, objections to the demands for preferential or concessional treatment of the developing countries ranked high. Soviet specialists criticized the notion of an automatic distribution of income from the developed to the developing countries, for this contradicted all the laws of international trade as well as theoretical principles of economics.

Possible U.S. Responses

How does the emergence of new trends in the three areas affect the overall U.S.–Soviet competition in the Third World? The answer depends, of course, on the way Soviet motivations are interpreted. If the observer believes that the USSR operates according to some blueprint for world domination, then all the recent departures in theory and practice do not alter the picture. They are nothing but Machiavellian tactics to enable the USSR to attain that goal by different, more subtle means. And the U.S. response remains the same: to keep the USSR out of the world market as a disruptive element that cannot have legitimate interests or pursue them in an acceptable manner.

But if the observer believes that the world and the actors on its stage change because of the force of circumstances and experience, that Soviet leaders—like other people—are capable of learning and innovating and are not predestined to pursue a set course, then the changes in outlook and actions described in this chapter offer prospects for reducing tensions. There are enough indications of change over the past decade to suggest that the USSR is in transition from acting as an outside challenger to becoming a candidate for core membership in the existing economic system. Unable to dominate either by virtue of its own strength or by manipulating the hostilities of the Third World, and incapable of retreating into a posture of isolation, Moscow now seeks admission to the global club without any reference to a special relationship between the LDCs and the Socialist bloc.

How should the United States respond to this more constructive (though naturally self-serving) turn in Soviet policies? If U.S. policy makers believe that the West can impose an effective economic quarantine on the East to undermine its strength and to discredit its overall challenge, then the answer is to continue economic warfare. But if analysts concede that neither goal is possible, then Western leaders can proceed to respond positively to Soviet attempts to become a participating member of the global economic community, acting in accordance with normal commercial interests and practices and not according to some systemic "socialist" (hence subversive and destabilizing) ways.

Steps toward an Improved Economic Relationship

The burden of recent changes in Soviet outlook and policies, as well as in the world situation, suggests four departures that would help reduce Soviet-American tensions.

First, the U.S. leadership should relax about the purported Communist economic threat in the Third World and begin to take account of how and where the demonstrable Soviet weaknesses have influenced the adoption of milder, less confrontational policies. Here we should take into account that the

USSR is not afraid to put its new thinking regarding economic aid on the record. The current version of the Communist party of the Soviet Union program (established in 1986 and replacing the Khrushchev text adopted in 1961) drops all reference to the USSR's "international duty to assist" peoples seeking to consolidate their independence. More than that, it instructs the radical states that "people build their new society mainly through their own effort," and it cautions them that the USSR will support them "only to the extent of its ability."

Second, the United States and its allies should consider policies that would encourage Soviet attempts to engage in perfectly legitimate economic pursuits on the assumption that the expansion of mutually beneficial trade relations will create an atmosphere more conducive to constructive negotiations in other areas. (Here it should not be forgotten that the question of opening up to greater participation in world trade is not a settled issue in the USSR. A positive Western response could encourage those political forces in the Soviet Union that advocate concentrating on normal economic ties with the LDCs, rather than on promoting revolutionary change, both for the sake of the Soviet consumer and for international peace.)

Third, the United States should encourage joint U.S.–Soviet specialized discussions and studies on various global problems touching the Third World and involving us all. These joint activities should aim to educate one another, identify areas of common concern, and publicize the results of joint deliberations. Suitable topics could cover humanitarian subjects (food or health), economic projects (joint exploitation of resources), or political problems (the economic effects of the military budgets in the LDCs). Many of these topics have already been explored in joint American-Soviet seminars, held under the terms of official cultural exchanges, but their results remain off the record.

Last but not least, planning should begin for joint U.S.–Soviet operations, both commercial and humanitarian, in the Third World to support economic growth in some LDCs and to avoid economic disasters in others. (The results were unintentional, but Soviet trucks facilitated the distribution of

American food in Ethiopia during the recent famine disaster. Neither side publicized this fact.) Here, too, normal trade relations and a common effort to eliminate sickness or poverty should contribute to establishing conditions on local and international levels that are conducive to stability and peace.

7

Military Aspects of U.S.-Soviet Competition in the Third World

FRANCIS FUKUYAMA

Introduction

It is common for Soviet observers of the Third World to assert that, in the final analysis, the influence of the two superpowers in the Third World depends on the relative attractiveness of the socioeconomic models they represent. This statement is profoundly true at some level: a country's foreign policy is ultimately shaped by the character of the domestic institutions it possesses or is seeking to build, which in the case of most developing countries follows one of the great world historical patterns. And yet, while it is comforting for the superpowers to think that they can derive influence abroad merely on the strength of the positive example they set at home, this is a "truth" that is valid only in the long run. In the short run, Third World states, regimes, and individual leaders

FRANCIS FUKUYAMA is a staff member of the Political Science Department, The Rand Corporation. Dr. Fukuyama's specialty in Middle Eastern and Soviet affairs has encompassed academic and U.S. Department of State experience. His numerous publications reflect his concentration on Soviet policy toward the Third World.

need to be able to survive long enough to build those very domestic institutions, and for that reason need security in the form of external military aid, weapons, advisers, training, and, in the last extreme, direct superpower military intervention. Much of the history of the postwar superpower rivalry in the Third World consequently revolves around military issues. Much as one might bemoan this fact, it has been an inevitable feature of the competition and is likely to remain so for the foreseeable future.

Military matters are important not only in order to understand the dynamics of the U.S.–Soviet rivalry in the Third World, but from the standpoint of the larger U.S.–Soviet relationship as well. While the central problem of that relationship has been the threat of nuclear war, the Third World has been the locus of almost all of the major U.S.–Soviet confrontations since World War II, and—in the cases of Korea, Vietnam, and Afghanistan—the only arena where Americans or Soviets have died in large numbers. Moreover, there are parts of the Third World, like the Persian Gulf, where superpower stakes are high enough to warrant direct military conflict and escalation to nuclear weapons. Indeed, one can make a strong case that nuclear war is more likely to be triggered in the Persian Gulf than in Europe, an argument that underlines the interconnectedness of Third World military matters to questions of global security.

Military factors affect the superpower competition in two respects: first, the United States and the Soviet Union to some extent seek influence in the Third World for the sake of military *ends* or objectives; and second, military force or assistance constitutes an important *means* by which the superpowers gain and consolidate political influence. Of course, strictly speaking there is no such thing as a purely military objective; force is always a means to some higher political goal, if only the protection of a country's territorial integrity and political institutions. When we speak of military ends in the present context, we refer to objectives external to the security of the particular Third World country or region in question, primarily related to the superpower's worldwide strategic nuclear posture. Of the two dimensions, the military factor as a means has been much more important than as an end for both the U.S. and the USSR. In the following sections, this chapter will look at both aspects of the problem in a historical perspective and conclude with several observations about the present and likely future character of the military competition between the superpowers in the Third World.

Superpower Military Objectives in the Third World

It is important to note at the outset that the primary strategic prizes throughout the postwar period have been Europe and Northeast Asia, and that the Third World has held a distinctly lower priority for both the United States and the USSR. While both superpowers have pursued military objectives there, these have been only one of several motivating factors whose significance has varied over time.

The United States

U.S. policy in the Third World was guided in a major way by explicit military objectives primarily during the 1950s. Over the following two decades it lost its larger global strategic coherence, until concern over access to oil in the late 1970s and early 1980s led to a modest resurgence of interest in a number of Third World countries for overt military purposes.

U.S. military strategy in the 1950s sought to create a series of interlocking "defensive" alliances around the periphery of the Soviet Union modeled after the North Atlantic Treaty Organization (NATO) in Europe. These included the Baghdad Pact, the Southeast Asian Treaty Organization, and separate bilateral security treaties between Japan and South Korea and the United States. Aside from their part in the desire to create a physical containment barrier to Soviet and Chinese expansionism, these alliances served as the political underpinning for a series of military bases which permitted the United States to execute its Dulles-era strategy of "massive retaliation." The ranges of early strategic systems like B-47 bombers,

Jupiter and Thor medium- and intermediate-range ballistic missiles (MRBMs and IRBMs), and carrier-based aviation were limited, requiring them to be physically deployed close to the Soviet homeland. Washington consequently sought to organize the states of the Middle East's so-called Northern Tier (Turkey, Iraq, Iran, and Pakistan) into the Baghdad Pact not simply for their own defense, but to permit the Strategic Air Command (SAC) to carry out reconnaissance and combat against a specified target set in the southern USSR in the event of war.

This clear-cut (if not openly admitted) military objective thus became one of the factors driving U.S. policy toward the Third World, and particularly in the Middle East, during the Eisenhower administration. In subsequent decades, Dulles-era "pactomania" became a much less salient factor for two reasons. In the first place, America's Third World alliances proved much more vulnerable to local political upheavals and instability than the NATO alliance; the Iraqi monarchy which had been the linchpin of the Baghdad Pact was overthrown in 1958 shortly after the signing of the treaty, while the United States gradually lost basing rights in Libya, Pakistan, Thailand, and eventually Iran. Other allies lost their strategic value as they nervously ended overt military cooperation and sought to distance themselves from Washington. Indeed, military cooperation between the local government and the United States engendered considerable nationalist resentment, and in the case of Iraq in the 1950s and Iran in the 1970s was itself one of the causes of instability.

The second reason for the decreasing salience of military goals in U.S. policy was advances in technology, which permitted vast increases in the range of strategic systems. B-47s were replaced with long-range B-52s and intercontinental ballistic missiles (ICBMs) were deployed in the continental United States in place of earlier generation MRBMs and IRBMs. It was no longer necessary to base American central strategic systems overseas, and consequently the need for facilities in the Third World was less pressing. Subsequent technological improvements such as space-based reconnaissance platforms and submarine-launched missiles of increasing range further decreased the need for forward deployments.

Between the late 1950s and the early 1980s it is hard to find a similar overarching strategic concept like massive retaliation which provided U.S. foreign policy in the Third World with a clear-cut military objective. The commitment of half a million U.S. troops to Vietnam was defended on the grounds of the "strategic importance" of Vietnam and the rest of Southeast Asia. By this it was generally meant that South Vietnam constituted the Free World's weak link, a link whose loss might undermine American credibility and trigger an uncontrollable series of Communist revolutions in other, more inherently important, countries. It was also a test of the broader U.S. willingness to back alliance commitments. Yet to accord Vietnam itself any kind of strategic priority in the scale of global American interests was to both misunderstand and abuse the term. U.S. military activities elsewhere in the Third World in this period generally were related to the security of the specific countries or regions involved, and did not serve global strategic purposes. One of the consequences of the U.S. Navy's costly investment in nuclear-powered aircraft carriers is that it is able to project power around the world without having to rely on bases in less-developed countries, with the sole exception of the Philippines.

It was only in the late 1970s, after the Iranian revolution and the Soviet invasion of Afghanistan, that U.S. policy toward the Third World again began to be guided by explicit military objectives. The vulnerability of Western economies to oil supply disruptions, which had been demonstrated so vividly during the 1970s, coupled with the endemic political instability of the Middle East/Persian Gulf, prompted the United States to undertake creation of the Rapid Deployment Force (later redesignated Central Command, or CENTCOM), designed to deter threats to Western access to oil. While eschewing formal basing rights, the United States did seek contingency access and facilities agreements with a number of countries near the Persian Gulf like Oman, Egypt, Somalia, and Kenya. These arrangements served the global objective of preserving European and Japanese access to the Persian Gulf, a goal whose significance went beyond the security of the countries in the region itself.

The Soviet Union

The USSR has also pursued military goals in the Third World. While these are an important factor explaining the direction and character of Soviet policy, they have never been Moscow's predominant motive and at times have been subordinated to other political objectives.

When the Soviet Union made its first foray into the Third World in the mid-1950s, it followed military objectives that were the direct counterparts of U.S. strategy at that time. Moscow's chief concern was to undermine the series of U.S.-sponsored pacts being erected around its borders, the most important of which was the Baghdad Pact with the SAC bases in the Northern Tier. This it did by supporting Egypt's Gamal Abdel Nasser and other Arab nationalists and encouraging their opposition to Iraq's military links with the West. Nikita Khrushchev was initially interested in Egypt and Syria less for their own sakes than for their usefulness as bargaining chips to be traded in for neutralization of the U.S. presence in the Northern Tier. This is evident from Khrushchev's repeated calls between 1956 and 1958 for a four-power conference on the Middle East that would have, in effect, traded the Western position in the Northern Tier for the Soviet position in Egypt and Syria. This Soviet strategy succeeded brilliantly with Nuri al-Said's overthrow at the hands of Nasserist officers in 1958; the Baghdad Pact and its successor, the Central Treaty Organization (CENTO), never possessed the same dynamism after the loss of its founding member.

From the early 1960s to the early 1970s the Soviet Union followed a different set of military goals related to the development of a Soviet bluewater navy. Changes in naval technology created two new missions for the Soviet navy by the early to mid-1960s: first, the neutralization (or attempted neutralization, since the goal remained technically elusive) of U.S. strategic nuclear systems at sea, that is, ballistic missile–carrying submarines (SSBNs) and aircraft carrier battle groups; and second, the protection of its own SSBNs from hostile Western antisubmarine warfare (ASW). Since the ranges of first- and second-generation U.S. and Soviet submarine-launched ballistic missiles were limited, the latter activity had to be carried out close to the U.S. coast and correspondingly far from Soviet home bases.

Since the Soviets possessed no aircraft carriers at this time and had relatively fewer nuclear-powered ships than the U.S. Navy, land bases for naval aircraft and port facilities were necessary for the stationing of permanent flotillas in distant oceans. The deployment after 1964 of a permanent Soviet naval squadron, the Fifth *Eskadra,* in the Mediterranean was intended to counter U.S. SSBNs and nuclear-armed carrier battle groups operating there, and led to a substantial requirement for overseas basing. Hence, the Soviet Union began searching for support facilities all around the Mediterranean littoral in the mid-1960s. Michael McGwire points out in U.S. *Naval Institute Proceedings/Naval Review* in May 1980 that the process was accelerated by their eviction from the Albanian port of Vlona in 1962. Admiral Sergei Gorshkov, founder of the modern Soviet navy, personally pressed Nasser on several occasions for access to naval facilities, a request that was ultimately granted in the aftermath of the June 1967 Middle East war. Particularly after the worsening of the Sino-Soviet conflict toward the end of the decade, the Soviets developed a greater interest in preserving the sea line of communication between European and the far eastern USSR, including the Indian Ocean and South China Sea. Demands for access to naval facilities have been a consistent adjunct of Soviet diplomacy, leading to arrangements with Algeria, Syria, and Somalia, and, in the 1970s, South Yemen, Ethiopia, and Vietnam.

But while naval access has been a regular theme in Soviet policy since the early 1960s, military objectives and, particularly, considerations related to the strategic nuclear balance played an increasingly smaller role in Soviet policy; such goals were but one of several competing motives behind the widespread and unprecedented burst of Soviet activities in the Third World that took place during the mid- and late 1970s, beginning with the intervention in Angola in 1975 and culminating with the invasion of Afghanistan in 1980. Political, ideological, and economic factors frequently weighed more heavily in the balance than did strategic ones, at least in the short run. This was most evident from Soviet behavior in the Horn of Africa, where Moscow put at risk and ultimately lost the large missile-handling facility they had established at Berbera, Somalia, in return for what they hoped would be an increase in their overall influence with larger and more influential Ethiopia. (Some observers have argued that the Soviets hoped to maintain relations with both Somalia and Ethiopia in spite of their support for Addis Ababa in the Ogaden war, and that, in any case, the Soviets have replaced Berbera with comparable facilities in Aden and Massawa, Ethiopia. This may have been true, but the Soviets were nonetheless taking a calculated risk in alienating Mogadishu.) Further developments in naval technology are in many ways decreasing Moscow's requirement for overseas basing. The long-range missiles carried aboard the fourth generation of Soviet Typhoon-class submarines permit these boats to be deployed in bastions near the Soviet homeland, like the Barents Sea or the Sea of Okhotsk. Moreover, increases in U.S. SSBN ranges vastly increased the ocean areas in which American missile-carrying submarines could patrol, complicating an already difficult task to the point of diminishing marginal returns.

Military Power as Means

While the superpowers have pursued military goals on and off in the Third World, it is clear that for both military power has been much more important as a means to other, essentially political, objectives. These objectives include the preservation in power of regimes of a particular ideological character, deterrence of threats from hostile neighbors, the inducing or bribing of clients to behave in certain specific ways, or the increasing of the superpower's general fund of influence with a particular state. Political influence is in some sense a fungible commodity which is both desirable in itself, and translatable into other, more concrete assets like military bases or votes in the United Nations at a later time. The distinction between means and ends is therefore not a hard and fast one. While there are times when military assistance serves specific political ends (as when the United States agreed to build two new air bases in Israel to induce the latter to sign the peace treaty with Egypt), in most cases the superpower simply desires to increase its general fund of good will (as in the case of the USSR's long-term cultivation of India).

Military power as an instrument for achieving political ends can itself take a variety of forms, which fall along a spectrum of increasingly direct involvement on the part of the superpower. At the low end of the spectrum lie arms transfers and military assistance, which throughout the postwar period have been the most typical form of military involvement by the Great Powers in the Third World. At the high end there is direct intervention by the superpowers' own combat forces, while in between lie use of allied or proxy forces, military training for internal and external security purposes, logistic support for overseas interventions, joint command arrangements, development of military organization and infrastructure, and other arrangements.

There are many similarities between the two superpowers' use of military force as a political instrument; indeed, much of their rivalry in areas of the Third World, like the Middle East, has consisted of the competitive arming of their respective clients (as in the Arab-Israeli conflict), or attempts to outbid each other in weapons supply for the favors of a particular country (as in the case of Egypt in the mid-1950s and again in the mid-1970s). Nonetheless, the two superpowers have in certain respects been moving in opposite directions throughout the postwar period, resulting in what might be termed a role reversal that will have important implications for their mutual relations in the future. In particular, the United States has shown a steadily decreasing willingness to employ military power directly in the Third World, while for the Soviet Union the reverse has been true. This development has been accompanied by corresponding changes in both the quantity and quality of the superpowers' respective influence. The consequence of this trend is that while in the past it has generally been the United States which has employed its military power in defense of the political status quo, it is now the USSR that is increasingly being called on to do so. The sections that follow will include a discussion of each of these trends in greater detail.

The United States Experience

The United States has consistently shown a much greater proclivity to use military power directly in the Third World than has the Soviet Union. The United States has not only fought two major wars in the Third World since the end of World War II, but it has intervened or made a show of force on more than 100 other occasions, as enumerated in *Iron Fist, Velvet Glove,* edited by Stephen Kaplan.

Direct Use of Military Power

The United States Position as World Power. There were several reasons for this use of military power. The first had to do with America's conception of its role in the world in the immediate postwar period. The United States emerged from World War II with an enormous confidence in itself and its ability to take over from Great Britain and other European powers the role of guarantor of a liberal world order. The United States position as the predominant economic power coupled with a desire to avoid a return to traditional isolationism led postwar American statesmen to fill with uncommon enthusiasm the vacuum left by the European colonial powers. While the Soviet Union also had global ambitions, it had been substantially weakened by the war and was preoccupied with the consolidation of its hold over Eastern Europe.

Defense of the Status Quo. The second factor was military capability. The United States, like Britain, was historically a maritime power with substantial overseas interests; it was the only Great Power to have a major service branch—the Marine Corps—dedicated exclusively to what is referred to as "power projection." (Britain, France, and the Soviet Union all possess marines or seaborne amphibious troops, but they are limited in number and totally dependent on outside logistical support. The U.S. Marine Corps, by contrast, has its own navy and air force.) The United States had long experience using military force to keep order in its own hemisphere, and as a result of the emerging Cold War it found itself with substantial forces already deployed overseas. The Soviet Union, by contrast, was traditionally a continental power whose strength lay in its ground forces; its only military forays were in areas like Korea, Turkey, and Iran, immediately adjacent to its borders.

Finally, in most Third World regions the United States was attempting to defend the political status quo, while the Soviet Union and its allies sought to challenge it. This was to be expected since the Soviet Union saw itself as the leader of an international revolutionary movement, and given the fact that at the start of the postwar period most of the Third World was still under the direct control of the European colonial powers. The United States, on the other hand, was allied in NATO to these very countries, and while it found itself supporting decolonization in former British, Dutch, and French territories, it tended to support established social classes and a conservative political order in the newly liberated countries. The most typical Third World military conflict in the first two or three postwar decades was a left wing insurgency supported by the socialist bloc against a local government supported by the West, as was the case in Malaysia, Laos, Vietnam, and Algeria. It is almost universally the case that substantially greater force ratios are required to fight guerrillas than conventional opponents; insurgents rely on a long-term political strategy which requires lower material and manpower inputs. Hence, it was natural that the United States or France should feel a greater need for direct intervention with their own forces than did outside powers supporting the Vietcong or the Algerian National Liberation Front.

Shift Away from Use of Force

As time progressed the United States became steadily less prepared to use its own military forces directly in Third World conflicts, and consequently began to rely more heavily on other means such as military assistance or allies to achieve its purposes. This situation has evolved not because of changes in military capabilities, but primarily because of a major shift in America's view of its own global role, induced largely by the high costs of direct intervention in Vietnam. In addition, the structure of Third World conflicts has shifted to some degree as well, and the United States by the mid-1980s faced an increasing number of opportunities to challenge a status quo supported by the Soviet Union through relatively low-level provision of military aid. But while the United States is much less prepared to use direct military instruments than it was twenty or thirty years ago, the debate over the use of force has been a dialectical process whose course was by no means predetermined.

Korea provided the first major occasion for the direct use of American military power in the Third World, and also engendered the first debate over appropriate military instruments. The fact that the United States lost close to 50,000 casualties in the defense of a country earlier declared outside the sphere of vital American interests and incurred a continuing ground force commitment to the defense of South Korea immediately engendered a search for alternative means of dealing with Third World security problems. The solution offered by the Eisenhower administration was the doctrine of massive retaliation, by which it was hoped the deterrent effect of American strategic superiority would be extended outside the European theater.

It is common now to scoff at massive retaliation as a strategic doctrine for dealing with Third World challenges, but it is in fact possible to document cases in which U.S. strategic power provided leverage in local crises. For example, Mohamed Haykal, in *Nasser: The Cairo Documents,* reports that when Egyptian

President Nasser appealed to Khrushchev for help during the 1958 Lebanon-Iraqi crisis, the latter told Nasser:

The Americans had gone off their heads and "frankly, we are not ready for a confrontation. We are not ready for World War Three. . . ."
Krushchev [sic] replied that Nasser would have to bend with the storm, there was no other way because Dulles could blow the whole world to pieces. . . .

Nonetheless, massive retaliation was a fundamentally flawed doctrine; its success depended on American strategic superiority, which was lost and never to be regained during the 1960s, and it was designed in response to a Third World conflict—the conventional invasion of South Korea by the North—which proved to be highly atypical of those actually faced by the United States in subsequent years.

It took the commitment of half a million men in the Vietnam War to force a major shift in American thinking about the use of direct military instruments in the Third World. The circumstances of that war and its effects on American willingness to employ force are well known and do not need to be detailed here. The most clear-cut shift in American policy as a result of popular opposition to the war was the so-called Nixon Doctrine enunciated on Guam in 1969, in which President Richard Nixon asserted that local American allies in the Third World would henceforth bear the major burden of combat, with the U.S. role being restricted to military and economic assistance. The war also led to the codification into American law of a number of measures designed to limit future U.S. involvement in Third World conflicts, such as the War Powers Act or the Clark Amendment (lifted in 1985), which forbade the provision of assistance to any of the rival guerrilla groups in Angola.

Use of Proxies. As a result of the Vietnam-induced constraints on the direct employment of U.S. combat forces, American policy in the 1970s began to search for proxies that could take over the burden of regional security. The most clear-cut application of the Nixon Doctrine occurred in Iran, where the Shah after 1972 was expected to assume many of the responsibilities for maintaining regional stability in the Persian Gulf in the wake of the withdrawing British. (Iran actually did play this regional security role in Oman, where it helped Sultan Qaboos suppress the Dhofar rebellion.) To facilitate his doing so he was given virtually free rein by the Nixon administration with regard to arms purchases. The problem of this approach was twofold: first, there were very few candidate proxies like Iran that were willing and able to guarantee their own security, much less the security of states around them; and second, the very act of conferring a regional security role on a state had disturbing internal consequences, as the eventual fate of the Shah proved. In spite of these shortcomings, the desire to find and exploit Third World proxies has proven very strong. The Carter administration early on emphasized "regional hegemonic powers," while the Reagan administration toyed for a while with the idea of building up Saudi Arabia as a security pillar. The identification of suitable candidates has proven elusive, however.

Arms Transfers. In the absence of full-fledged proxies, the United States came to rely increasingly heavily on military assistance as a policy tool during the 1970s. The American desire to shift some of the regional security burden away from itself coincided with several other developments reinforcing this tendency. The substantial increases in the level of U.S. arms transfers that took place in that decade are traceable to four countries, all of them located in the Middle East: Israel, Egypt, Saudi Arabia, and Iran. The oil crisis of the early 1970s underlined the Persian Gulf's importance and put considerable amounts of cash into the pockets of the oil producers, who were nervous about their own security and, therefore, eager customers of weapons. American contractors and the U.S. Department of the Treasury had a corresponding interest in repatriating petrodollars. The October 1973 war demonstrated the region's continuing political instability and the Western world's vulnerability to oil supply disruptions.

In this period the United States came to see weapons supply

as a major source of leverage in pursuit of concrete diplomatic goals like settlement of the Arab-Israeli conflict. Examples of this abound: the threatened or actual withholding of arms induced Israel to break its blockade of the Egyptian Third Army in 1973 and to sign the Sinai II withdrawal agreement in 1975, just as the previously mentioned promise of substantially higher levels of assistance was crucial in inducing Egypt and Israel to agree to the Camp David Accords and the Egyptian-Israeli peace treaty. The Reagan administration argued in 1981 that while provision of military assistance to Pakistan (including F-16 fighters) might not head off a Pakistani nuclear weapon entirely, it would at least give Washington greater leverage in delaying its introduction than was the case under the Carter administration when Pakistan was cut off entirely under a Symington Amendment embargo.

Problems. In terms of the quality of influence provided, however, arms transfers were a much weaker instrument than were direct forms of intervention. American allies like Israel and Turkey have been notably uncooperative on issues like Cyprus or West Bank settlement activity and often have been able to exert a kind of reverse leverage on Washington. The reasons for this are straightforward, if not always clearly understood. If the United States is truly interested in the security and well-being of an ally, there are limits to the severity of the sanctions—usually in the form of withholding arms deliveries —it can impose in order to secure compliance with its political wishes. If the limits are not observed, the sanctions can begin endangering the larger end that the security relationship was meant to serve in the first place. Generally speaking, the regional ally will have a greater stake in the particular issue involved than the United States has, and in a contest of wills is much more likely to try to "go it alone" than give in. Hence it is not surprising that the congressional arms embargo imposed on Turkey after its 1974 invasion of Cyprus was totally ineffective or that the aid ban to Pakistan after 1979 failed to slow the momentum of its nuclear weapons development program.

Policy in the Mid-1980s

Under the Reagan administration there was something of a reassertion of U.S. willingness to intervene directly, as the cases of Grenada and Lebanon demonstrated. In addition, plans for CENTCOM begun under the Carter administration were carried forward. It would be a mistake, however, to see in these events a surmounting of the "Vietnam syndrome" or a return to the earlier prointervention consensus. The Grenada intervention was popular only because it was quick, low-cost, and, most important, successful: in these respects it is likely to be highly atypical of other conflicts that the United States will face in the Third World. The Reagan administration's difficulties in building congressional and popular support for its Central American policies are more indicative of the constraints that will continue to limit future U.S. involvements.

Opposition to Use of Force. Moreover, the conventional wisdom that post-Vietnam restraints on U.S. use of force have been imposed largely by Congress and left-of-center public opinion ignores the fact that in recent years one of the most resolute institutional opponents of the direct use of military force in Third World conflicts has been the U.S. military itself. There were many in the armed forces who responded to public criticisms of their role in Vietnam by arguing that they were unfairly hobbled by the country's political leadership, which forced them to fight under political constraints that did not permit exercise of the military means that in their professional judgment were deemed necessary to win. These views have been most forcefully expressed by Colonel Harry G. Summers in his book *On Strategy: A Critical Analysis of the Vietnam War.* Summers feels that Vietnam was misconstrued as a counterinsurgency war when in fact it was a conventional conflict subject to the solutions of conventional military strategy, solutions that the U.S. military was not permitted to carry out by successive administrations. Summers's book has been widely acclaimed and is the nearest thing to a consensus retrospective view of Vietnam within the armed forces.

The military's consistent position since Vietnam is that the United States should employ force only when there is a strong public consensus behind intervention *and* when the military is permitted to use whatever means are needed to win clearly and quickly. If these conditions cannot be met, the military's strong preference is not to get involved in the first place. This perspective is accurately reflected in Secretary of Defense Caspar Weinberger's well-known opposition to the U.S. Marine presence in Lebanon in 1982–84 and in the secretary's November 1984 speech to the National Press Club outlining six tests which the United States should pose prior to future interventions. Those conditions include: (1) forces should not be committed unless the situation is deemed vital to our national interests; (2) we should only commit combat troops with a clear intention of winning; (3) when committing forces we should have clearly defined political and military objectives, and we should know how our forces can accomplish those objectives; (4) when combat forces are committed we must constantly reassess the situation to determine if our vital interests are still at stake; (5) before committing forces we should have reasonable assurance of support from the American people and their representatives in Congress; and (6) the commitment of U.S. forces should be a last resort. (It should be noted that the invasion of Grenada would not have been attempted under these ground rules, particularly in view of conditions 1 and 5.)

While the Weinberger conditions appear on the surface to be a formula for more selective direct intervention, the fact is that there are virtually no Third World conflicts that will meet all six of the Weinberger tests, i.e., will be short, popular, low-cost, and winnable. Third World conflicts almost by definition are messy and politically ambiguous; political considerations will inevitably predominate over military ones and restrict the unbridled use of military means. Thus the Weinberger conditions are in fact a more or less disingenuous formula for avoiding Third World intervention altogether, reflecting a strong policy preference on the part of the uniformed military.

The Soviet Experience

Soviet use of military force as an instrument of Third World policy has followed an evolution reverse from that of the United States. Starting out as a continental power with virtually no friends or interests in the developing world, the Soviet Union began by using arms transfers and economic aid to build ties to Third World states, then moved to increasingly direct forms of intervention, including military training, combat advisers, and proxies (primarily Cuba and East Germany), culminating finally in the massive and direct intervention by Soviet combat forces in Afghanistan. This evolution went through four distinct phases, corresponding to the political strategies of the first four postwar general secretaries of the Soviet Communist party.

Postwar Policy

In the first period, from the end of World War II until Joseph Stalin's death, the USSR showed little interest in the Third World, much of which was still under European control. During the period beginning in 1947 known as the *Zhdanovshchina,* the Soviets understood international relations in highly bipolar terms, with countries belonging to either the capitalist or socialist camp. Stalin recognized only orthodox Communist parties in the Third World as allies, classifying non-Communist nationalist leaderships as bourgeois or petty-bourgeois and writing them off as puppets of the imperialist powers. Since local Third World Communist parties were quite weak in this period, this effectively stunted the growth of Soviet ties with the developing World. The only two Soviet Third World initiatives of this period, the establishment of an independent pro-Soviet republic in northern Iran in 1946 and their go-ahead for Kim Il-Sung's invasion of South Korea in 1950, took place in regions directly contiguous to the Soviet Union and made use of orthodox Communist allies and/or Soviet forces.

A Second Phase of Soviet Policy

It was Khrushchev who undertook a major policy innovation in 1955. Khrushchev recognized the anti-imperialist potential of non-Communist nationalist leaders like Nasser, Nehru, Sukarno, Ghana's Nkrumah, and Keita of Mali. These leaders all followed vaguely left wing ideologies, heavily overlaid with local nationalist doctrines like pan-Arabism or African social-ism, but united in their resentment of Western colonialism. Beginning with the famous Soviet-Egyptian arms deal of July 1955, the USSR began to reach out to this group of what it called bourgeois nationalists, supporting them in conflicts with the West such as the crisis over Egypt's nationalization of the Suez Canal.

In this second phase of Soviet policy, which lasted roughly from 1955 through the early 1970s, arms transfers were the primary instrument by which Moscow sought to build political influence. While the Soviets also supported a number of ex-pensive, high-visibility economic projects like the Aswan High Dam in Egypt, their competitive advantage with the West lay in the realm of arms supply, where they were able to provide large quantities of cheap, advanced arms from their own mas-sive inventories. While sophisticated by Third World stan-dards, Soviet weapons have generally been less advanced than their American counterparts, and therefore more readily us-able by Third World military organizations. The Soviets ob-tained their initial foothold in Egypt when the United States was slow to respond to an Egyptian request for military assist-ance following a destructive Israeli raid on Gaza in 1954; when the bulk of the Egyptian army was destroyed in the tripartite Anglo-Franco-Israeli intervention in 1956, the Soviets rebuilt it virtually overnight. Arms supply similarly underlay Soviet ties with Indonesia, India, Syria, and Ghana in this period.

Apart from military assistance and diplomatic support of-fered in times of crisis, the Soviets did not possess other significant instruments of influence and leverage. Soviet economic assistance has always been limited, and concentrated in the hands of a few clients. In spite of their shared anti-imperialism, Moscow's new Third World allies were an ideologically heterogeneous group which frequently sought to assert their independence from Moscow and suppressed local Communist parties without remorse. The Soviets were for the most part indifferent to the internal political character of their client regimes and did not seek to interfere directly in their domestic politics. Ties were maintained at a state-to-state level and usually did not extend below the single charismatic nationalist leader at the top.

Problems. Khrushchev's opening to non-Communist nationalists in the Third World led to an enormous broadening of Soviet influence there, heightening Soviet political prestige and leading to direct benefits like basing rights for the Soviet navy. But relationships built around arms transfers also suffered from several critical weaknesses. The first had to do with the limitations of arms supply as an instrument of political leverage, mentioned already in the American context. Arms transfers proved to be a very blunt tool that, experience showed, could not be manipulated to fine-tune the policies of client states; more often clients were able to exert reverse leverage and force the Soviet Union to do things it would have preferred not to do.

The best example of this was Egypt, Moscow's oldest and most important Third World client. Following Egypt's defeat by Israel in the June 1967 war, Soviet policy sought two objectives: first, restoring its tarnished prestige as Cairo's patron and building Egypt's bargaining leverage, and, second, pushing Egypt gently toward a negotiated political settlement with Tel Aviv while preventing the outbreak of another war. (The Soviets were not opposed to conflict per se so much as conflict leading to another defeat for its Arab clients, carrying the risk of heightened Soviet involvement and confrontation with the United States.) These aims were mutually contradictory. The massive Soviet resupply of Egypt and Syria following the June

war served to restore Soviet prestige to some extent, but undermined the second objective by encouraging President
Nasser to believe that he had a military option against Israel.
Moscow was unable to prevent him from undertaking a war of
attrition along the Suez Canal in 1969; when the Israelis responded by engaging in deep penetration bombing of the
interior of Egypt, the Soviets found themselves having to dispatch 20,000 of their own combat troops in early 1970 to assist
in Egypt's air defense, the first time that Soviet forces had been
deployed on that scale in a Third World country.

Soviet attempts to impose sanctions on an ally through the
withholding of arms have proven no more successful than in
the American case. Following the August 1970 cease-fire along
the Suez front, the Soviets reduced the flow of weapons to
Egypt in hopes of compelling the new president, Anwar Sadat,
to give up the military option and move toward a political
settlement. Sadat had recounted four occasions in 1971 and
1972 on which he vainly traveled to Moscow in search of what
he termed a "deterrent" weapon. Sadat responded to Soviet
cautiousness by dramatically expelling the 20,000 Soviet advisers in Egypt in July 1972. The Soviets were suddenly faced
with the choice of upping the ante with regard to Egypt, or
losing their most important Third World client altogether.
The Soviets had no other alternative than to flood Egypt with
weapons and implicitly give Sadat the go-ahead to launch the
October 1973 war, thereby finding themselves dragged into
war and a confrontation with the United States that they had
sought to avoid for six years.

Numerous other examples of the weakness of the arms
transfer instrument can be adduced. Soviet control over weapons supply was not sufficient to prevent Syria from intervening
in Lebanon in 1976 contrary to Soviet wishes, or to head off
Iraq's attack on Iran in September 1980. Moreover, arms
transfers could do nothing to address the problem of the stay-
ing power of Soviet Third World clients. The Soviets suffered
a number of setbacks when Khrushchev-era clients were overthrown in coups, as in the case of Algeria's Ben Bella, Ghana's
Nkrumah, Indonesia's Sukarno, and Mali's Keita, or when they

defected to the Western camp altogether as in the case of Sadat after the October war. Few Soviet clients had an institutional base like a vanguard party that would guarantee the long-term maintenance of a pro-Soviet orientation, and since Soviet ties were only with the top leader, they often did not survive that leader's passing.

Recent Policy

In the third phase of Soviet Third World policy, which began roughly in the mid-1970s and spanned the period of intense activism associated with the second half of Leonid Brezhnev's tenure, Moscow sought to address these earlier weaknesses by supplementing arms transfers with a number of other policy instruments, including the substantially heightened degree of direct Soviet military involvement in the internal affairs of client states.

Proxies. The first of these innovations was the development and use of proxy or cooperative forces like Cuba or East Germany. While Soviet collaboration with other states of the socialist community developed haphazardly at first, by the time of the intervention in the Horn of Africa in 1977 it had the marks of a well-organized enterprise involving a clear-cut division of labor among the different members of the "Soviet collective security" system. Within this system, the Cubans provided combat personnel and training, the Soviets contributed logistic support and materiel, the East Germans provided internal security personnel and training, the Czechs, technical support, and so on. Cooperative forces permitted the Soviet Union to intervene directly in Third World conflicts like the Angolan civil war or the Ogaden conflict and decisively influence their outcome in its favor, while avoiding the provocation of the direct deployment of Soviet combat forces.

Moscow's ability to make use of cooperative forces like Cuba is ultimately made possible by ideology, i.e., by the fact that Marxism-Leninism is an explicitly internationalist doctrine which provides an elaborate justification for proletarian coop-

eration across national boundaries. While liberal internationalism plays something of a similar role in justifying collective
security arrangements in the West, there has not to date been
a small capitalist state that, like Cuba, has agreed to send large
contingents of troops to distant continents to fight for causes
that have no conceivable relationship to its own national security.

On the other hand, simple adherence to Marxism-Leninism
does not guarantee common policies; Soviet-Cuban collaboration in the Third World was made possible only by important
shifts in the ideological positions of both countries in the early
1970s. Havana and Moscow were in fact at odds through most
of the 1960s. The former criticized the USSR for excessive
conservatism, arguing that it ought to support armed struggle
and guerrilla warfare as a means of promoting revolutionary
change in Latin America, and predicting that Cuba would ar-
rive at communism sooner than the Soviet Union. The dispute
became sufficiently severe that in 1968 Moscow actually cut off
oil shipments to Cuba. The Cubans were forced to move right
as a result of the evident failure of the Cuban path to communism, while the Soviet Union moved left to prove that its
search for detente with the West did not imply a diminution
of its revolutionary vigor. The two countries thus met some-
where in the middle, making possible the Soviet-Cuban collaboration of the mid-1970s.

Marxist-Leninist Vanguard Parties. The second, and arguably
more important, innovation of the 1970s was the Marxist-
Leninist vanguard party (MLVP). During this decade, the Soviet Union and its socialist bloc allies supported the coming to
power or consolidation of self-proclaimed Marxist-Leninist
regimes in Angola, Mozambique, South Yemen, Ethiopia,
Benin, Guinea-Bissau, Vietnam, Laos, Kampuchea, Afghanistan, and Nicaragua. Soviet writers are quick to emphasize the
difference between this "second generation" of radical socialist-oriented states and the earlier generation of bourgeois nationalists. While none but Vietnam is fully socialist, the ideological commitment of these later clients to scientific socialism

and socialist internationalism makes them far more likely to be reliable allies of the USSR than non-Communist Khrushchev-era clients like Syria or India. As China and Yugoslavia demonstrated, declarative Marxism-Leninism is not sufficient to guarantee reliability; but, all things being equal, such a state is less likely to insist on its independence from Moscow than is a regime committed to, say, pan-Arabism or Islamic Marxism. As one Soviet author, Rostislav Ul'yanovsky, put it in *Narody Azii i Afriki* in March 1984:

In the practical aspect [the new generation of Marxist-Leninist states] enhance cooperation with the socialist countries to a new level and deliberately promote the expansion of such cooperation. They do not mistrust the socialist commonwealth or fear a "communist penetration," which is still experienced by the national democrats and occasionally even by the revolutionary democrats of the older generation.

A client's adherence to scientific socialism rather than a syncretist doctrine like African socialism has military implications as well. Bourgeois nationalists and older generation "revolutionary democrats" tended to resist military cooperation with the Soviet Union for its own sake, to demonstrate that they were not "tools" of Moscow. The new generation Marxist-Leninist states are less sensitive to this charge and have proven relatively more ready to provide the USSR with port and base access, overflight rights, and other military advantages.

More important in Soviet eyes than their adherence to scientific socialism is that client regimes be led by disciplined, centralized Marxist-Leninist vanguard parties. With Soviet encouragement the Popular Movement for the Liberation of Angola (MPLA) in Angola and Frelimo in Mozambique transformed themselves into formal vanguard parties in 1977, the Yemeni Socialist party in the People's Democratic Republic of Yemen (PDRY), in 1978, and the Ethiopian Worker's party in Ethiopia, 1984. (The People's Democratic party of Afghanistan [PDPA] began its existence as a formal Communist party.) The vanguard party was seen by the Soviets as a solution to the weaknesses inherent in the Khrushchev-era bourgeois nationalists whose rule was often charismatic but highly person-alistic and unstable. The vanguard party creates a permanent institutional basis for continued ties to the socialist bloc, and permits the Soviets multiple entry points into the country's leadership besides the single leader at the top.

Increasing Direct Military Involvement. Emphasis on MLVPs in the third phase of Soviet policy toward the Third World required substantially higher levels of direct Soviet interfer-ence in the internal affairs of client states and consequently accelerated the above mentioned trend toward increasing di-rect Soviet military involvement. The USSR was no longer indifferent to the internal ideological character of its Third World clients, but was interested in actively encouraging what might be called Leninist state-building, that is, consolidation of political power in the hands of a revolutionary democratic party and its eventual transformation into a vanguard party, creation of powerful internal security organs to preserve it in power, and the establishment of centralized Leninist state or-gans to gain control over the national economy, for example. Control over the client's internal security forces was particu-larly important, since it gave the Soviets a means of actually removing the local leadership and replacing it with a more compliant one. It is clear that these sorts of ambitious objec-tives could not be achieved through simple arms transfers and other instruments of the Khrushchev era.

Promotion of MLVPs thus went hand-in-hand with the use of proxies like Cuba and East Germany. Proxies provided the Soviets with a means not only of supporting existing clients but of helping them to come to power in the first place, and thereafter of shaping their internal socioeconomic character. Hence Cuban military forces with Soviet logistic support were crucial in helping the MPLA win out over its National Union for the Total Liberation of Angola (UNITA) and National Front for the Liberation of Angola (FNLA) opponents in An-gola; after the MPLA victory, the East Germans were active in restructuring the Angolan internal security apparatus, while Soviet, Cuban, and East German advisers helped in a variety of state-building tasks ranging from the writing of a socialist constitution to the training of MPLA party cadres. Once in power, states ruled by MLVPs were more likely to cooperate with the Soviet bloc in military matters and to play the role of proxy in turn, as when South Yemen assisted in the Soviet resupply of Ethiopia in 1977–78.

The logical outcome of this heightened Soviet willingness to interfere actively in the internal affairs of its clients was direct intervention by Soviet combat forces, which is what in fact happened in Afghanistan in December 1979. The PDPA, which came to power in a bloody coup in April 1978, was an orthodox Communist party organized from the beginning as a vanguard party. Indeed, the very orthodoxy of its socialist internationalism guaranteed it a very narrow base of support; by the end of 1979 the Soviets had no choice other than direct intervention if they were to preserve Communist rule in Kabul. Afghanistan was only the most blatant instance of Soviet use of military power to preserve the ideological character of a client regime. When PDRY President Selim Rubai Ali made overtures to the conservative states of the Persian Gulf in 1978, he was removed in a coup probably staged by the East Germans (who at the time were helping reorganize South Yemen's internal security forces), and his followers were suppressed by Cuban troops ferried in from Ethiopia.

The Soviet turn to MLVPs in the third phase led to an intense period of Third World activism in the mid- to late 1970s and a substantial expansion of the Soviet client base. This expansionism had certain negative consequences for Moscow as well, however, and appears to have brought on a fourth phase of reassessment, particularly under the brief tenure of Yuri Andropov. Soviet political leaders like Andropov, as well as other writers and specialists on the Third World, pointed to three specific problems with the activist legacy of the late Brezhnev period.

Problems. First, Soviet military and economic aid to Third World countries was an increasing burden on the Soviet economy at a time when the overall rate of growth in output and productivity was slowing markedly. Second, Moscow's expansionist behavior in the Third World proved destructive of the larger East-West relationship, bringing on a return to tense superpower relations that made further initiatives more dangerous and costly. While Soviet spokesmen continually assert their right to support revolutionary movements at the same time that they pursue arms control with the United States, many have realized that as a practical matter the two are incompatible. This lesson was brought home by the Carter administration's withdrawal of the SALT II treaty from Senate consideration after the Soviet invasion of Afghanistan. Finally, the new generation of Marxist-Leninist clients acquired in the past decade has fared very poorly as a group. Far from being models of economic development, states like Mozambique and Ethiopia have become international charity cases, dependent on the West for aid and resources that the Soviet bloc has been unable or unwilling to supply. Moreover, a number of these countries, including Afghanistan, Angola, Mozambique, and Nicaragua, have become mired in anti-Communist guerrilla wars, reflecting their narrow political base and lack of legitimacy. From a Soviet perspective, for all of their "declarative" Marxism-Leninism, not one of these states has made the transition to socialism successfully.

Whether these misgivings have been or will be translated into policy remains to be seen. While the Soviets appear to have been relatively quiescent in the Third World in the early 1980s, this may simply reflect a lack of opportunities; there is no evidence of a cutback in the monetary resources being devoted to Third World clients. Preliminary indications are that Gorbachev is a follower of Andropov in policy toward the developing world as in other areas and that he will concentrate on internal economic development; but it would be foolhardy for anyone to predict with confidence the course of future Soviet policy.

Military Power and Future U.S.–Soviet Interactions

Although they have done so in the past, neither the United States nor the Soviet Union currently pursues significant military objectives in the Third World. It is clear, however, that both superpowers have used military force in a variety of ways as an instrument of policy and leverage in the Third World, and are likely to continue to do so. While the use of military power has been costly, dangerous, and frequently counter productive, it is too valuable a tool to expect either side to renounce its use any time in the foreseeable future.

Role Reversal

Even as the United States has moved from more to less direct forms of military involvement in the decades since World War II, the Soviet Union has moved in the opposite direction. In certain ways this has happened because the Soviet Union has been on the same learning curve as the United States, but with a ten- or twenty-year delay. The United States began the postwar era by committing itself to a wide array of overseas alliances and clients, requiring intervention and direct application of military power at many points around the globe. In Vietnam the United States became seriously overextended and found that it simply did not have the will to expend the resources required to achieve what in the end were peripheral objectives in a not terribly strategic part of the world. The Soviet Union began this same period as a largely landlocked power that only gradually developed the doctrine, economic resources, and military capabilities to project influence into distant parts of the Third World. As the United States retreated from its globalist posture in the 1970s, the Soviet Union rushed in to fill the vacuum—in the case of Danang and Cam Ranh Bay in Vietnam, both literally and symbolically. Thereafter, it was the turn of the USSR to be bogged down in a number of unpleasant Third World conflicts in places like Afghanistan, Angola, and Kampuchea. The consequences of these involvements have thus far been limited, and it would be foolish to suggest that their impact on Soviet attitudes and society is anything comparable to that of America's fifteen-year involvement in Vietnam. Nonetheless, there are some signs that recent developments have compelled some within the Soviet leadership to consider whether the gains available in the Third World are worth the price.

In light of the Soviet Union's belated rise as an imperial power, it is not surprising that there has occurred something of a role reversal between it and the United States. Instead of being the advocate of revolutionary change, the USSR now finds itself the defender of the status quo in a number of regions in the Third World. This is the result not simply of the quantitative expansion of the Soviet client base, but of its qualitative aspects as well. The MLVPs promoted by the Soviet Union during the 1970s have everywhere turned out to be weak, narrowly based, lacking in internal legitimacy, riven by ethnic and sectarian conflicts, and generally unable to maintain themselves in power without substantial military assistance from the Soviet Union, Cuba, and the other states of the socialist bloc. The very features which made them attractive to Moscow as clients—their commitment to scientific socialism and proletarian internationalism—disqualified them as authentic representatives of local nationalism.

The Future

This reversal in roles suggests that future U.S.–Soviet military interactions will look considerably different from those of the previous three decades. The Soviet Union has already been forced to deploy a contingent of over 100,000 men to Afghanistan, with constant military pressures to up the ante, and together with Cuba may be forced to make a similar decision with regard to Angola. The Soviet military has had to participate in or provide its clients advice in counterinsurgency warfare, something that no professional military organization enjoys doing or does particularly well.

The United States will face several unfamiliar policy choices as well. While the Soviets have a well-developed doctrine for bringing about revolutionary change and supporting wars of national liberation, as well as much direct experience in this area, the United States is accustomed to dealing with established states in the framework of international law. It feels uncomfortable supporting subversive guerrilla organizations,

even when they represent the majority of the country's population (as is arguably the case in Afghanistan and Angola). The
United States military has virtually no experience in supporting insurgencies, and the machinery of the United States government is notably inept at handling operations that require
discretion and finesse. While certain anti-Communist insurgent movements like the Afghan *mujahedeen* will attract considerable popular and congressional support, others like the *contras* in Nicaragua will be targets of continuing controversy for
human rights and other reasons. Most importantly, proper
handling of an insurgent movement requires a great deal of
tactical flexibility. After defining its objectives clearly (i.e.,
whether to wean away or overthrow the pro-Soviet regime),
the United States must be able to mix both military force and
political means like negotiations to secure its ends. A certain
legalistic strain in U.S. foreign policy predisposes Americans
to regard "peaceful solutions" and the use of force as an
either/or choice; the realpolitik application of both simultaneously sits poorly with many.

This reversal of superpower roles will of course not be universal. In many parts of the world, such as Central America
and potentially in the Philippines, the Soviets will find opportunities to support guerrilla organizations seeking revolutionary social change against an American-supported status quo.
The Third World will then be a kind of mixed place, with both
superpowers backing military challenges to each other's interests. And in areas like the Middle East there is every prospect
for further conventional confrontations between U.S. and Soviet clients.

Reducing superpower tensions in such a world will not be
easy. There are good reasons why many proposed solutions
for doing so, such as negotiation of regional arms control
agreements or division of the Third World into superpower
spheres of influence, will be no more workable than in the
past. Nor does a solution lie in the unilateral American renunciation of its interests in the Third World or the disavowal of
military means to secure them. The Soviet Union was able to
run free in the Third World in the late 1970s in no small part

because of the United States' post-Vietnam retreat. If the Soviets are to be deterred from doing so in response to future opportunities, they must understand that there are definite costs to activism. This is not a formula for an American return to the globalism of the 1950s, but rather for a prudent and selective application of military force in conjunction with other instruments of policy. While Vietnam may have taught us that the United States does not need (and cannot afford) to win every round, it is no more the case that the United States can afford to lose all of them. For it is only if the problem of military security is addressed in the short run that the force of the American example in the social and economic spheres can exert its influence in the long run.

Final Report of the
Seventieth American Assembly

At the close of their discussions, the participants in the Seventieth American Assembly, on *East-West Tensions in the Third World,* at Arden House, Harriman, New York, November 21–24, 1985, reviewed as a group the following statement. This statement represents a general agreement; however, no one was asked to sign it. Furthermore, it should be understood that not everyone agreed with all of it.

Introduction

The "scourge of war" did not end with World War II. By any measure, the lives lost, the explosives dropped upon human beings in the many wars fought in the Third World over the past forty years add up to an awesome and terrible human catastrophe. There can be no doubt that conflict in Asia, Africa, Latin America, and the Middle East is a matter of the most direct and immediate concern to the majority of the people on this earth.

The military competition between the great powers, particularly in nuclear weapons, necessarily commands our central attention because of its potential fateful consequences for all mankind. But we must also be concerned about the competition between East and West in the Third World.

Wars in the Third World have not only been brutal and costly, but local conflicts in the Third World contain the ever-present risk of escalation. Moreover, the high levels of tension resulting from superpower competition in the Third World affect the climate for arms control. Conversely, tensions that flow from an unregulated military competition—whether in strategic or conventional weapons—impede efforts to moderate the tensions and level of conflict in the Third World.

Judgments may differ whether what is involved is mainly a competition between different ideologies and social systems or a rivalry between powerful nation-states seeking to advance their interests. In either perspective, it matters greatly whether that competition is conducted at a high level of tension with its ever-present risk of widening conflicts, or at more moderated and less dangerous levels.

If there is to be any possibility that superpower relations can ultimately evolve in a less dangerous and more productive direction, ways will have to be found to set restraints on outside intervention and to achieve some degree of cooperation to avert costly and terrible conflicts.

This is the problem to which the following discussion is directed.

Background

The two world wars radically transformed the terrain of international politics. The old balance of power, which had created a degree of stability in international politics for almost a century, was shattered by the emergence of two new giants on the international stage; the nations that had formerly dominated the power balance had been grievously weakened; and the introduction of nuclear weapons called into question the traditional relationship of war to politics. At first, the world appeared starkly bipolar, but in time it became clear that another factor of change—the rapid process of decolonization—had created a molten fluidity in what came to be called the

"Third World." The turbulent process of nation-building, of shifting allegiances, of transient groupings into regional power centers tempered bipolar dominance with multipolar complexities.

The complexities are enormous. Generalizations about the Third World fail to convey the differences among the regions involved, the differences in their histories, their levels of development, their political cultures, their problems. Manifold sources of conflict beset these developing states—tribal and religious differences and boundaries inherited from the colonial period. These countries struggle with the problems of nation-building in the face of a perilous imbalance between population growth and food supply. The result is unpredictability and turbulence on a terrain where the interests of the Great Powers meet and sometimes conflict.

Perhaps later historians will be able better to define and describe the character of the phenomenon we call "nationalism," which has emerged as a dominant political force in these areas. Forged in the period of struggle for independence, Third World nationalism is a complex but powerful force, sometimes integrative, sometimes disruptive and irrational. No efforts to deal with these parts of the world are likely to be effective that do not take into account the powerful emotional force of local nationalism.

Economic problems, sometimes described as the "North-South" conflict, clearly cut across East-West competition. Despite brave starts in the immediate post-war period toward assisting the new nations in their development, mounting debts, famines, and consequent political instabilities are constant reminders of the variegated unsolved problems of the individual countries which we lump together in the term the "Third World."

Economics is also becoming more important in another aspect of the Soviet Union's relations with the Third World in that the declining competitiveness of the Soviet economy is placing an important constraint on its capacity to implement economic strategies in the Third World.

The Soviet Union's economic efforts in the Third World

should be viewed as an instrument of overall global strategy more than as an end in itself. Involvement in the Third World could be positive in that it could offer additional markets for the Third World. Soviet aid to encourage development could be positive in itself and thereby contribute to stability. Moreover, there is some new evidence that the Soviet Union is being motivated increasingly by economic more than political objectives, e.g., to obtain foreign exchange and markets for oil, arms, gold, etc.

The United States has little capacity to influence the Soviet Union's policies concerning its involvement in the Third World, nor the Third World's response to such Soviet efforts.

The Soviet Challenge

There are unresolved differences in the West about the nature of the Soviet challenge. Those who see the Soviet Union as inherently aggressive tend to see upheavals in the Third World as the product of ideologically driven Soviet actions. This view emphasizes the containment of Soviet ambitions in the Third World as the primary objective of Western policy, often with an emphasis upon the military instrumentality. At the other end of the spectrum are those who see the Soviet Union essentially as a nation-state in a mounting phase of its national development as a Great Power, pressing against the existing configuration of power in the world, pragmatically exploiting favorable opportunities for the increase in its influence. This latter view emphasizes local conditions that give rise to these opportunities as the main focus for Western efforts. Between these two views there are many who see a combination of these factors at work.

As the subsequent discussion demonstrates, strategic, political, and economic considerations are intermingled in varying degrees in the different regions involved. In sorting out these considerations, we are prone to be influenced by unresolved assumptions about Soviet motivations that lead to different policy preferences. Is every increase of Soviet influence in the Third World to be challenged, or only those that threaten the

independence of the countries involved? Are there some areas
where the Soviet Union and the West have common interests,
and where some degree of collaborative effort to attenuate
local conflict situations may be possible? The answers to these
questions depend upon a clarification of Western interests, as
well as a greater degree of agreement about common purposes than yet exists between the United States and its allies.

There are also choices to be made by the Soviet Union. Has
it learned that the exploitation of opportunities in the Third
World can not be pursued without disrupting its relations with
the West? Will its concern with domestic economic problems
cause it to question its capacity to support costly commitments
in the Third World of uncertain benefit? If these considerations enter into the current Soviet reexamination of its options, and if the Soviet leadership perceives a Western readiness to collaborate in codifying practical restraints in at least
some of the turbulent areas of the Third World, then some
possibilities for moderating tensions in the Third World may
warrant further exploration.

Assembly Findings

The following sections address the particular circumstances
to be found in four principal regions of East-West competition.

Middle East

Conflict in the Middle East has local roots. East-West competition and rivalry color the playing out of events but are not
the driving forces. Nevertheless, the region as a whole is likely
to remain a major arena for U.S.–Soviet competition and one
of potentially high risk.

American interests focus on the availability of energy resources both for the United States and for its allies (and those
states which produce oil and gas) and on the security of Israel.
Views differ on the comparable weight of Soviet interests in
the area (e.g., security against external threats close to its

borders) and even whether Soviet objectives lie primarily in threatening or unsettling U.S. interests in the region. There is wide agreement, however, on the volatility of the region, both in terms of shifting alliances and allegiances and in the interplay of religion, nationalism, and personality. These are extremely difficult for outside players to understand or control.

There is also little agreement on the implications of these factors for U.S.–Soviet relations and for American policy. There are differences, for example, on whether or not the ambiguities in the Arabian/Persian Gulf warrant efforts by the United States and Soviet Union to clarify their primary interests. Clarification would "draw lines," which might induce the Soviets to take unacceptable actions in some areas; on the other hand, failure to clarify issues could also lead to miscalculations. There are similar differences over whether to convene an international conference to deal with the Arab-Israel conflict and whether the Soviets should be included. Some believe that the United States would risk giving the Soviets status in the region they have long sought as well as an opportunity to frustrate constructive action by those most directly involved. Others argue that no agreement is possible without Soviet involvement. It is clear to all that, regardless of the forum, the ultimate resolution of the Arab-Israel conflict will be agonizingly difficult and in the long run will depend primarily on local and regional judgments, not the decisions of the Great Powers.

U.S. policy in the gulf area has on balance been cautious, well conceived, and successful. It has focused on avoiding expansion of the Iraq-Iran war, preventing U.S. (or Soviet) involvement in that conflict, preserving U.S. options in dealing with its aftermath, and assuring U.S. security capabilities in the region. The Soviets have also been cautious in the area. The dangers for East-West conflict envisaged a few years ago have not thus far emerged. It is unclear how the war will ultimately end. If, however, the United States is well informed about events and personalities, makes clear that it is not hostile to Islam, and is prepared to improve its relations with all parties, it will be as well positioned as it can be to deal with events.

Soviet intervention in Iran does not seem likely under present circumstances.

Terrorism is a major and continuing concern for the United States in the region. Soviet attitudes toward terrorism are less clear. Opinions differ as to whether the Soviets believe they gain from the instability and uncertainty produced by terrorists (whom they have even supported in some instances). There are divided views on whether the United States should offer to work with the Soviets in combating terrorism. Better intelligence, defensive measures, cooperation with those local forces that may help to inhibit terrorist activities, and—on occasion—precisely targeted, swift, and effective response are the best available options for dealing with terrorist actions. Some even urge a broad reduction in the region of U.S. presence, both official and private.

There is broad agreement that umbrella-type conferences and meetings on Middle East issues with the Soviets have not been seen as fruitful. It is important, however, for the parties concerned to establish and maintain a regular dialogue with the Soviets through diplomatic channels, such as the talks at the assistant secretary level that are already established.

Latin America

The Soviet Union is not a major threat to U.S. interests in South America, but Cuban and Soviet military and subversive activities in Central America are a matter of grave concern. Therefore, a key U.S. objective in Central America is to halt those Cuban and Soviet activities.

Aspects of the problem which need to be considered before setting policy include the following:

—Cuba remains committed to intervention in Central America and has the capacity to expand its military and revolutionary presence.

—Cuba is a Marxist-Leninist state allied with the Soviet Union, but the United States is attempting to prevent other countries in the Western Hemisphere, particularly Nicaragua, from following this path.

—The Soviet Union has supplied arms not only to Cuba, but also to Nicaragua. The U.S. has made it clear that it would not accept the introduction of certain categories of sophisticated weapons into Nicaragua.

Present U.S. policy of isolation and pressure is not succeeding in removing Cuban presence, nor is it likely to do so in the future. However, the alternative approach of conciliation has not worked in the past either, and there is considerable doubt of its likely success in the future.

Some believe that consideration should be given to reestablishing diplomatic relations and lifting the trade embargo, but it is not anticipated that these steps alone would persuade the Cubans to desist. Even a guarantee against U.S. invasion of Nicaragua is unlikely to achieve that.

Some believe that normalization of relations with Cuba should serve as part of a long-term process of trying to change Cuban policy. Some others argue that Cuban understandings with other Latin American states (e.g., Venezuela and Mexico) have relieved these states of Cuban pressure. Still others believe that increased U.S. assistance to Latin American countries might inhibit Cuba's courting of those countries with revolutionary ideas. Lastly, there are those who believe that continuing sanctions are needed.

As for Nicaragua, there was disagreement as to how to attain the objective of moving the regime toward democratic pluralism and independence. Some believe that it would be best to support fully the Contadora process. Others believe that continued support of the *contras* would actually further this process. Others considered that this support would have the opposite effect. But if the primary U.S. objective is merely to prevent Nicaragua from supporting insurgencies in the rest of Central America, then various ways of sealing the Nicaraguan border might be sufficient (e.g., an inter-American patrolled demilitarized zone around Nicaragua).

The introduction of U.S. *combat* troops should only be considered as an ultimate last resort. Some suggest that the Kissinger Commission is an appropriate elaboration of principles to apply.

However, U.S. military trainers and advisers are a necessary factor in the Central American nation-building process to show our support for our interests and values and help prepare our allies and friends for self-defense. Nonetheless, the military instrument is useless unless the political regime being defended is also supported by its people. Care needs to be taken to avoid ending up with a military oligarchy, which has been, and could be, as much a cause of the problem as its solution.

Asia

The regional balance in Asia is stable and remains militarily sound for the United States. The sources of strength lie in the economic dynamism and political stability of most of the countries of the area, in intraregional political cohesion, and in the extensive economic interrelationships amongst the countries of the region.

Soviet military power has grown steadily in Soviet Asia and the Pacific, but this has not as yet had a significant political impact on the countries of the region. The measured increase in U.S. capabilities and force flexibility has been appropriate to the increased Soviet military challenge. There is no reason for the United States to contemplate dramatic changes in force dispositions. Nevertheless, continuing careful reassessment of this military balance is important and would become urgent should U.S. access to bases in the Philippines—Subic Naval and Clark Air Force—be called into question as a result of political changes in that country.

The Soviet Union remains at a strong political disadvantage in the region except for a handful of countries—Vietnam and Afghanistan. Moscow is politically suspect in most other countries, except for India, and has little to offer the region as a major trading partner or source of technology. However, a shock to the economic growth of the region, which might be inflicted by a change in trade or other economic policies by the United States, Japan, or the European Economic Community, or by a general breakdown in international trade relations, would be seriously damaging to U.S. interests in the area. It also might increase political and economic instability in the region, and provide opportunities for the Soviet Union to strengthen its own political position. Nevertheless, Japanese–U.S. relationships are probably sufficiently strong to withstand even such major shocks.

The most urgent cause for U.S. concern is the Philippines. Mounting political unrest, a growing insurgency, and intractable economic problems threaten national stability and integrity there as well as broad U.S. interests in the region. Emergence of a Philippine government that has both the confidence of the population and the will and determination to undertake the political, economic, social, and military reforms to restore stability and growth is critical. A visibly free and fair democratic election process actively encouraged by the United States and other concerned countries is a first step in this process and a prior condition for substantial economic assistance by the United States, Japan, other concerned nations, and private and public financial institutions.

The limited improvements in Sino-Soviet relations have not yet been of serious concern to the United States. More substantial improvements are likely to be constrained both by continuing political and strategic policy differences and by limits to the economic and technological benefits for both sides from the relationship. A return to a strategic relationship by the USSR and China is unlikely.

Nor does a substantive strategic shift in Japanese ties with the Soviet Union appear likely, although there may be some easing in the relationship. The United States and Japan share an interest in assuring that the USSR does not gain unduly from the transfer of high technology, which may be one of its objectives in improving ties with Japan. Opportunities for major expansion of economic relations are likely to be limited by economic factors as well as by strongly held Japanese views of the USSR, concern over mounting Soviet military dispositions, the Soviet occupation of four islands at the northern tip of Japan, and by Japan's broad associations with the West.

While the Soviets would probably profit from political and

economic instability in the region, they also share a common interest with the United States in avoiding major conflict in the volatile areas of Korea and Indochina. A political and low-level military struggle continues in Kampuchea where the Association of Southeast Asian Nations (ASEAN) and the great majority of the United Nations membership seek to replace the Vietnam-dominated government with a more truly neutral one. Some believe it will be useful to maintain a continuing exchange of views with the Soviets on these areas, perhaps through established diplomatic channels for periodic consultation. In any dialogue with the Soviets on these areas, however, it is essential that the views and interests of other U.S. friends and interested parties in the region be closely consulted.

The problems which most concern the countries of Asia, as well as U.S. interests in the area, however, are not primarily related to East-West issues and are not likely to find their resolution or amelioration through the channel of U.S.–Soviet talks.

Africa

Angola, Namibia, and South Africa are central to the political life of the continent. Different premises with respect to U.S. foreign policy in these areas lead to different actions.

Issues relating to them focus on apartheid and race rather than on the U.S.–Soviet relationship. In the meantime, racial violence and political and economic disruption have moved South Africa to center stage. The dilemmas of U.S. policy are evident. Some strongly urge sanctions and disengagement, which dissociate the United States from South African repression and align American policy with the overwhelming sentiment of Africa and the world. Others still argue that constructive engagement may yet encourage peaceful change, build bridges to moderate blacks and white opponents of apartheid, and avoid furthering the interests of Soviet allies in the area.

Regarding Angola, the first question is whether the U.S. goal is to bring down the Luanda government or to encourage a settlement resulting in the withdrawal of Cuban troops. Some believe that the goal is to topple the Luanda regime, and, therefore, Savimbi should be supported. A disadvantage of this course of action is that it associates the United States with South Africa through the Savimbi link. Moreover, Savimbi's effective challenge to the Popular Movement for the Liberation of Angola (MPLA) means that Luanda continues to need Cuban troop support and justifies the growing Soviet presence in the country.

The bargain the U.S. government has been trying to bring about is a balanced withdrawal of Cuban troops from Angola and of South Africa from Namibia. Concern over continued Cuban presence might be regarded by South Africa as justification to maintain its presence in Namibia and to delay progress towards Namibia's independence. All parties involved in the negotiation process have accepted, on principle, Security Council Resolution 435 as the basis for Namibian independence, and they should be encouraged to continue doing so. Whether the South Africans will ultimately agree to such a bargain and take practical steps to implement it remains moot.

The Soviet Union has not played a significant role in this situation. Perhaps this is because the Soviets see their prospects as brightening even without the necessity of their taking more vigorous action. It may also be that the USSR, having backed the losing horse in Zimbabwe, is moving cautiously to avoid a repetition of that misjudgment. Perhaps the Soviets want to be able to play a "constructive" role. This may change if the violence gets further out of hand.

No U.S. policy in Southern Africa has been notably successful in years past. While primary U.S. security interests do not appear to be at stake in the short term, there are those who believe that fundamental U.S. interests in many parts of the world will sooner or later be seriously affected.

Conclusion

As the preceding sections illustrate, it is not an easy task to reconcile the vigorous and effective prosecution of our interests in our competition with the Soviet Union with the necessity we also face for maintaining a less dangerous international environment.

It is beyond dispute that the primary obligation of Western governments must be to defend their vital interests, to maintain a military balance, to protect and advance democratic and pluralist values in the world, and to seek to strengthen the international system against the chaos and violence that threaten it.

But it is also true that an enlightened understanding of our own self-interest compels us to seek to manage the competition with the Soviet Union in ways that reduce the risk of war and that will encourage the evolution of this relationship over what may be a long period of time in directions that are less dangerous and that may be more productive.

This requires us, in the first instance, to protect our security by a rational management of the nuclear military competition, to seek a nuclear military balance at as stable and moderate a level as we can. It also requires us to manage the East-West competition in the Third World so that it does not lead to violent conflict.

This latter task, which is the central subject of this report, is made more difficult by the residual apprehensions created by actions of the Soviet Union marked by a lack of restraint. Although the Soviet Union has not created the turbulence and the upheavals that characterize large areas of the Third World, it has been prepared to exploit the opportunities that arise for the advancement of its interests and the expansion of its influence. The Soviet Union now has a number of client states and military facilities in the Third World. Nevertheless, it has not appeared to appreciate its own enlightened self-interest; many of its actions have generated hostility and suspicions; some have been costly and self-defeating.

But the world they and we inhabit is increasingly dangerous; situations abound that can lead us into involvements that neither of us may intend, that may be beyond our power to control. Whether the generational change that has now taken place in the Soviet leadership will lead the Soviet Union, in its own self-interest, to conduct itself with greater restraint and responsibility is a possibility that should be encouraged.

Although both superpowers seek to weaken the other's influence in the Third World, many of the present and potential conflict situations in the Third World are not zero-sum situations; both may lose if the conflicts widen, and both may gain if they can be contained or settled without violence. So may the third parties affected by the outcome of the bipolar competition. If in non-zero-sum cases, we can agree to conduct our competition within the limits of practical restraints—on the kinds and levels of weapons to be introduced into such areas, the numbers of military personnel—the benefit would be equally shared, and certainly no less with the people of the area involved. The evolving pattern of regions taking conflict resolution into their own hands may contribute to such restraint.

Beyond such limited measures of cooperation could come, with time, broader measures. In the Third World, the Soviet Union is not invariably a status quo power, and in this world of change, it would be vain for the United States to seek to be the undiscriminating defender of the status quo. The direction toward which we must work is to gain common acceptance of the principle of non-intervention by force, either to produce or to prevent political change, so that the people of the Third World may accommodate the process of change without violence.

It may be a long time before the Soviet Union or the West are prepared to move in this direction. But if they and we come with time to appreciate that their security and their own self-interest, and ours as well, depend upon the strengthening of the international system against the violence and the chaos which now threaten to engulf it, logic and reason will propel us in this direction. Although they may be far from present-day realities, the compelling argument is that the alternative is terrible to contemplate, for them, for us, and for the billions who inhabit the Third World.

Participants
The Seventieth American Assembly

ARCHIE E. ALBRIGHT
President and Chief Executive
Officer
Foreign Policy Association
New York, New York

DAVID E. ALBRIGHT
Air War College
Maxwell Air Force Base
Montgomery, Alabama

JOHN B. BELLINGER
Director
Defense Guidance Staff
Office of the Under Secretary
of Defense for Policy
Department of Defense
Washington, D.C.

EMIL CASTRO
Chief
Trade and Foreign Policy
Control Division
Office of East-West Trade
U.S. Department of State
Washington, D.C.

*NATHANIEL DAVIS
Alexander & Adelaide Hixon
Professor of Humanities
Harvey Mudd College
Claremont, California

WILLIAM DOHERTY
Executive Director
American Institute for Free
Labor Development
AFL-CIO
Washington, D.C.

JORGE I. DOMINGUEZ
Department of Government
Harvard University
Cambridge, Massachusetts

FRANCIS FUKUYAMA
Rand/U.C.L.A.
Center for the Study of Soviet
International Behavior
Santa Monica, California

CHARLES GRAY
Executive Director
Asian-American Free Labor
Institute
AFL-CIO
Washington, D.C.

PETER GROSE
Managing Editor
Foreign Affairs and Senior
Fellow, Council on Foreign
Relations
New York, New York

CLAUS M. HALLE
President
Coca-Cola International
Atlanta, Georgia

RICHARD HELMS

President
Safeer Company
Washington D.C.
*Discussion Leader
**Rapporteur
†Delivered Formal Address

RICHARD HERRMANN
Department of Political Science
Ohio State University
Columbus, Ohio

**TED HOPF
Harriman Scholar
Department of Political Science
Columbia University
New York, New York

†ROBERT JERVIS
Institute of War & Peace
Studies
School of International Affairs
Columbia University
New York, New York

JOSEPH JOHN JOVA
Meridian House International
Washington, D.C.

PETER H. JUVILER
Department of Political Science
Barnard College
New York, New York

JAMES A. KELLY
Deputy Assistant Secretary
(East Asian & Pacific Affairs)
Department of Defense
Washington, D.C.

DAVID KILGOUR, M.P.
Parliamentary Secretary to the
Minister of External Relations
House of Commons
Ottawa, Ontario
Canada

**RIINA KIONKA
Harriman Scholar
Department of Political Science
Columbia University
New York, New York

*PAUL H. KREISBERG
Director of Studies
Council on Foreign Relations
New York, New York

LT. GEN. RICHARD D.
LAWRENCE
President
National Defense University
Fort McNair
Washington, D.C.

SUSANNE S. LOTARSKI
Director
Office of Eastern European &
Soviet Affairs
International Trade
Administration
U.S. Department of Commerce
Washington, D.C.

B. WILLIAM MADER
Deputy Chief of
Correspondents
Time
New York, New York

MURRAY McLEAN
Counselor
Embassy of Australia
Washington, D.C.

**SCOTT MONJE
Harriman Scholar
Department of Political Science
Columbia University
New York, New York

WILFRIED NARTUS
Political Counselor
Embassy of Belgium
Washington, D.C.

LILLIAN PUBILLONES
NOLAN
Staff Consultant
Subcommittee on Western
Hemisphere Affairs
Committee on Foreign Affairs
U.S. House of Representatives
Washington, D.C.

GARDNER G. PECKHAM
Minority Staff Consultant
Committee on Foreign Affairs
U.S. House of Representatives
Washington, D.C.

GERALD A. POLLACK
Coordinator-Financial
Economics
Exxon Corporation
New York, New York

CAPT. BARRY PLOTT
Military Fellow
Council on Foreign Relations
New York, New York

EDMUND W. PUGH, JR.
Rye, New York

WILLIAM B. QUANDT
The Brookings Institution
Washington, D.C.

CHALMERS M. ROBERTS
Bethesda, Maryland

†SERGEI ROGOV
Institute on the U.S.A. &
Canada
Embassy of the Union of Soviet
Socialist Republics
Washington, D.C.

ARTHUR H. ROSEN
President
National Committee on United
States-China Relations
New York, New York

STANLEY O. ROTH
Staff Director
Subcommittee on Asian &
Pacific Affairs
Committee on Foreign Affairs
U.S. House of Representatives
Washington, D.C.

HENRIK SCHMIEGELOW
Counselor
Embassy of the Federal
Republic of Germany
Washington, D.C.

*DANIEL A. SHARP
Director
International and Public Affairs
Xerox Corporation
Stamford, Connecticut

MARSHALL D. SHULMAN
Director
The W. Averell Harriman
Institute for Advanced Study of
the Soviet Union
School of International Affairs
Columbia University
New York, New York

GARY SOROKA
Policy Development Bureau
Department of External Affairs
Ottawa, Ontario
Canada

ANNE C. STEPHENS
Associate Director
Fund for the Future
Foreign Policy Association
New York, New York

About The American Assembly

The American Assembly was established by Dwight D. Eisenhower at Columbia University in 1950. It holds nonpartisan meetings and publishes authoritative books to illuminate issues of United States policy.

An affiliate of Columbia, with offices at Barnard College, the Assembly is a national, educational institution incorporated in the state of New York.

The Assembly seeks to provide information, stimulate discussion, and evoke independent conclusions on matters of vital public interest.

American Assembly Sessions

At least two national programs are initiated each year. Authorities are retained to write background papers presenting essential data and defining the main issues of each subject.

A group of men and women representing a broad range of experience, competence, and American leadership meet for several days to discuss the Assembly topic and consider alternatives for national policy.

All Assemblies follow the same procedure. The background papers are sent to participants in advance of the Assembly. The Assembly meets in small groups for four or five lengthy periods. All groups use the same agenda. At the close of these informal sessions participants adopt in plenary session a final report of findings and recommendations.

Regional, state, and local Assemblies are held following the national session at Arden House. Assemblies have also been held in England, Switzerland, Malaysia, Canada, the Caribbean, South America, Central America, the Philippines, and Japan. Over one hundred forty institutions have cosponsored one or more Assemblies.

The American Assembly
COLUMBIA UNIVERSITY

About the W. Averell Harriman Institute for Advanced Study of the Soviet Union

Columbia University's W. Averell Harriman Institute for Advanced Study of the Soviet Union is the oldest (founded as the Russian Institute in 1946) and largest center devoted to the study of Russia and the Soviet Union in the United States. Governor W. Averell Harriman endowed the Institute in 1982 in order to meet three critical areas of need in this country: the preparation of graduate students for scholarly and professional careers in Soviet studies; the promotion of advanced research on Russia and the Soviet Union; and the dissemination of information, analyses, and insights concerning the Soviet Union to academics, the business community, policy makers, and the general public.

The Harriman Institute fosters an interdisciplinary approach to the study of Russia and the Soviet Union. The Institute strives to maintain a reputation for independent objectivity. It eschews any orthodoxy and is hospitable to a range of views.

The W. Averell Harriman Institute for Advanced Study of the Soviet Union
NATIONAL ADVISORY COUNCIL

Index

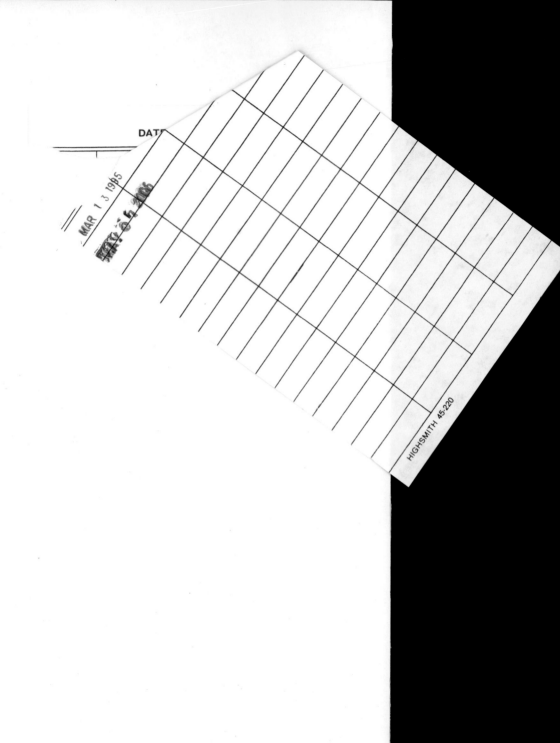